STRINGING
Rosaries

Volume 2 of the Contemporary Voices of Indigenous Peoples Series
Michael Yellow Bird and Suzzanne Kelley, Editors

STRINGING
Rosaries

*The History, the Unforgivable, and the Healing
of Northern Plains American Indian
Boarding School Survivors*

DENISE K. LAJIMODIERE

North Dakota State University Press
Dept. 2360, P.O. Box 6050, Fargo, ND 58108-6050
www.ndsupress.org

North Dakota State University Press
Dept. 2360, P.O. Box 6050, Fargo, ND 58108-6050
www.ndsupress.org

Stringing Rosaries: The History, the Unforgivable, and the Healing of Northern Plains American Indian Boarding School Survivors
By Denise K. Lajimodiere

First Edition, Third Printing

David Bertolini, Director
Suzzanne Kelley, Publisher
Zachary Vietz, Publicist
Angela Beaton, Graduate Editorial Assistant
Amanda Watts, Graduate Intern
Taylor Flakker, Bryan Keidel, Samantha Soukup, and Grace Rivard, Publishing Interns

Cover photo courtesy of Bureau of Catholic Indian Missions
Cover design by Jamie Hohnadel Trosen
Interior design by Deb Tanner

International Standard Book Number: 978-1-946163-43-1
Library of Congress Control Number: 2018967346

Printed in the United States of America

Publisher's Cataloging-In-Publication Data
(Prepared by The Donohue Group, Inc.)

Names: Lajimodiere, Denise K., author.
Title: Stringing rosaries : the history, the unforgivable, and the healing
   of Northern Plains American Indian boarding school survivors / Denise
   K. Lajimodiere.
Other Titles: Contemporary voices of indigenous peoples series ; v. 2.
Description: First edition. | Fargo, ND : North Dakota State University
   Press, [2019] | Includes bibliographical references and index.
Identifiers: ISBN 9781946163103
Subjects: LCSH: Off-reservation boarding schools--Great Plains--History--
   20th century. | Indian children--Education--Great Plains--History--20th
   century. | Indian children--Abuse of--Great Plains--History--20th
   century. | Indians, Treatment of--Great Plains--History--20th century.
   | Boarding school students--Great Plains--Interviews. | BISAC: HISTORY
   / Native American. | HISTORY / United States / 20th Century. | HISTORY
   / United States / State & Local / Midwest (IA, IL, IN, KS, MI, MN, MO,
   ND, NE, OH, SD, WI) | EDUCATION / General.
Classification: LCC E97.5 .L35 2019 | DDC 371.829/97078--dc23

∞ This paper meets the requirements of ANSI/NISO Z39.48-1992
(Permanence of Paper).

To my parents and grandparents who are boarding school survivors.

For my children, grandchildren, and great-grandchildren that you may understand the events that shaped my life.

HEAR MY VOICE

by Ramona Klein

Hear my voice
and hear the pain
that sears my soul,
feel the pain of the little girl,
smell the air,
smell the scent of Brylcreem
that brings back memories
in a flash,
taste the salt,
know that tears
help heal.
See the hands
that reached for the little girl,
know that it will not be forgotten.
Embrace the love
that should have been there.
Set me free to live
a life without pain.

CONTENTS

PREFACE

My interest in American Indian boarding school survivors' stories evolved from recording my father and other family members speaking of their experiences. I never knew these stories existed, because my family members had all maintained silence on their experiences until I began asking questions. My research helped me gain insight, a deeper understanding of my parents, and how and why my siblings and I were parented the way we were. That insight led me to an emotional ceremony of forgiveness, described in the last chapter of *Stringing Rosaries*.

The journey to record survivors' stories led me through the Dakotas and Minnesota and into the personal and private space of boarding school survivors. While there, I heard stories that they had never shared before. I came to an understanding of new terms: historical and intergenerational trauma, soul wound. Through their stories, I witnessed the tragic legacy of the boarding school era and an astonishing resilience.

I am haunted by the resounding silence of abuses that happened at boarding schools across the United States. I want these survivors' stories told uninterrupted, so each survivor tells their own story in their own words. The majority wanted their names kept anonymous but wanted the world to know what happened to them. The youngest survivor interviewed was fifty years old, and the oldest was eighty-nine. I traveled to their homes or wherever they were most comfortable with being interviewed. In the tradition of my Turtle Mountain Chippewa tribe, I offered them tobacco and gifts. To set a tone of safety, I told them my parents' and grandparents' boarding school stories and that I was considered intergenerational, someone who did not go to boarding school but was a survivor of boarding school survivors.

The journey was emotionally exhausting. Often, after hearing their stories I had to sit in my car for a long while, sobbing, waiting to compose myself for the long drive back across the plains to the university. Over the course of interviewing and writing, I would need to take months, and even several years, away from the manuscript. Family, friends, and ceremony, along with my promise to the survivors that I would let the world know what happened to them kept me coming back to the manuscript.

ACKNOWLEDGEMENTS

I humbly acknowledge the boarding school survivors in this book who were courageous enough to break their silence. Their experiences shared here are told as they remember. Some interviewees wish to maintain their anonymity. In such instances, the reader is advised that the name used is a pseudonym. My vision for this book was to present each interviewee's story as told from birth to present, thus the reader is able to understand, or be aware of, life events before boarding school, the reasons for attending boarding school, what happened at the boarding schools, and the current effects of their time at the boarding schools.

The poem, "Hear My Voice," is used with permission of the author, Ramona Klein.

Special recognition must be given to the Boarding School Healing Project founders—Andrea Smith, Sammy Toineeta, and Rosemary Gifford—for their vision; the Native American Rights Fund; and lawyer Donald Wharton, for providing the vehicle and legal counsel to move their vision forward by organizing the initial 2011 symposium where the National Native American Boarding School Healing Coalition (NABS) was formed. Kudos to the first NABS Board of Directors—myself, Jerilyn DeCoteau, Andrea Smith, Patsy Whitefoot, Edna Brillon, and Don Coyhis—for their intense work in developing the vision, philosophy, and goals of the Coalition.

Thank you to North Dakota State University School of Education, the Seventh Generation Fund, and NABS for providing travel funds and small grants.

Migwech to Lea Roberts, who diligently and patiently transcribed all of the interviews, chuckling—and just as often weeping—as she listened and typed.

A special thank you to Suzzanne Kelley, publisher, who immediately embraced and supported my vision for this book. I am forever grateful.

PART I:

The History

"How shall we reach the full-blooded Indians?" a Quaker missionary *was once asked. She replied, according to a story in which Bishop Hare took pleasure, "To reach the full-blooded Indian, send after him a full-blooded Christian."*

— The Life and Labors of Bishop Hare: Apostle to the Sioux
William Hobart Hare, Mark Antony De Wolfe Howe

Savage and civilized life cannot live and prosper on the same ground. One of the two must die.

— Report of the United States Commissioner for Indian Affairs (1881),
found in *The Red Man and the White Man in North America from Its Discovery to the Present Time*, by George Edward Ellis

Captain Richard Pratt. *Courtesy Hampton University Archives.*

Author's mother, Lola Plante (far right), and friends Gladys Delorme and Martha Jeanotte, at boarding school. *Author files.*

New recruits (the before photo), Spokane Indians.
Courtesy Pacific University Archives.

New recruits (the after photo), remaining Spokane Indians after seven months at school (one student died), Forest Grove (later called Chemawa). Pratt liked to boast of "before" and "after" photographs to show the progress of civilizing the savage.
Courtesy Pacific University Archives.

AMERICAN INDIAN BOARDING SCHOOL HISTORY

The history of the American Indian boarding school era is one of the United States' best-kept secrets. This major federal policy has largely been written out of the history books. The boarding school policy represents a shift from genocide of American Indian people to a more defensible but no less insidious policy of cultural genocide — the systematic destruction of American Indian communities through the removal and reprogramming of their children. Boarding schools physically, emotionally, and culturally removed students as young as two years old for a minimum of four and up to twelve years away from their family and tribe. This approach was thought to be less costly than wars against the tribe or eradication of the American Indian population.[1]

My research and interviews reveal that children were literally stolen from their family. I also reviewed hundreds of student folders and found that the line for parent signatures had the same handwriting throughout the entire form. Indian agents most likely signed for the family, forging their signatures.

Stringing Rosaries contains sixteen qualitative interviews of Northern Plains American Indian boarding schools survivors, adding to a growing body of information documenting boarding schools and their devastating consequences for American Indian families and communities.[2] Although I

---

[1] David W. Adams, *Education for Extinction: American Indians and the Boarding School Experience, 1875–1928* (Lawrence: University Press of Kansas, 1995); Brenda Child, *Boarding School Seasons: American Indian Families, 1900–1940* (Lincoln: University of Nebraska Press, 2000); Teresa Evans-Campbell, "Historical Trauma in American Indian/Native Alaska Communities: A Multilevel Framework for Exploring Impacts on Individuals, Families, and Communities," *Journal of Interpersonal Violence* 23 (3: 2008): 313–38.

[2] See also: Adams, *Education for Extinction*; Child, *Boarding School Seasons*; Clyde Ellis, *To Change Them Forever: Indian Education at the Rainy Mountain Boarding School, 1893–1996* (Norman: University of Oklahoma Press, 1996); Michael C. Coleman, *American Indian Children at School, 1850–1930* (Jackson: University Press of Mississippi, 1994); S. Colmant, L. Schultz, R. Robbins, et al., "Constructing Meaning to the Indian Boarding School Experience," *Journal of American Indian Education* 43 (3: 2004): 22–40; Basil Johnston, *Indian School Days* (Toronto: Key Porter, 1988); K. T. Lomawaima, "Educating Native Americans," in *Handbook of Research on Multicultural Education*, ed. J. A. Banks (New York: Macmillan, 1995), pp. 331–47; John Reyhner and Jeanne Eder, *Indian Education: A History* (Norman: University of Oklahoma Press, 2004); Morton Beiser, "A Hazard to Mental Health: Indian Boarding School," *American Journal of Psychiatry* 131 (3: 1974): 305–306; Maria Yellow Horse Brave Heart, "The Historical Trauma Response among Natives and Its Relationship with Substance Abuse: A Lakota Illustration," in *Healing and Mental Health for Native Americans: Speaking in Red*, eds. E. Nebelkopf and M. Phillips (Altamira Press, 2004), pp. 7–18; Eric Dlugokinski and Lyn Kramer, "A System of Neglect: Indian Boarding School," *American Journal of Psychiatry* 131 (1974): 670–73; Marc H. Irwin and Samuel Roll, "The Psychological Impact of Sexual Abuse of Native American Boarding School Children," *Journal of the American Academy of Psychoanalysis* 23 (3: 1995): 461–73; J. Noriega, "American Indian Education in the United States: Indoctrination for Subordination to Colonialism," in *The State of Native America: Genocide, Colonization, and Resistance*, ed. M. A. James (Boston: South End Press, 1992), pp. 371–402.

interviewed many more survivors, the parameters of this book—attempts at gender, geographic, and school representations—limited the number of accepted interviews. The purpose of this study is to investigate the experiences of those attending boarding schools during the years 1921 to 1986 in the Northern Plains region of the United States.

***

An article in a national tribal magazine stated that the National Boarding School Healing Project (now the National Native American Boarding School Healing Coalition, or NABS) was looking for researchers to document boarding school survivor stories. I contacted the organization to let them know that I had already been doing informal interviews with my family members. The Project had an interview protocol that I adopted for my research. As an academic researcher, I received International Review Board status and permission from North Dakota State University to conduct a qualitative interview study of boarding school survivors. Qualitative interview research methodology allowed me to capture the essence of how the survivors viewed their experience. Qualitative study is "an inquiry process of understanding a social or human problem, based on building a complex, holistic picture, formed with words, reporting detailed views of informants, and conducted in a natural setting."[3]

I put a notice about my research in tribal newspapers throughout North Dakota, leaving my phone number and university email address. I received responses from survivors living in the Dakotas and Minnesota. I traveled to the survivors' homes to conduct the interviews. I would introduce myself in my Ojibwe tribal language and offer, as is customary in my tribe, asema or kinnickinnick—a traditional tobacco made of red willow—as a respectful way of asking for information. At the end of the interview, also following my tribal tradition, the participants were gifted with blankets, red willow baskets, and wild rice.

***

---

[3] John W. Cresswell, *Research Design: Qualitative and Quantitative Approach* (Thousand Oaks: Sage Publication, 1994), pp. 1–2.

Historical Trauma Theory — as proposed by social worker, psychiatry professor, and mental health expert Maria Yellow Horse Brave Heart — describes the collective emotional and psychological injury over a lifespan and across generations, resulting from the cataclysmic history of genocide. Historical trauma is the legacy of numerous traumatic events a community experiences over generations and encompasses the psychological and social responses to such events.[4] Over successive generations, American Indian people have experienced traumatic assaults that have had enduring consequences for families and communities. These assaults include forced removal of children through Indian boarding school policies and prohibition of spiritual and cultural practices. Historical trauma has become increasingly important in considerations of wellness among American Indian communities.

The Historic Trauma Transmission model of study describes possible social and psychological manifestations of historical trauma. According to the model, there is no single historical trauma response. Rather, there are different social disorders with respective clusters of symptoms such as post-traumatic stress disorder, dissociative disorders, and maladaptive social patterns (suicide, domestic violence, sexual abuse, and interpersonal maladjustment). Historical trauma disrupts adaptive social and cultural patterns and transforms them into maladaptive ones that manifest themselves in symptoms, causing deep breakdowns in social functioning that may last for years, decades, or even generations.[5]

Historical Unresolved Grief Theory describes the grief resulting from the historical trauma of genocide, grief that has not been expressed, acknowledged, and resolved. Like trauma, it can span across generations. When we look at multi-generational trauma, and how it has been passed on from generation to generation, virtually every US tribe has its own stories of attempted genocide, warfare, relocations, and boarding school trauma.

***

On March 3, 1819, the US Congress passed an Act to provide education "for the purpose of providing against further decline and final extinction of the Indian tribes . . . to instruct them in the mode of agriculture suited

---

[4] See Brave Heart, Josephine Chase, et al., "Historical Trauma among Indigenous Peoples of the Americas: Concepts, Research, and Clinical Considerations," *Journal of Psychoactive Drugs* 43 (4: 2011): 282–90; Les Whitbeck, G. Adams, et al., "Conceptualizing and Measuring Historical Trauma among American Indian People," *American Journal of Community Psychology* 33 (3-4: 2004): 119–30.
[5] The Aboriginal Healing Foundation Research Series, 2004, www.ahf.ca/publications/research-series.

to their situation, and for teaching their children in reading, writing and arithmetic."[6] The $10,000 appropriation was commonly known as the Civilization Fund. The federal government allowed day schools and mission schools run by churches and missionary societies to be located on the reservations they served. Assimilationists of the time viewed this as a disadvantage, as the students remained in their home communities under the influence of parents and tribal elders and often went "back to the blanket," sloughing off "civilized" habits in favor of maintaining tribal traditions and language.

President Ulysses S. Grant announced his Indian Peace Policy in his first inaugural address on March 4, 1869, declaring, "The proper treatment of the original occupants of this land, the Indians, is one deserving of careful study. I will favor any course toward them which tends to their civilization and ultimate citizenship."[7] His policy allowed religious denominations to undertake the work of civilizing the Indians. The Bureau of Catholic Indian Missions, created in 1874, also established boarding schools on and off reservations.

Boarding schools physically separated children in the formative years of their lives from the influence of family and tribe.[8] Imposed upon American Indian children was a Eurocentric educational system, based on an Anglo-conformist assimilationist approach. As historian David W. Adams states, "The word was civilization . . . Indians . . . were savages." The term, civilization, "served as a legitimizing rationale for the hegemonic relationship that had come to characterize Indian-white relations."[9] Carl Schurz, former Commissioner of Indian Affairs, concluded in 1881 that Indians were confronted with "this stern alternative: extermination or civilization."[10]

In March 1891, Congress authorized the Commissioner of Indian Affairs "to make and enforce by proper means such rules and regulations as will secure the attendance of Indian children of suitable age and health at school established and maintained for their benefit."[11] Two years lat-

[6] Civilization Fund Act, 1819, Ch. 85 § 1.3 Stat. 516.
[7] Ulysses S. Grant, Inauguration Day Speech, 4 March 1869.
[8] See Adams, *Education for Extinction*; Lomawaima, *They Called It a Prairie Light: The Story of Chilocco Indian School* (Lincoln: University of Nebraska Press, 1994); Child, *Boarding School Seasons*; Margaret Archuleta, Child, and Lomawaima, eds., *Away from Home: American Indian Boarding School Experiences, 1879–2000* (Phoenix: Heard Museum, 2000); Clifford Trafzer, Jean Keller, and Lorene Sisquoc, eds., *Boarding School Blues: Revisiting American Indian Educational Experiences* (Lincoln: University of Nebraska Press, 2006); Michael Cooper, *Indian School: Teaching the White Man's Way* (New York: Clarion Books, 1999); Esther Horne and Sally McBeth, *Essie's Story: The Life and Legacy of a Shoshone Teacher* (Lincoln: University of Nebraska Press, 1998).
[9] Adams, *Education for Extinction*, p. 12.
[10] Carl Schurz, "Present Aspect of the Indian Problem," *North American Review* 258 (4): 7.
[11] Statutes at Large of the United States of America, 1891, p. 1014 (found in Adams, *Education for Extinction*).

er, Congress authorized the Indian Office to "Withhold rations, clothing and other annuities from Indian parents or guardians who refuse or neglect to send and keep their children in some school a reasonable portion of each year."[12]

***

Captain Richard H. Pratt's boarding school experiment began in the late nineteenth century after the Arapaho, Cheyenne, Comanche, and Kiowa prisoners incarcerated at Fort Marion in Saint Augustine, Florida, became subject to Pratt's newly devised civilization program. Pratt's program of half days in the classroom and half days spent at some form of manual labor soon became standard boarding school curriculum. A staunch nineteenth-century assimilationist, Pratt's position differed slightly from the popular slogan in the west that held that the only good Indian was a dead one. "In a sense," he said, "I agree with the sentiment, but only in this: that all the Indian there is in the race should be dead. Kill the Indian in him, and save the man."[13] Pratt believed the solution to the perceived problem of students reverting "back to the blanket" was to remove Indian children from their homes to off-reservation boarding schools, ensuring they would be "thoroughly Christianized, individualized, and republicanized."[14] Pratt was allowed to found a school in 1879 at the site of unused cavalry barracks at Carlisle, Pennsylvania. He organized his school along rigid military lines, including harsh disciplinary tactics. The years between 1874 and 1920 are important to the history of American Indian education because of the period's dramatic effect on Indian children across the United States and, in turn, the tribal cultures they came from. Historian Jeffrey Hamley explains,

> During this time-span, boarding school education for Indians
> was conceived, inaugurated and developed into a large-scale and
> complex system of schooling unrivalled in American education for
> what it attempted to accomplish—the destruction of tribal cultures
> as a means to assimilate Indians into the lower levels of American
> society.[15]

***

---

[12] Statutes at Large, p. 635.
[13] Richard Pratt, Official Report of the Nineteenth Annual Conference of Charities and Correction, 1892, p. 46.
[14] Adams, *Education for Extinction*, p. 335.
[15] Jeffrey Hamley, "Cultural Genocide in the Classroom: A History of the Federal Boarding School Movement in American Indian Education, 1875–1920" (PhD diss., Harvard University, 1994), p. 15.

By 1887, about 14,300 American Indian children were enrolled in 227 schools run by the Bureau of Indian Affairs or by religious groups.[16] Rations, annuities, and other goods were withheld from parents and guardians who refused to send children to school after the compulsory attendance law for American Indians was passed by Congress in 1891.

Indian boarding schools, or industrial schools, prepared boys for manual labor or farming and prepared girls for domestic work. The schools also extensively utilized Pratt's Outing program, where boarding schools kept students for the summer, sending the children to white family homes in nearby towns to be further schooled in domestic chores. Rather than sending students home during summers, they were involuntarily leased out to white homes as menial labor during the summer months.[17]

Additionally, government expenditures for boarding schools were always small, and the schools exploited the free labor of Indian children in order to function. Due to overcrowding in these schools, tuberculosis, trachoma, and other contagious diseases flourished. Historian David Adams states that "epidemics of tuberculosis, trachoma, measles, pneumonia, mumps and influenza regularly swept through overcrowded dormitories, taking a terrible toll on the bodies and spirits of the stricken . . . thus, disease and death were also aspects of the boarding school experience."[18] The boarding school, whether on or off the reservation, became the institutional manifestation of the government's determination to completely restructure the Indians' minds and personalities. Boarding schools were established for the sole purpose of severing the Indian child's physical, cultural, and spiritual connection to his tribe.

There is no definitive list of US boarding schools. My decade-long search for American Indian boarding schools currently lists three hundred sixty-five on and off reservation boarding schools that were located in twenty-nine states. An example of the challenges faced in this research is a question I had regarding Catholic boarding schools. No one had ever asked the Catholic Bureau how many on- and off-reservation boarding schools they operated. More research needs to be done on the number and names of other Christian denomination boarding schools. In 1872, the Board of

[16] J. R. Feagin and C. B. Feagin, *Racial and Ethnic Relations*, 7th Edition (Prentice Hall, 2002).
[17] See Andrea Smith, *Conquest: Sexual Violence and American Indian Genocide* (Cambridge: South End Press, 2005).
[18] Adams, *Education for Extinction*, pp. 124–25.

Indian Commissioners allotted seventy-three Indian agencies to the Methodists, Orthodox Friends, Hicksite Friends Reformed Dutch, Presbyterians, Episcopalians, Baptists, Congregationalists, Unitarians, and Lutherans.

I present my research on boarding schools to non-Native audiences of educators and students at schools and universities throughout the Northern Plains. With few exceptions, the majority of the attendees have never heard of American Indian boarding schools, perhaps a reflection of a colonial mindset of selectively forgetting this chapter in US history.

***

Five major themes emerged from this qualitative interview study. First, the survivors experienced loss, which can be subdivided into five sub-elements: loss of identity, language, culture, ceremonies, and tradition; loss of self-esteem; loneliness due to loss of parents and extended family; feeling of abandonment by parents; and feeling lost and out of place when they returned home. Second, survivors attending boarding school experienced abuse, subdivided into corporal punishment and forced child labor; the Outing program; hunger/malnourishment; and sexual and mental abuse. Third, survivors experienced unresolved grief, mental health issues, relationship issues, and alcohol abuse. Fourth, survivors expressed that they felt they had an inferior education at the boarding schools they attended. Fifth, survivors expressed ways for community and personal healing such as a government apology, returning to tribal spirituality practices, forgiveness, and therapy.

Fundamental human rights of American Indian children were violated in boarding schools as documented by this study. What remains poignant to me is the resounding silence the survivors have maintained throughout their lives regarding their boarding school experiences. Whether positive or abusive, they have refused to — or were unable to — talk to their parents, siblings, or their children. The stories told here are laden with sorrow, pain, and lasting trauma. The majority of survivors in this study had either never spoken of their boarding school experiences or had only told spouses. Nearly all had been sexually abused, and many lived in silence and shame, telling no one. They stated, "I have to live with these memories; I don't want to pass them on to my children and grandchildren." One survivor whispered to me about being sexually abused by a priest: "I haven't told anyone; I don't know why I'm telling you." I told her, "I know why. You are telling me because I asked." No one had ever asked them to talk about the boarding school experiences.

Several survivors stated they had a good time at the boarding school they attended. I saw a pattern in their stories in that they saw horrific beatings and disciplinary actions, so they resolved to behave and thus were treated differently by nuns, priests, or school officials. Most survivors also didn't understand that boarding school policy was one of forced assimilation and forced Christianity and that they were being trained only in labor trades, although many, like my father who learned carpentry skills, were able to support their family.

Even though they were asked about positive experiences, favorite teachers or mentors, and friendships, these interviewees related a majority of negative experiences. These boarding school survivors' stories reflect the traumatic legacy of the US government's policy of accelerated forced assimilation into white culture. The survivors were treated as undeserving of respect and dignity as children, as human beings, and as members of an ethnic group.

Most boarding school survivors in this study attended, or were sent to, boarding schools hundreds of miles away from their home reservation. At these schools they experienced severe beatings or they witnessed the beatings of fellow students by staff, were caused mental and emotional harm, were sexually abused or witnessed sexual abuse, were forced to do manual labor, were hungry, and they experienced the forced loss of language, culture, tribal traditions, and spirituality. These boarding school survivors continue to experience emotional trauma. They all believe they had a poor education at boarding schools they attended.

The survivors have expressed that an individual way for each to heal their *soul wound*, both personally and as tribes, would be through either a governmental apology, therapy, or a return to American Indian spirituality, including language and ceremonies.[19] Their stories are told with a look to the future, a future filled with American Indian traditions, language, culture, and most importantly, forgiveness. Although boarding school experiences have taken a toll on their individual mental health and also on the healthy function of their families, these survivors have demonstrated enormous resilience in light of their personal experiences and their tribal history.

---

[19] See Eduardo Duran, Bonnie Duran, Brave Heart, Susan Yellow Horse-Davis, "Healing the American Soul Wound," *International Handbook of Multigenerational Legacies of Trauma*, ed. Yael Danieli (New York: Plenum Press, 1998) and Andrea Smith, *Soul Wound: The Legacy of Native American Schools*, Amnesty Now, Summer, pp. 14–17, http://www.manataka.org/page2290.html.

***

It has taken extraordinary courage for these boarding school survivors to come forward to speak about the abuse they suffered. Increasingly, the damage from boarding school abuse, loneliness, and lack of love and lack of parenting is being seen as a major factor in ills that plague tribes today, passing from one generation to the next and manifesting in high rates of poverty, substance abuse, domestic violence, depression, and suicide.[20] We look to our Canadian First Nation relatives for models of healing from boarding school trauma and historical trauma. The Aboriginal Healing Foundation (AHF) report, "Historic Trauma and Aboriginal Healing," prepared in 2004 by Cynthia Wesley-Esquimaux and Magdalena Smolewski, proposes a new model of historic trauma transmission "to create a better understanding of the actiology of social and cultural diffusion that devastated Aboriginal communities for so many years."[21] The AHF research has shown that it takes

> approximately ten years of continuous healing efforts before a community is securely established in healing from boarding school trauma. Impacts of programs reports positive improved family relationships, increased self-esteem and pride, achievement of higher education and employment; to preventions of suicides. Community impacts are growth in social capital indicators such as volunteerism, informal caring networks, and cultural events. One of the notable impacts reported by case study communities is that the "silence and shame surrounding boarding school abuses are being broken, creating the climate for ongoing healing."[22]

In Roderick McCormick's study, First Nations people utilized several healing modalities to heal their communities and themselves.[23] These modalities included exercise and the expression of emotion to restore balance and establishing social connections to create inter-connectedness between family, community, culture, and nature. McCormick concludes that three aspects—balance, inter-connectedness and intra-connectedness, and transcendence—are the most important means and ends of the healing process. For American Indian people, the definition of health evolved around the

---

[20] Donald Warne and Denise K. Lajimodiere, "American Indian Health Disparities: Psychosocial Influences," *Social and Personality Psychology Compass* 10: 1–13.
[21] Cynthia C. Wesley-Esquimaux and Magdalena Smolewski, *Historic Trauma and Aboriginal Healing* (Ottowa: Aboriginal Healing Foundation, 2004), p. 65.
[22] Ibid., p. 4.
[23] Roderick McCormick, "Culturally Appropriate Means and Ends of Counseling as Described by the First Nations People of British Columbia," *International Journal for the Advancement of Counselling* 18 (3: 995–1996).

whole being of each person; the physical, emotional, mental, and spiritual aspects of a person being in balance and harmony with each other as well as with the environment and other beings. Many American Indian counseling programs already use the concept of inter-connectedness in their initiatives, using the symbolism of the Medicine Wheel or the Healing Circle that integrate different elements of American Indian philosophy of life. Also important to community healing is partnerships with elders' groups, shelters and assault centers, youth organizations, police, addiction services, social services, education, and health, with the last two being the most needful of utilized resources.

The Canadian healing model is a holistic, community-based approach that emphasizes training and capacity building in healing, with reliance not only on professional healers, but healers with lived experience and cultural knowledge. Maria Yellow Horse Brave Heart developed a Lakota grief experience questionnaire and the semantic differential, as well as a self-reported evaluation instrument and a follow-up questionnaire.[24] The Aboriginal Healing Foundation Research Series states,

> Based on this assessment, an experimental curriculum intervention has been delivered to a group of ten Lakota parents and two Lakota parent facilitators on a Lakota reservation. Similar healing modalities can be devised and successfully implemented to help American Indian people negotiate and successfully practice their social and cultural knowledge in a contemporary world, and use their disastrous experience of de-population and forced assimilation to their benefit.[25]

***

According to the 2009 Evaluation of Community-Based Healing Initiatives Supported through the Aboriginal Healing Foundation final report,

> The majority of respondents felt that the Government's formal apology had had a significant impact at the personal, community and national level. For some Survivors, this was the recognition and acknowledgement of their suffering that they had been awaiting for a long time; some reported that the heightened awareness caused by the Apology made them feel at last entitled to come forward for healing; Survivors said the government Apology in a sense gave public

---

[24] Brave Heart and Lemyra M. DeBruyn, "The American Indian Holocaust: Healing Historical Unresolved Grief," *National Center for American Indian and Alaska Native Research* 8 (2: 1998): 56–78.
[25] The Aboriginal Healing Foundation Research Series, 2004, p. 77.

authenticity to the private pain and shame many had endured for most of their lives.[26]

In like manner, the US Congress passed Senate Joint Resolution 14 in 2009, acknowledging "a long history of official depredations and ill-conceived policies by the Federal Government regarding Indian tribes." Resolution 14 further recommends that an apology be made "to all Native peoples on behalf of the United States." The resolution, titled Resolution of Apology to the Native Peoples of the United States, was incorporated into the Defense Appropriations Act of 2010 where it became buried in Title VIII, Section 8113. Although the resolution "urges the President to acknowledge the wrongs of the United States against Indian tribes in the history of the US in order to bring healing to this land," no apology has occurred. As a result, there is to date no meaningful apology from either Congress or any president.

***

Stringing Rosaries provides a vehicle for sixteen boarding school survivors to tell their story. The stories told here are filled with sorrow, pain, and lasting trauma. Yet they are stories told with a look to the future, a future filled with American Indian traditions, language, culture, and most importantly, forgiveness. These survivors have demonstrated enormous resilience in light of their personal boarding school experiences and their tribal history. These events have taken a toll on their individual mental health and on the healthy function of their families.

Maria Yellow Horse Brave Heart, as described in her 1998 article, "The Return to the Sacred Path: Healing the Historical Trauma Response among the Lakota," has developed historical trauma and unresolved grief interventions among American Indians.[27] These interventions have shown to be effective among a small segment of the population with elevated psychosocial issues. Other studies show the importance of incorporating culturally specific assessments, allowing for traditional healing approaches.[28]

---

[26] Evaluation of Community-Based Healing Initiatives Supported through the Aboriginal Healing Foundation, 2009, p. 42.

[27] Brave Heart, "The Return to the Sacred Path: Healing the Historical Trauma Response among the Lakota," *Smith College Studies in Social Work*, 68 (3): 287–305.

[28] See, Fisher & Ball, 2002; Strickland, Walsh & Cooper, 2006; Glen McCabe, "The Healing Path: A Culture and Community-Derived Indigenous Therapy Model," *Psychotherapy: Theory, Research, Practice, Training*, 44 (2: 2007): 148–60.

To paraphrase the words of Paula Gunn Allen in her 1986 publication, *The Sacred Hoop: Recovering the Feminine in American Indian Traditions*, the next step will be to change American Indian people's social and cultural status from an isolated, dispossessed victimhood to one of incorporation into the fabric of society as knowledgeable, empowered, and belonging equals. "In the transformation from one state to another," Gunn Allen notes, "the prior state or condition must cease to exist. It must die."[29] As individuals, American Indians can continue the healing process through group and family therapy as well as by attending to their own spiritual development. Further, American Indian tribes will need to facilitate communal grief rituals, incorporating traditional practices.

***

There is still work to be done to increase our understanding of how current life stressors and traumatic events are experienced within the context of boarding school trauma. Scholars of trauma are committed to developing effective treatments for current and historical trauma. Future scholarship might directly investigate resilience and healing around the continuum of boarding school trauma in American Indian communities. Scholars should give consideration to the occurrence of intergenerational trauma, unresolved grieving, post-traumatic stress disorder, and their effects among boarding school survivors and their descendants living today.

At conferences, gatherings, and trainings across the United States, current research and production of historical materials must promote the awareness and understanding of the needs and issues surrounding boarding school trauma and its legacy. There are thousands more boarding school survivors that need to be interviewed and asked about their experiences, good or bad. The survivors I interviewed have told me they want the world to know what happened to them. *Stringing Rosaries* provides a means for these survivors to tell their stories in their own voices, as I promised them.

---

[29] Paula Gunn Allen, *The Sacred Hoop: Recovering the Feminine in American Indian Traditions* (Boston: Beacon Press, 1986), pp. 79–80.

PART II:

In their own voices.

The silence is broken.

Instruction by Father Prantauer, SD. *Marquette Archives.*

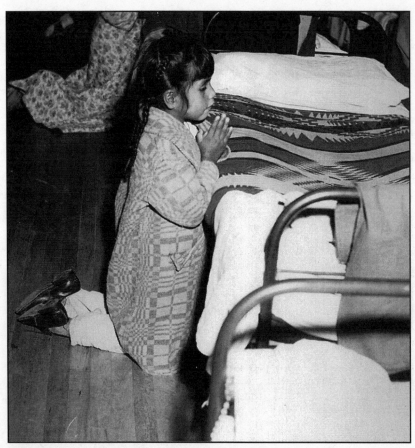

Young girl praying. *Bureau of Catholic Indian Missions.*

THE PRIEST

Josephine (born 1946, pseudonym), sixty-three, was living in Minneapolis at the time of her interview. She was born on the Turtle Mountain Indian Reservation in north central North Dakota. Her first home was a log cabin with a mud, or gumbo, floor, packed hard. She is one of five siblings born to Native parents from the same tribe. Her father died when she was around four years old, and she has little memory of him. Her mother died in 1996. Both of her parents attended boarding schools at Chamberlain, South Dakota, and Wahpeton, North Dakota. Josephine is married with four children. She has a tenth-grade education. She spent eight years at St. Joseph's Indian Boarding School, Chamberlain, and two years in the public school at Dunseith, North Dakota. Josephine grew up hearing the Chippewa language but does not speak it. She has worked in the potato fields and as a waitress. We interviewed in a quiet room, separate and away from her family.

When I was little, there was a lot of drinking and we used to hide in the woods. My family struggled financially and I was often hungry. Half the time I was starving to death, never anything to eat at home. I remember my biggest meal was fried berries and sometimes gallette with lard.[30] We lived in a log cabin, had to mow more grass on the roof than we did in the yard! We didn't have to sweep the floor because it was a dirt floor, it was packed hard.

I would come home in the summer months but my mom was usually not around, so I stayed with an aunt instead. My aunt would tie us to the tree and treat us the way she was treated at boarding school. I decided to stay at boarding school throughout the year after that. I went to Chamberlain boarding school in South Dakota, a Catholic-run school. I was five years old. The first day I couldn't have been there more than half an hour and already one kid had drowned, by the lake. I went over there and he was blue; they got us out of there and told us to get in the dorms and stay there.

---

[30] Gallette is a type of bread, similar to a large biscuit. Also called bannock bread.

Then they immediately separated me from my brother. I saw him once in a great while, like on Christmas.

We had to march everywhere. It was something that you had to do. After a while it comes natural. They were very strict and very disciplined and they wanted everything their way, and if they didn't get it you got disciplined. In the morning we'd get up early, brush our teeth, fix our bed — no matter how small you were you fixed your bed, got yourself together. We went to church, then we went and ate breakfast. Usually it was cereal or oatmeal and coffee. Yeah, I think they'd give us coffee because we never had nap times. It was a boarding school, so they didn't want you to mess up the beds during the day, keep giving you coffee to keep you active so you didn't have to sleep until night-time.

We went to lunch, and then had a little Mass, a little prayer session in the afternoon. And then at night we'd have supper and went to church. I was constantly kneeling and my knees are sore, I mean, I've had a lot of problems with my knees since. I don't remember any games I played. I did a lot of praying. I don't remember a favorite subject or happy memory. Nothing was fun.

They'd make you kneel on a broomstick if you were bad. Oh God, that hurt. And you better not move because they'd come over and pull your hair or slap you in the face. Sometimes me and my sister — we were really small — and there was a big locker. They'd stick us up on top of the locker so we couldn't get down, couldn't go no place. We were being punished. If we'd have fallen off the locker we'd get hurt. The nuns put us up there until they came back, and we didn't dare move because it was too high. Yeah, those nuns were mean. They'd just pull your hair, slap you in the face, do whatever they wanted to, and push you, tell you to put your hands palms down on the table and [they would] hit [them] with the sharp edge of a ruler, and beat you with a belt across your bare butt and your back, and — they were *mean*.

I got put in a closet, dark, no lights, just pails, brooms, and mops. I don't remember why or for how long. When you're small everything seems like forever. If you peed your pants the nuns made sure that all the kids were around you so they could tell them what you had done so the kids would laugh at you.

There was a nun, Sister Naomi, I remember because she had one blue eye and one brown eye and red hair. I caught her one time when she was brushing her hair. I was so small I didn't know I wasn't supposed to go in her private bedroom. I opened up the door and she was brushing her long red hair. She beat me for that with a razor strap.

There was a girl; she had to be nine or ten years old. She was really sick and anytime she'd wet her bed, the nuns would rub her face in it, and she would be crying and screaming. They had her casket right down in the main entryway and I could see the casket when I walked up stairs. They buried her there. Why did they have her funeral there? How come her parents didn't take her or anything? She was really nice and she used to cry all the time. I think that's how she died because they didn't give her the care she needed and they abused her so much. After seeing that I just had to concentrate on me. Even now, I'm, you know, I'll take care of me.

I remember that we had to clean the bathrooms with tooth brushes and get on our hands and knees. Things weren't round, they were square, and you better not leave anything in the corners. I never got enough to eat. I remember the dry buns. We got packages from home but the nuns used to go through it I guess; I never got it.

I wore a uniform — a little skirt and a white blouse. You had to keep your own stuff, and usually they had numbers on everything so when they washed it everything was put in your locker. The dorm was just so open, it was beds one right after another. It wasn't private rooms; [the] beds were very close together. I remember [some] people having measles, and then everybody did. And then they would have lice, and we'd have to take care of each other. That was an ongoing thing. The nuns put kerosene on our heads and put plastic bags on there. My scalp used to burn. Then after about twenty minutes or so, they'd wash it off. They cut my hair. I had really long hair. I'm glad they cut it because the nuns used to pull it all the time.

I remember having to serve the priest wine, but never in the wine hall. I remember being brought to the priest's room, but I never really remembered leaving. You know, I'd wake up, and how did—I never really thought about it, but you know, now that I think about it, what did they do? Get me drunk? Well, why would they want a bunch of young girls serving them wine anyway? I was six years old. I had a lot of problems "down there," you know? Then the priest—not a nun—would take me to the doctor, drive me there in his car. I don't know, I was wondering because a lot of times I think that stuff had to do with, like when, I, with me and my husband and stuff, you know, don't touch me, you know, I don't really like hugs and stuff, people holding me.

I was too scared to try to run away. Where would I go? I was little. If you got caught they used to shave your head and put overalls on you, shave the girls' heads. When I finally returned home I felt like I was just taking up space, like I was in the way.

I think about the time I spent in boarding school all the time; it's not something you forget. I can remember all the bad things that happened. To this day as old as I am, it still hurts. It's something that you don't forget. The memories of the sexual abuse are deep inside of me. It wasn't like it happened just once; it was almost every day. That's why I try to make my life as good as I can. That's why I don't want anybody interfering in my life; I do things I want to do within the law. I don't drink, I don't smoke, I don't swear. I never abused my kids; I protected them with my life, trust me, in school and when they were at home.

As far as therapy, I don't think I want to remember because I think it would hurt too much. If I start to remember things that happened when I was small I try to do something else and try to get it out of my head. I kind of deal with it in my own way. I do other things every time I think of something. I've got my kids and grandkids around me, so I usually do something with them and it goes away. My kids always came first; I don't care if I went bankrupt, I made sure they had the best of everything, and my grandkids, they get everything.

When I retired I had a major heart attack and I have diabetes. Today I go to casino once in a while. I have no patience for anything. I don't read, takes up too much of my time. I used to draw, but I don't have any patience for that either. I can't sit for long periods of time. I'm not too big on just laying around. I want to do stuff. I like to get out, I don't care if I got a dime, and I want to go looking to see what's out there. I drive all over the place, any place and every place. I don't really have friends, I don't have time. I have to wrap myself around my kids and grandkids, make sure that they have everything I didn't have. I made sure they weren't abused.

I had a nervous breakdown last year because of my boarding school and childhood experiences. I was in the psychiatric hospital for five weeks. I never told the doctors about the priests sexually abusing me. I was too ashamed. What would they think about me because I'm Indian? I should have stopped that priest.

In eighth grade I was pulled out of Chamberlain to work for my mother. I'd been working in fields ever since I was young, eight or seven years old. Every fall we'd go to the valley and pick potatoes. You wake up and you picked from the time it got light in the morning until it got dark. My mom was alcoholic and she was just greedy. I remember getting a whole hundred twenty-five dollars and she took it all. When I was fourteen my mother slapped me and told me to get out, handing me a quarter. My sister sent me twenty-five dollars. The train ticket cost twenty dollars. I moved to Minneapolis and worked as a waitress, passing for sixteen. I never went back to the reservation to this day.

I told my husband about what happened to me; he's not really sympathetic because he's a veteran of the Vietnam War. He went through a lot in the war. He has three Purple Hearts, so he almost died.

I'd like to see a lawsuit against the boarding school in the United States, but then how would I go about it? It's my word against theirs, and me taking on Chamberlain, South Dakota, is like me taking on the government.

Lined up for drinks at the Preventorium, Fort Totten Indian Boarding School, ND. *National Archives at Kansas City.*

Girls setting tables in dining hall, St. Francis Mission, SD.
Marquette Archives.

POSTUM COFFEE

It became difficult to hear Julia (b. 1939, pseudonym) over the noise of the busy restaurant she chose to meet at. She then suggested we move to her daughter's home nearby, a spacious late model house. As we settled on the couch, Julia's daughter came home. After a brief introduction, she moved to the kitchen and turned on a radio.

At this point in the interview, I asked Julia about sexual abuse. She leaned in close to me and began to speak in a nearly inaudible whisper. Motioning toward her daughter, she said she did not want her daughter to hear or to ever know that she was sexually abused at the school. Julia did not want a copy of her interview transcript mailed to her for review or to keep as a document of her boarding school interview.

Julia was seventy years old at the time of our interview. She was born on the Turtle Mountain Indian Reservation, Belcourt, North Dakota. Her parents were patients at the San Haven tuberculosis sanatorium located in Dunseith, North Dakota, when they met. Her mother had TB when Julia was born. Julia attended the Chamberlain, South Dakota, Catholic boarding school from ages five to ten. Both of her parents are from Turtle Mountain. English is Julia's second language; her first language is a mixture of Cree, Chippewa, and French, known as Michif.

When I was born, I weighed less than a pound, and everyone thought I was dead. My aunt fixed up a shoebox and put me in there. They were going to bury me, and my aunt said I started blinking my eyes. I still keep blinking my eyes hard to this day to remind myself I'm alive! After I was born my mother was sent back to the sanatorium, and I went to live with my grandparents. My parents didn't marry, and my father moved to the West Coast.

I spent my early years on my grandparents' farm living in a one-room home. I thought my grandparents were my parents. There were four beds, and then there was our bed, a big huge bed and we all slept in that one big bed. We had a wood-burning stove, no electricity, just kerosene lamps, and no running water—yeah, you ran after it! We had a well, and Grandma would make homemade butter. She would put that butter and eggs in a pail and drop them way down in the water so it would keep nice and cool in the summertime. I loved playing in the hills, and we played hide and seek in the nearby church cemetery. My uncles would go out and shoot birds and I and my sister would clean the birds and we'd eat them; sometimes that's all we had to eat. We had a garden, and Grandma would can stuff and put it down in the cellar for wintertime. My grandfather drank. He'd go to town and he'd buy booze and the next thing you know it would be one cow gone, two cows gone, the horses would be gone, pigs would be gone, until all we had left was chickens.

When I was five years old, I was put on a bus that took me to St. Joseph's Catholic Boarding School in Chamberlain, South Dakota. When I first saw the place it was so big—not used to seeing big buildings like that. It looked so scary, and the nuns were so mean, yelling at us, "Get off the bus, get off the bus!" I didn't speak English very well, so we'd look at each other, because we didn't know what she was talking about, you know? They grabbed us by the arm and dragged us off the bus, and I cried, "No, no we want to go back home!" They lined us up and they asked what our grandparents' names were, so I said Kookum and Mooshum, and the nun hit me over the head with her hand, knocked me to the floor. She said, "You're not going to be talking that way by the time you leave here! You're gonna be talking English!" Course we didn't know what they were talking about then, we didn't understand, but we eventually learned. They'd take us in a room and tell us, "You can't talk that language anymore, this is what you have to do; this is how you pronounce *mother* and *father*." They wouldn't let us go to bed until we learned at least one or two English words.

I don't recall having my hair cut or cleaned for lice, but shortly [after] other kids came the nuns would give us two or three girls, and we had to use kerosene to clean their heads with these really fine combs. I was only five years old! The nun would come over to check the head: "No, you didn't do this clean, get that hair clean or you're not going to bed 'til you get that done!"

We had to wear a uniform, but I remember seeing a big semi come in to the school with clothes and toys, new and used. They had people coming from town and they'd sell all that stuff. We had to help sort it out. I'd say, "Oh, look at this nice stuff," and the nuns would say, "Oh, no, no, that's not for you." Soon all these cars would come and people would go in and take the stuff away, pay the nuns. Brand new toys and all! I don't know what they did with that money.

We always had shoes, not always the best, and thin coats, sometimes we'd just have sweaters. The school had an outhouse up the hill; sometimes we had to go out there in the wintertime.

In the dorm there was about enough room for you to walk through. There was a bed here, and a bed here, and you had a hard time squeezing into your bed. A lot of the girls cried all the time. I wanted to go home, because I loved my grandparents. I thought they were my mother and dad. We just thought our folks deserted us.

We made our beds every morning. Our bed[sheet]s had to have [tightly folded] corners; if they didn't they'd take everything and throw it and you'd have to redo your bed. We had to sweep the bedroom, clean up the showers, clean the classrooms, desks, and wipe the doors down, the windows. Seems like we were always working. The only time we got a little bit of time off was on Sundays. We'd go outside and play on Sundays.

My favorite subjects in school [were] math and geography. There was actually a nun that was real nice to my older sister. She'd come and get us at night out of bed and take us down to a room where there was a piano, and she'd play piano for us. She'd take her habit off and she'd let my sister comb her long brown hair. One of the priests got her pregnant, and she had to leave. We all just cried and cried. The other nuns were mean. If anyone got into trouble, they would have to put their nose on a broomstick handle and hold it against the wall. Didn't dare let it fall, that's how mean they were. They'd take them rulers and hit you on your knuckles; sometimes your hands would just bleed. I had to sleep with a girl because we didn't have enough beds. She wet the bed and the nun blamed it on me, and I got a whipping and she rubbed my nose in that urine. I heard from the boys that the brothers were mean to them, got beat up every day.[31] They had a paddle and [the brothers would] make them pull their pants down and just beat them until they were red. They had to work at the barn with the animals, cows, horses, pigs, and chickens. One priest had a strap, and he'd sharpen knives with it. He'd take that thing, and when the boys were bad, he'd beat them. He was so mean.

For breakfast they'd put a box of cereal on the table, and there was like ten people and they all had to share that cereal, and if there wasn't enough, whoever got the end of the box there was nothing there, they didn't get nothing. If the pitcher of milk came around and it came to you and there

---

[31] Catholic "brothers" commit themselves to following Christ in Consecrated life of the Church, usually by the vows of poverty, celibacy, and obedience. They are considered laymen in the sense of not being ordained.

was no milk you didn't get milk; you ate your cereal dry. I was hungry all the time. We had sandwiches for dinner, but that's all we had; we never had anything else. For supper we'd have a potato and maybe some meat, and more coffee. Coffee, every day we had coffee—Postum coffee, had it for breakfast, lunch, and you had it for supper.[32]

Fresh vegetables! Are you kidding? The priests did. They had fresh vegetables and fruit every day. We had our great big room where we sat and ate, and right next to it was the priests' room where they ate. They had fresh fruit and fresh vegetables. Sometimes I had to go take food in there. Their tables were . . . Oh! Oh! . . . you should see their tables! It was so fancy—fancy plates and dishes and coffee cups—and Oh my God, the food! We used to stand there and look at it. I would steal food whenever I could.

One time a nun said, "You have to help me in here. We got to cook some eggs for the priests." I told her I was too tiny to cook. She said, "I don't care how tiny you are, you're going to help me." I picked up an egg and accidently broke it. She grabbed me by the back of my neck, opened the door, and threw me down in the cellar. She yelled, "You're staying down there until you can behave yourself." All I did was crack a stupid egg. She threw me down in the pantry; for three days I stayed down there. I was only five years old. She locked the door so I couldn't get out. It was dark in there. At first I cried and cried because I tried to get out and she wouldn't let me out. It was chilly and I didn't have a blanket, just the clothes I had on. I slept on top of the potatoes since the cans or the floor was too cold. Finally, some girls came down to put bread away, and they said, "What are you doing down here?" I was so weak, I got put into the infirmary, and then the nuns came once a day and brought me food until I got my strength back. After a while, I started getting kind of aggressive and the nun would throw me down in the pantry. So after the third or fourth time I started talking to myself, "Yeah, I guess I'm stupid," and then after a while I thought, "Hmmm." I found a can opener. So what I'd do? I'd get them cans and I'd open them up and I started eating. I thought, boy, this girl isn't going to starve any more. There was a window way up high and I'd take these cans, and I'd have a hard time lifting them, but I got them so I had a stairway up to that window. I could see legs go by. What the heck! So I hollered out, and there was boys. I said, "Hey, hey, you guys want to do something for me? I'm down here, and I've been locked down here for a couple, three

---

[32] Postum is a powdered roasted-grain beverage once popular as a coffee substitute. The caffeine-free beverage was created by the Postum Cereal Company founder C. W. Post in 1895 and marketed as a healthful alternative to coffee.

days. I can't get out. I peed and crapped in a can." I put it up there and the boys hauled it away. I'd give them fruit and stuff. I'd give them bread, not too much though. These were the boys the priests would beat, so when I gave them boys that food, oh, they were really thankful. Sometimes the nun that locked me in the pantry would let me out, saying, "Oh, I forgot you."

I was molested by the priests. I don't like to talk about it. It was two different priests. Sometimes one would come get me out of my bed. Or, if we were in the gym to watch movies, one of them would come after me, because no one played with me. I was the littlest one in the school. They'd call me out of school and the nun would say, "Father wants to see you," and I'd say, "No, I don't want to go," and I was told, "You have to go." They'd pull my pants down and fondle me. There was no one I could tell, couldn't tell the nuns.

I still haven't told anyone; I just keep everything to myself. I don't know why I'm talking about it now. Some things you just don't talk about, just don't talk about. I don't want to talk to a therapist. I told you so somebody would know. I often blame myself; I should have been more aggressive. The only time I was happy was one time it was one of the priest's birthday. The nuns put me and this boy in a box, and it was all wrapped up, and put us on stage, and they were singing Happy Birthday to him, and then the nun came and undid the bow and I and the little boy jumped out of the box. We were his birthday present. But that's when it started happening, him molesting me. Sometimes I think about it and I can't sleep at night. And I shouldn't have to think about these things, you know? A lot of times things will come back. Like now that we are talking I remember I'm claustrophobic, you know why? Because when the nun would bring me to the priest's room, another priest would come in and he didn't want that priest to know I was there, [so] he would put me in his closet.

I'm still a Catholic, absolutely. I've raised my kids Catholic. I'm still a strong Catholic. I say the Rosary every day, go to Epiphany. But, even now when I go to church, if a priest comes up to me to shake my hand, I back away, I don't want nothing to do with him.

I think as the years went by when I was at Chamberlain, I got so frustrated, as young as I was. I couldn't tell anybody what was going on, so I got sort of aggressive. So, like when the nuns would do stuff to me I'd fight back. When I was around nine years old, I got so sick and tired of the nuns beating on these kids with their hands bloody and one day I thought, "I've had enough of this crap." So I took that ruler away from that nun and

I hit her with it and I said, "See how you like it," and I chased her around the room and I kept hitting her and hitting her, I was so mad! After that she never touched them kids again in that room.

When I was around ten years old, my mother started having kids and wanted me back home to babysit. Mom and my stepdad would go out drinking two or three weeks at a time, and we'd be left home alone. My sister would watch the babies inside, and I'd go outside and I'd snare rabbits, chop wood. With a lot of drinking in the home, an uncle attempted to molest her, but I beat him with his army boots. When my stepdad was home, I had to go with him deer hunting, carry a gun. I could hardly lift it, I was so tiny and skinny. We picked berries and nuts in the summertime. One summer when I was eleven, we went to pick potatoes in the valley. Ma let me have my own check, so I went to Grafton and I bought me this really cute sweater. I've still got it.

At the reservation school, we would make lard sandwiches with gallette, and take them to school. Oh, God, sometimes I would have deer meat inside and everybody would say, "I want some of that!" In the summer, Grandpa would go and get our commodities.[33] One year we went to get our commodities, and they were giving out this kind of fruit that we didn't have any idea what it was. It was a great big yellow fruit, huge, big as a football. It was a grapefruit. We didn't know how to eat them. My grandma tried cooking them. She tried canning them! She fed them to her pigs; the pig wouldn't eat it!

When I was little, I had to go out there and chop wood and bring it home because my mother and stepdad were out drinking. My sister did all the housework, and I was the "boy"; I had to go outside and do men's work. I had to haul water out of the lake. When my sister decided she's going to wash clothes, I had to run and run back and forth [to haul the water]. To curl your hair we would take them old bed sheets and make strips, and we'd put them in our hair and roll them up and tie a knot. In boarding school, everybody would be running around with rags in their hair.

I left Chamberlain when I was ten and returned to the reservation and went to the government school, or, the "big school," until tenth grade. Then I left the reservation at sixteen and moved to Minneapolis. I said, "I can't live on this reservation anymore." I was so sick of everything that I went through when I was younger, and for as young as I was, I thought like an older person, you know? I met another girl, and we went to Washington

---

[33] Commodities are supplementary food staples distributed monthly by the government.

state for about a year. I lived with my aunt. We picked mint and asparagus, carrots . . . apples, cherries, apricots, then I came back here to Minneapolis. I've worked in a restaurant, a factory, and [I] worked for an insurance company.

I told my husband about being sexually abused at boarding school. He served in the Korean War and survived, so he just tells me all that stuff happened a long time ago and I should just get over it. My sister was older than me but died when she was just fifty years old. I don't know how I lived to be seventy. How come I'm living to be so old?

I have five children and would never have sent any of them to boarding school, absolutely not. My kids couldn't go outside and play for two or three minutes and I was out there making sure I knew where they were all the time.

I don't want my kids or grandkids to ever read about this. I've had to spend my life thinking about it. I don't want anyone in my family to have to think one minute of it.

Shoe-making class, Holy Rosary Mission, SD, 1900.
Bureau of Catholic Indian Missions.

Boys digging trench, St. Joseph's Mission, SD. *Marquette Archives.*

WHITE BEAVER

*To interview Roger White Owl (b. 1953), I traveled from Fargo across
the Dakota plains to the Fort Berthold Indian Reservation in New Town,
North Dakota, where he grew up. Driving into the heart of the Bakken
oil field activity, I was intrigued and fascinated by the numerous oil rigs
dotting the barren landscape. I was also terrified by the huge oil trucks
tailgating me on the narrow road leading from the main freeway to the
reservation.*

*We met in his tribal home, surrounded by beautiful art. Roger has
a degree in social work, but he is also a self-taught, well-known Native
artist.*

*Roger's father was Hidatsa and had a third grade education. He was
also a Hidatsa Code Talker during WWII, serving under General George
S. Patton. Roger's mother was Ojibwe. She attended Stephan Mission,
Catholic Boarding School located on the Crow Creek Reservation in
South Dakota, and completed the eighth grade.*

I wanted to go to school with my older brothers and sisters, and I started
crying because I couldn't go. I was too young. My mother talked to me
saying, "Roger, there are things that you have to learn first before you can
go to school. One of the things you have to learn about is art, or drawing."
I started drawing a painting of a horse hanging on the wall my uncle had
done. I finished my drawing and I took it to my mom, and she said, "Oh,
Roger, what a beautiful cow!" She saw the look on my face and she realized what she had said. She also had the presence of mind to say, "Roger, if
you want people to know what you are drawing then you have to practice
and practice." I did, and now I'm a professional artist. I travel all over the
world with my art.

My dad gave me my work ethic. The things my parents taught me
when I was young about the ways of our people are still with me. I was
taken in by the Old Warrior Society. They said the reason I didn't go to
Vietnam at that time was because I was not to go over there and fight. They
saw in me a long time ago that my war would be here, and that war would
never end. The Society taught me to just watch and learn. I never started

drinking and I never did drugs. All the things I've gone through, like the abuse in boarding school, have been geared towards bringing me to where I am at right now. A lot of people see these abuses as bad things, which they are. The things that happened to me also taught and prepared me to go in the direction that I'm supposed to go.

I would wake up in the winter with snow inside of our kitchen from the holes in the building. I remember my brother climbing up a snowbank and going on top of the house and falling through the roof. I remember the sardine beds. We only had a few beds. All together there was fourteen of us, so we would lay head to toe on the length of one bed. We would be lying sideways; that's why I call it a sardine bed. The youngest ones were always kept in the middle where it was the warmest all the time. The older ones had to be on the outside. It wasn't hard on me. It was a lot of fun because we would do things with the snowbanks and that kind of thing. Actually, we didn't really miss anything as far as material-type things. My dad would make us toys out of shingles that were laying around. Our toys were things like the weeds that were growing. We had our own imagination and we used it, and it didn't cost us anything. My mother went to boarding school and she didn't have any problems there, so she thought it was a good thing for us. My father never did go to boarding school, so he didn't have anything against it.

For one and a half years, I went to St. Joseph's Catholic School in Chamberlain, South Dakota. My two older brothers came with me. My first impression of the school was that it was cold and scary. We got up before the sun came up. We fixed the bed military style with hospital corners, got dressed, went to church, back to the dorm, made sure everything's where it's supposed to be, and then went to eat. Breakfast was oatmeal, and I remember once in a while having eggs, but they always tasted powdery, not real eggs; it was almost like the commodity eggs.

My hair was never cut by the school. My dad was ex-military so he always cut our hair short anyway. I hated it. We called it a hiney because your head was as bare as your hiney! We had kerosene put in our hair. Even though my hair was short they still put kerosene in it. I remember it burning my scalp.

After breakfast, we went to school. We had to march everywhere, like one two, one two. We were done at school about four o'clock. We marched back to the dorm, and then we got ready to go to Mass, again. Lunchtime, too, we went to Mass before we went to lunch. After supper, we had what they called "free time," which was about an hour or two. We could go to the playground where there were swings and some teeter-totters. Mostly what we did was talk to each other because that was one of the chances I got to see my brother. The playground has a hurricane fence around it. I knew I couldn't get out. It was too tall, and then there was barbed wire on top. It was meant to keep you in, that's for sure.

The dorm attendants had their own room, which was like a doctor's room. They had curtains so if they wanted to they could look out and see the whole dorm. Our dorm was like army barracks where you had rows and rows of beds. It was just one big room as a bedroom. I didn't cry, but I heard kids crying at night wanting to go home. We had church early in the morning, in the afternoon, and in the evening before you went to bed again. It was mandatory that you went.

When I was younger, I always wondered why my parents hated me, why they did that to me, sent me there. As I got older, I realized why they did it. They thought they were helping, but they were trusting at the same time. They trusted the school to do what it's supposed to do and not do what it did. So, when they found out what was happening, they jerked us out of there.

I'm one of these people that is very observant, and I watch and learn things from my listening and watching. One of the things that the Old Warrior Society taught me was to just watch and learn, and when I do that I see things for what they really are. So I would see things such as my uncle, my aunt, or my brother, or my sister, or relatives, and all these other adults going and drinking and stuff like that. I would see what would happen to them and their families. I was always against drinking because of that. I knew that if I started myself that I would end up the same way, so I never did start drinking or anything like that and I never did drugs. I guess I could say I never went under the influence of "the man with fire around his ankles" and "man with no head." We have in our ancient stories, creation stories, spirits that were doing bad things to the people. "Fire around the ankles" is the same thing as alcohol or firewater. "Man with no head" is the same thing as a person that's taking drugs. They don't think, because they have no head. It's just the reaction of their bodies; they are reacting to the chemicals. We have "old woman with basket," which is another disease or the same thing as a bad spirit, which is diabetes, because it involves the food. She would capture other spirits such as the Great Buffalo Spirit and different spirits, and then she would eat them, so it deals with food. However, I did fall under the influence of the one called White Beaver, which is abuse. If you take a look at the characteristics of a beaver, a beaver is self-centered. It will build itself a dam not caring whether it destroys other people or other things, as long as it gets what it wants. If you look at abusive behaviors, a person that is abusive is also doing the same things. They're only interested in what they want, and that's all.

These are the four major evils. I hate to use the word evil, because it's a Christian thing. The four evils were fought long ago by two spirit warriors. They were brothers called Two Men. This goes back to the creation. They did the same thing as Michael the Archangel did. They put things into terms where people can understand, whether they're Christian or whatever. Everybody knows Michael the Archangel and what he's done. It's to fight these things that these two men did—drinking and drugs, diabetes and abuse. If you take a look at anyplace around the world, or even in here in the United States, those are the four major things, and it's the same four things that we are fighting.

I fell under the White Beaver in two ways. One of them was my experience at the boarding school in Chamberlain, South Dakota, St. Joseph's Catholic School. I was in first grade. I always heard stories from the other boys that were there about kids being taken out in the middle of the night, then coming back and crying. That kind of thing never happened to me at that school. What happened to me there was that I went sliding on this really steep hill. At the bottom of that steep hill was a big wire-mesh hurricane fence. I only went down once, but I kept going and my feet were forward on the sled and I ran into that fence. When I ran into that fence, I fell over because it stopped me pretty fast, pretty hard and pretty good. I knew that I was hurt. I told Brother Thomas that I was hurt and that I was going to go back to the dorm. I got ready for bed, laid down, and went to sleep.

I woke up in the morning and I couldn't move. We had to get up early at that time to get ready and go to Mass. All the other kids were getting ready. I couldn't move my legs and couldn't even move my arms that much either. The boys kept saying, "Get up, get up, the Brother's going to get mad!"

I said, "I can't, I can't move."

They said, "Well, what's wrong?"

The next thing I knew I heard the Brother hollering, "Roger, what are you doing lying in bed? Get out of bed! Get ready for Mass."

I said, "I can't move," and he said, "You're just faking!"

"No, I'm not, I'm not faking. It hurts and I can't move."

He said, "You don't want to go to Mass, and you're nothing but a sinner! If you don't get out of that bed I'm going to whip you right now!" He took off his belt and I started crying. I couldn't say anything because I was scared. He threw my blankets off, started hitting me, and he was hitting and hitting and hitting and hitting me. I was crying, but I couldn't move my body or anything. Finally realizing that I wasn't moving, he stopped. Then he said to one of the boys, "Go down and get the infirmary nurse." He was standing there looking at me and I was crying. He doesn't say anything.

The nurse comes up there and she takes a look at me and she says, "I need him to be down in the infirmary." That was downstairs a couple of flights of steps. The nurse said to have two of the other boys pick me up and take me down there. They took me to the hospital from the infirmary.

The nurses and doctors at the hospital looked at my welts but said nothing about it to anyone as far as I know. They told me that I had dislocated both my hips and that's why I wasn't able to move or anything. I wasn't put in a body cast. They just kept me in bed, and they would carry me to wherever I had to go all the time. It was the boys, not the Brothers or anybody else, that did that. They assigned a couple of the bigger boys to carry me all that time, which they didn't care for and I don't blame them. It kind of put me in a bad place with them, too.

It took a long time for me to be able to stand and walk. It still affects me yet today. When I was a teenager, it could be raining and I'd be walking along and all of a sudden my legs would just stop working and I'd fall over. So it still bothers me, especially when the humidity is high. I will still fall sometimes to this day; otherwise my health is fine.

At that time I had been taught by the elders. I realized the people involved in running this place were not what they were saying they were. If they weren't what they were saying they were, then they had to be the opposite of that. I didn't want to go back there again, and I told my parents that. They came that spring and found out what had happened. They kept the rest of us out of that school after that.

At first, when I was younger, I despised the Catholic Church. I despised the Brother. I wished that he was dead for all the things he did. It wasn't done to just me. The sexual abuse and beatings were done to the other students as well. Some of my other brothers were there and they got the beatings too. They don't really talk about it much at all, but I knew that it had happened to them.

The sexual abuse would happen late at night when all of us were sleeping or were supposed to be sleeping. The Brothers would come in and they would take somebody out. When the kids would come back they would be crying. They didn't want to be touched and they were always scared. No one ever talked about it.

They beat us with a thick leather belt, maybe about the same size that I'm wearing, about an eighth of an inch thick and about two inches wide. He would just fold it in half, hold the end and use that. It was about a foot or so long.

My brother did something and they shaved all of his hair off. He wanted to go and visit with his girlfriend. He kind of snuck out of the dorm but got caught. His girlfriend was in the girls' dorm, so he didn't leave the campus or grounds. He just wanted to go and visit with her. It was during early evening, but their rules were that we couldn't leave building at certain times of the evening because we had church. He just wanted to go and talk to his girlfriend. He got caught and they shaved his head. My other brother that's two years older than me, they did something to him; he never did say, he wouldn't talk about it.

For students that ran away, they would also do a lot of isolation. Isolation was just a closet that they were kept in. If there was more than one they used a different closet. I never ran away. The river is just a little way away from the school itself. The other side of the river was home, the direction of home. We had the fence, and then you had the river with no bridge in sight at the time that I could see. There were these obstacles where it wouldn't do me any good.

My spiritual health is where everything is coming from. That's why I said that I'm at where I'm at now. One of the things was when I was younger, I hated them and I wanted them to die, that kind of thing like that there, but as I got older, I guess it's the training of the elders that brought me on the path where I'm at now.

I was born and baptized Catholic, but I'm not a Catholic. I believe in our Native American spirituality. Its true meaning is the way of our ancestors, so I live that way. I live the way that was taught to us by the elders and the Old Warrior Society. All the things that happened to me, such as my wife divorcing me, and moving here in 1995, was actually a test of my faith and my ability to do what's right and to see things for the way it should be seen. She was the first woman that I had allowed myself to love again after all the things that happened to me. That is one of the things I had to do—to learn how to love again. I had to learn how to cry again; I had to learn how to live again. It was at that time that I had allowed myself to love again. I really did love her and I was able to pass that test.

It was in 1995 that I received a vision that I was going to be receiving a bundle from the spirit world. I drew what happened, and all the things it showed me was in this vision. I told my family about it and then I just let it go. About eight months later I was asked to be a keeper of a bundle. This bundle that I have, which I accepted of course, because I was asked and because of the vision that I was given. The bundle that I have is the Two Men Bundle, the two brothers that fought those four evils.

I wouldn't have been able to do this or be here and know the things that I know if it wasn't for the things that had happened, the bad as well as the good, because now that's what I tell people. I teach people these things. I teach them how bad things happen to us, we are going to experience bad things, but wherever there's bad, there's good as well. It depends on us as to what we are going to dwell on and how we are going to let that affect our lives. Where there's good there's bad, where there's bad there's good. If we decide we're going to dwell on the bad, or keep the bad, that's when bad happens. It's just going to keep happening and that's all you're going to see. It's going to affect your life in a way where it's going to consume you.

There are some things that happened in my life that basically caused my heart to die, caused me a lot of resentment, bitterness, and hatred. When a person is being abused, that person may also become the abuser. I believe that's part of what happened with me as well. I became abusive to women, verbally and physically. At the time that it was happening, I couldn't stand myself and came close to killing myself. I went and got help. I needed to learn how to trust, how to cry, and how to be honest again. I had to kill my old self to bring back my new self, to be renewed again. The counselor was a really good friend and that is part of the reason I went into social work.

In high school back on the reservation, I went to see the school counselor and I said I wanted to go to college. He said, "Why, you're not going to be any better than a ditch digger. You're not going to be anything better than that." My Indian name in Hidatsa means Eagle Who Dared to do Difficult Things and Accomplishes Them. I made it a challenge to prove that counselor wrong, and that's exactly what I did.

I would never send my kids to boarding school. I never wanted them to have to go through what I did. Healing from the hurts of boarding school is hard to do. What's necessary for us to do to get better is we need to forgive, to get rid of that hatred. Once you can forgive, then you can truly heal. To help heal the reservation would be a return to our ancestral ways, to the Four Ways of Life that were given to us by the Creator. I'm not a holy man; if you have to call me anything, call me a messenger. I'm just giving a message. The message is to return to what you were given in your ceremonies. Return to the Four Ways of Life. It's not only being honest with others but getting honest with yourself. You have to face yourself and what's really taking place within you. Then those things will be revealed [and] then you can get rid of it. A lawsuit against the government will never cause healing. It's mostly spirituality that needs to be brought back to the person.

U. S. GOV T. INDIAN SCHOOL, WAHPETON, N. D. 701.   COPYRIGHT 1911 JOHNSON-OLSON

Wahpeton government school, ND. Still operating as a boarding school and renamed Circle of Nations School. *North Dakota State University Archives.*

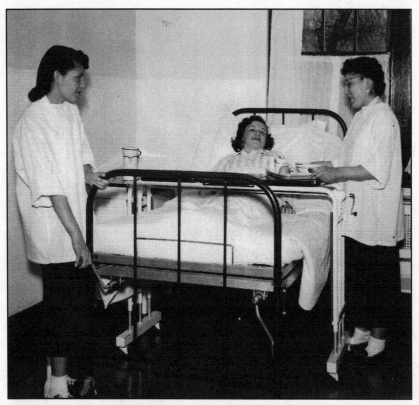

Nursing class, Flandreau. *National Archives at Kansas City.*

STRINGING ROSARIES

Genevieve (b. 1953, pseudonym) and I sipped on hot tea as we sat at her kitchen table for the interview, the room bright with the afternoon sun. I was delighted to see we both loved strong black Lipton tea, an homage to our mothers and grandmothers. Warm and friendly, Genevieve, at fifty-six years old, is fast-talking and laughs easily with sparkling eyes. She describes herself as having an outgoing personality with lots of energy and as a mover and shaker. She grew up on the Turtle Mountain Indian Reservation in Belcourt, North Dakota. Both her parents are Chippewa. Genevieve has three children and nine brothers and sisters. She mentions her mother went to boarding school in Wahpeton, North Dakota, and her father stayed on the reservation, attending St. Ann's Catholic Mission school. She had just finished her doctorate degree when we sat for this interview.

When I was a little kid, my uncles used to set up a wrestling ring with my brother and me. I was really fast and strong. I could move those farm boys around! I always had a sense of my own power, and I have to this day. We were dirt poor. Our house burned down when I was three. The pot-bellied wood stovepipes got hot. So we were absolutely destitute then, because everything we had, had burned. We then lived in the granary. Dad and Mom cleaned out the granary and we lived in that until winter came, and they had no choice but to send us to the boarding school. It was stark poverty that forced them to have to send us there. It was that or let us starve. But we were hard working people. We had our own cattle, our own milk, chickens, eggs, and we had a huge garden. We were strong, physically active kids. I could milk four cows in the morning before school, and we'd throw bales. Our family was dirt poor, but we were close, and in a lot of ways we were happy in those growing up years before boarding school intervened.

I returned to the reservation and attended Dunseith Day School.[34] I went to boarding school at Stephan, South Dakota, for high school, gradu-

---

[34] By 1893 Congress appropriated $2.3 million for Indian education. The bulk of the money went to establishing day schools on or near Indian villages or reservations. By 1900, one hundred forty-seven day schools were in operation, the majority on reservations in the Great Plains.

ating from there. I didn't go home during my years at boarding school. My father was a farmer and my mother a homemaker, taking in foster children.

I attended St. Joseph's Indian Boarding School in Chamberlain, South Dakota, during second and third grade. On the bus, kids were crying, sitting on the bus in shock. Some of the kids would get sick and throw up on the bus, they were so emotionally distraught. The trip there itself was traumatic. I was six or seven; my brother was five. We came from a very caring, very loving home, raised in a clean, very well taken care of home; we were always nicely dressed.

The nuns treated us like we were little animals because our dad was a farmer. They treated us like we were cattle. We were raised very prim and proper, raised very modest, and the first thing they did is, in military style, dip all of our heads in this bug juice. We called it bug juice, and we said, "We don't have bugs." Didn't make any difference. Everybody had to go into the shower. This is when you first arrived. Some things you have to blot out in order to self-protect, so I don't know if we were given towels or if we were group showered. Then they cut our hair, got a bowl cut so we all come out looking the same, like cookie cutter kids. My mom, as a way of compensating her grief for sending us to boarding school, sent me with three or four real beautiful little dresses. They were all taken away from me, and we were given uniforms. We had little beanies, which were round and they had like four different colors. Then you went into this room, and there was just row after row of new shoes. They lined us up for supper, and again, I'd never seen anything like this, we'd all march into this big dining room, sit down at these long military-style-type tables, and they'd bring us whatever grub they were serving. It wasn't good stuff.

The priests ate like kings. Some girls would get selected to go serve the priests, and their food was like night and day of what we got. They had a chef that cooked their food, and they had fresh vegetables, lots of fresh fruit, and steaks and fancy food, very well prepared that looked very appealing on the plate, and we got some kind of slop in a bowl. We weren't hungry, but nothing ever excited you. You ate to survive. It kept you alive. On the playground, we ate like real soldiers ate. They'd figure we were hungry, so a nun would come out with a big tin garbage can, and she'd walk out to the playground and sit down and hand every kid a slice of bread. Some kids would have their family send them peanut butter. They'd put peanut butter on their plain slice of bread. Otherwise, you just had a plain slice of bread and that was your treat.

Kids tried to run away. We had a lot of kids run away. They would send dogs after them and track them down. There was one kid that gave the other kids hope, because he constantly challenged the rules and broke them, and then he got severely punished, but he had so much spirit, they kept trying to squash his spirit. He was the one that gave the other ones hope. We couldn't call home. Your parents had to call you. The nun would go round up all the brothers and sisters and bring you into a little broom closet with the phone. Each kid was given a lecture before they could answer the phone of the things we were not allowed to tell or say. We'd all just say everything was good, everything's fine, everybody's nice to me, and there'd be tears streaming down our cheeks.

When I was in third grade, I got sick. One of my sisters claims that they tried medication on us. My cheek started off with a little bump on my jaw line. That thing grew and it kept growing until all of a sudden it was rock hard and it was almost touching my neck and was pushing up on my eye. It must have been some kind of goiter or something, I don't know. They kept trying to do remedies to make it go away and it wouldn't go away. My brothers and sisters were worried about me, but the school wouldn't let them tell Mom and Dad. Finally, they put me in the hospital for over three weeks. My parents never were allowed to be told. Here I was, a little kid, and I was traumatized by watching the doctor and the nurse get sexual in front of me! They were pawing each other and kissing each other and doing things in a child's room that they had no business doing. They figured I was just a little Indian kid. I was an innocent little kid; I mean, we were raised in a very good home with good morals.

After I survived that, I ended up getting some kind of injury on my arm and I got blood poisoning and I had a bright red line going from my wrist and all the way up my arm until it passed my elbow. If it would have hit my heart, I would have been dead. The nuns sat up with me all night long putting hot compresses on it, but they refused to bring me to the hospital because it would cost money, and they refused to call my parents. How I survived that I don't know, but we were threatened, all of us were threatened not to tell what happened to me, either incident.

We were raised in a real clean home, and within six weeks of being there we had all these impetigo sores. We had these big goopy sores on us. I got athlete's foot from there, and they wouldn't treat it. My brother broke his arm, and rather than take him to the doctor, they made him carry a pail of sand with that broken arm. And then, they'd take us to the dentist, and he would just fill our teeth, randomly. Practically every tooth in my head is filled, because they didn't care if there was a cavity there or not. It was what they got paid for, so most of what I've seen of other boarding school kids is whole mouths of teeth filled.

We had all kinds of rebellion. We would go into the supply room and steal supplies. Then we'd sneak out to behind the playground and we'd go bury these supplies, just lots of them. It was maybe our way of saying "up yours."

The dorm was row upon row of little beds, and when the lights went out, you had to be in your bed and the nun would walk the floor and check for you. If you weren't in there, there was hell to be paid. One time I crawled out of my bed and was crawling around underneath the beds. What I was up to I don't know, but she noticed me missing. Some of the kids tried helping me then, "She's in the bathroom, we think she's in the bathroom," trying to give me enough chance to get out from under the bed and back in my bed.

Some of the nuns were mentally ill. One time we were walking to Benediction in the evening and the little girls were giggling and kind of restless and I was talking. This young beautiful nun, physically very beautiful, probably early twenties, came up to me. I was just a little tiny girl. She comes up to me, took my skin, and she turned it and turned it with her long fingernails until she drew blood.

I know in retrospect now, as a psychiatric nurse, I think the kids that ended up being resilient and survivors were the ones that were able to somehow engender some adult to care take for them. I was always able to do that. I had a nun that was my guardian angel. She was a very lacking adult herself, but she used to come and get me and take me out of the dorm to the boys' dorm where she worked. I would sew with her, and she'd give me little treats and was kind and gentle with me. She just gave me a time out from the scary place, because when I was with her I felt safe and secure. I darned socks and we'd do embroidery, and we got paid for stringing rosaries every day, like a penny. I mean we got just dirt. It was like slave labor. They had these little white plastic rosaries and you'd string them on a card, and then they'd put those in those begging letters and send them out all across the country. They would choose the most pitiful, pathetic looking Indian kids to paste on those begging letters, and send those little rosaries out that we all had to string. You might get like a penny for five rosaries, and you wouldn't get actual money, but you'd get points to go to the candy store on Sunday. We also used to have those great big polishers and polish the floors. We baked bread and helped with the meal. If you got punished, you literally had to scrub with a toothbrush.

Bed-wetters would have to take their sheets and hang them out the window to advertise, and they'd tell who wet the bed, humiliate them throughout the whole school, and they'd get beat besides. The nun would take you into a little closet. She had a little red stick and you'd have to bend over this bench, and she'd literally beat you with the stick. If she really got into it, she'd break the stick. One time we were all lined up and the big girls were ahead of us. This one girl was talking in line and the big girls had to have their hair in rollers. All of a sudden the priest lost his temper in the confessional and he came out and he started slugging her in the head, slugging her rollers. I mean, he physically assaulted her right in front of us. You could hear an audible gasp, and everybody was horrified.

We were light-skinned, so we were treated a little better than the Sioux. So the Sioux and the Chippewa began to dislike each other. What we ended up with was gang warfare. If you didn't have a gang, somebody was going to beat you up. We were farm kids and we were so physically in good shape, we were really strong. We weren't brought up to fight though. We weren't the fighting type of kids. But these girls were after me. It was like they hunted you, and you feel like an animal. I was on the merry-go-round once, and I'm just a little tiny kid, maybe eight years old, and this girl tripped me as a way to fight. If she could beat me, then she would move up in gang stature. I lost my temper, so I just doubled back my fist, and I was powerful and I caught her in the stomach, lifted her right off her feet, knocked the wind out of her, knocked her down. I had never resorted to violence before and it broke my heart, so I started a little PR thing on myself; anybody mess with me, they get one chance and they were going down. So it turned out that I became the leader of the little girls and I was left alone. I didn't participate in the gang stuff, and I didn't abuse other kids; I was more like a lone wolf. But I did see them terrorize other kids, and I didn't have enough power to go in and protect the other kids. It was horrible to watch. It was absolutely like a gang.

We'd go to the big gym where they'd have some kind of social. If you were five or six years old, dying of loneliness, you could see your brothers and sisters maybe once a week, for like two hours. They were always insinuating that there was something going to happen of a sexual nature. These were brothers and sisters, Indian people, that wasn't even in our brains!

When the lights came on in the morning, we made the bed and did whatever was our cleaning to do. Then we went to Mass. You know, you got to hate Mass. We had to stand there doing these mindless rote prayers. It was an insult when a lot of the children came from such rich spiritual traditions. I'm not a practicing Catholic to this day. After church, we went to school. Every day was the same; it was all routine. On their playground there were merry-go-rounds and swings; we had some time that was play time, not a lot, everything was regimented. It was like the military. To this day, I can't stand a schedule where I know what's going to happen every moment of the day. It bores me to death.

I believe every single one of my brothers and sisters have some form of post-traumatic stress disorder. Some of my PTSD is that I can't drive alone very far, and if I'm not driving and somebody's taking me someplace, I panic. Because when you got put in the bus, you were going away from home and not coming back for a year. And I still can't be in [an] institutional setting. I was offered a job at the psychiatric hospital. I can't even be in that building; it brings flashbacks of boarding school to the degree that there is no way I can be in that setting.

There were kids that were rewarded for ratting on each other; those were the snitches. You know in Indian Country, when you give your word, your word is as good as gold.[35] The system stole those kids' honor, their word of honor, and they rewarded them for being snitches. They meant to divide us.

The sister that was the principal knew that I had a good mind and a lot of abilities. She used to take me out of class and expose me to a higher level of learning that intrigued me. She let me learn about Viktor Frankl and his survival during the Holocaust. I think that was part of my own survival; I knew that something else was possible.

In my own journey to healing, I've been a psychiatric nurse for a lot of years now, so I think it's in my past. Not completely though; I still deal with Post-Traumatic Stress Disorder. I've witnessed kids drinking lethally. I've never had a problem with alcohol.

I told my parents how bad it was at Chamberlain and that they had almost killed me twice, and then my brother with his broken arm, and then one brother, Raleigh, was so lonesome he got sick and they had to actu-

---

[35] Indian Country is defined at 18 U.S.C 1151 as: all land within the limits of any Indian reservation under the jurisdiction of the US government; all dependent Indian communities within the borders of the US whether within the original or subsequently acquired territory thereof, and whether within or without the limits of a state; all Indian allotments the Indian titles to which have not been extinguished, including right-of-way running through the same.

ally take him home. You can physically die from that. It's called failure to thrive. My parents were able to get another house and were able to financially keep us home; they did that by keeping foster kids, so that was hard, too.

My siblings and I don't discuss our boarding school years, and I don't want to hear some of their stories, because if they were painful I think I'd feel it at a deeper level than my own stuff. I think they do have worse stories than me. It would be like being traumatized all over again, so we don't do that to each other. I was the first one to break the code of silence and talk about it, and I got in trouble for talking about it. Then I'd talk to others, and one of the ladies that went to a boarding school told me about having to go to the dentist and he would make her strip down; while he was working on them he would feel her up. She must have been from a family where her parents showed no interest; they didn't call or check on her or nothing. My other three oldest siblings went to Wahpeton. That was an experience, too. They don't talk about it.

I put myself in boarding school at Stephan. I got there and realized how much I hated it, all those bad feelings and icky memories, but I managed to stay there. Literally, by that age, I was running my own life. I had friends from the reservation that went with me to boarding school; you get to know them in a way. Once you know somebody at that level . . . and you always know them that way. I had maybe four guys that were the closest friendship I've ever had with a male in my life, and they were not sexual relationships. They were the truest form of friendship that a male and female could have. One I'd just lean on him and drape on him and it was closeness, it was a familial comforting, and those guys were like my brothers. Even throughout my adult life, there is still those connections I made at boarding school. I'll walk in and there's somebody from boarding school, so it's been an invaluable connection throughout life, too.

When I graduated, I went to see the guidance counselor, and if I could see her today I'd bop her alongside the head. She said to me, "Well, looking at your grades and how you've done throughout your educational experience, if I were you I don't think I'd consider college. You might try a year or two, but if you did I would encourage you to go more for social reasons. You should be looking for a nice man to marry instead. You're a very nice looking girl; why don't you consider marrying someone white? You'd have a much nicer life." That one got burned into me, and so I went to Bottineau, and guess what I did? I married the white man! And I stayed with him for twenty-six years.

I had married into a farm family who didn't think college was necessary at all, so they pretty much put barriers up, wouldn't let me go back to
school. I became very ill when I was close to thirty years old and almost
died. I thought that does it, I'm going to school. I got into a competitive
nursing program in Grafton. We started off with three hundred people that
tested down to one hundred fifteen and then down to eighteen. I kept test-
ing in, and I still didn't know that I wasn't stupid. I graduated with honor
and got my LPN degree. But I kept wanting to do more things. It wasn't
until I was halfway through my master's program that it finally occurred to
me, "You know what? Maybe I'm not too dumb." I had a 4.0 GPA, and did
all the way through school. Even to this day though, you know, that was
so ground into who you were, that you were less than, that you were not
as smart as, and could never be as good as the others. To this day, I have
to keep telling myself, baloney, you did it and you are going to continue
to do it.

I literally ran from the reservation when I was eighteen and never
went back. It was a place that was full of pain. Growing up there was a
lot of pain, although I had some of the best times of my life there. But it's
that intermingling with the pain and the poverty. It just felt safer to me to
stay away from there. I return to attend pow wows. There is a beauty in the
people that is extraordinary, there is a resilience there, cohesion, and there
is a natural inbred sense of the spiritual. I'm very connected to the spiritual.
That's how I survived. I have an outgoing personality and a lot of energy.
I'm a mover and a shaker, and have been all my life. I always had a sense
of my own power, and have that to this day. I like being peaceful. I'm a
teacher, so when I teach and have done it well, you know you've made an
impact in somebody's life. I'm also a nurse and a healer. I have all kinds of
ways of healing, and I'm good at that.

Boarding school affected me because I had to numb my emotions. And
then you didn't express them. And then the trust, trust was destroyed. You
just had a lack of safety, and that very negatively impacted all of that. I
have three children and three grandchildren. I never wanted to send any of
them to attend school. They are too precious.

I would like to see an apology from the Catholic church and an apology from the federal government and ownership of what was done, get the
issue out of the darkness. It was done, and I mean, voice after voice can't
tell these stories and then have them deny it.

Boarding school affected how I parented my kids. I raised my kids Catholic; I married a Catholic farmer. The more I came into my own em-powerment as an adult woman I literally couldn't be Catholic anymore. I had learned closeness from my own parents. I was able to reconnect with the closeness that was in our family. As far as discipline though, when our dad was punishing us, it was actually abuse. He didn't know it and we didn't know it. He literally raised welts on our little butts and legs. It was too extreme. Native people didn't punish their kids like that before. That was taught to us. I never hit my kids like that. I didn't regain my self-esteem as a Native person until mid-life adult. It took going back to the culture and sitting with the elders to re-learn who I was. Even when I was married to the white man, everybody knew I was Native. That was part of my standing up for who I was, but it took me into my forties to have the power to win back my culture, to really be proud of being a Native person.

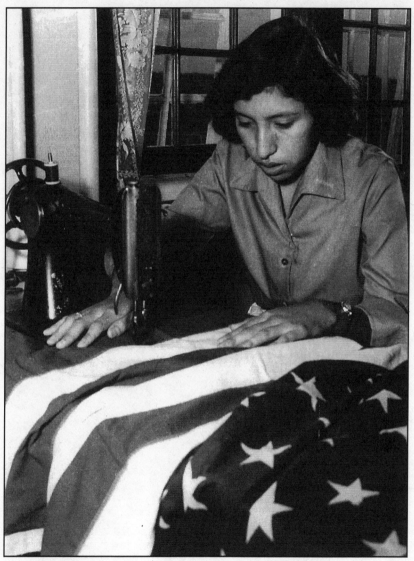

Girl sewing American flag, St. Michael's Mission, ND.
Marquette Archives.

Girls peeling potatoes, Pierre, SD. *National Archives at Kansas City.*

NERVOUS BREAKDOWN

*On a warm summer morning, I sat with Cecelia (b.1950, pseudonym), age
fifty-nine, and three of her daughters outside her rambling South Dakota
farmhouse as her husband, a farmer, lumbered off on a tractor. As we
moved our chairs to keep in the shade, swatting flies and mosquitoes, her
daughters melted away into the house one by one. Cecelia is a citizen
of the Sisseton Wahpeton Oyate. Both of Cecelia's parents are Native
American from Sisseton. She did not know if they had been to boarding
school. She has six children. She attended three boarding schools at
Flandreau and Pierre in South Dakota and Wahpeton in North Dakota.
As an adult, she worked thirty-one years in a poultry factory, a job she is
proud of.*

I wanted to go to boarding school to get away from problems at home. My
parents were alcoholic, and my mom would beat me with a strap, leaving
welts, and my grandfather had been molesting me since I was three. I got
placed with my grandmother. As long as I had my grandma I was OK. I had
an unhappy childhood, too much trouble. Sad, because my mother couldn't
take care of me or my sisters, so we were all taken away. My grandmother
couldn't take all of us.

I went to Wahpeton Indian Boarding School in North Dakota for my
first five years of school. When I first arrived I saw a girl on a swing, and
her feet went in the water by accident. The matron took her and beat her
with a horsewhip on the legs and then on her back. She was cut open and
all the welts on her were bleeding. After seeing that I tried to avoid misbe-
having and getting disciplined by the matrons. I ran into a matron that kept
picking on me. She kept nagging at me and nagging me saying this and
saying stuff to me. She had a habit of slapping me in the head. Finally, I
just couldn't take it, and I had a nervous breakdown. I was seven years old.
I couldn't stop wringing my hands. I spent three months in the hospital at
Breckenridge [MN]. They gave me medication to take; I have no idea what
that was. They kept monitoring me. I couldn't get out of bed; my legs were
so weak they just gave way, and I almost collapsed on the floor. I thought it

was the floor opening up . . . it got to the point where I couldn't feed myself. I tried but would drop the spoon. One of the orderlies came and fed me. I only weighed sixty pounds. I could stand behind that utility pole over there and you wouldn't know I was there. When I got out of the hospital, I had to stay and recuperate for three days in the dorm. Couldn't go back to my classroom until I got stronger. My teacher and classmates welcomed me back, but I didn't want to talk about it.

If anyone ran away, they made them cut all their hair off. Some of the girls ran away. Made all of them stand in front of us and tell us, "If you run away this is what we're going to do to you." I was scared and didn't try to run away. I was punished once for not listening to a teacher. I had to take a pail of water and go do the floors and outside steps with a small round scrub brush.

There was this one matron who was Indian. She was a mean one. I saw her get into a fight with one of the girls. She took her and knocked her on the floor and literally beat her with her fist. I said, "Is she going to kill her?" I thought to myself, "I'd better behave before she does that to me."

We wore Government Issue dresses, brown, green, and blue one-piece, sleeves, and button in the front, no pockets. They took our home clothes and locked them up. In the morning, a bell would ring and we'd get up and fix beds. The bed had to be fixed neat or they tore them all apart and made you redo them. We'd stand in line, brush our teeth and wash up. They'd check our hands over and if they weren't clean, they took that ruler and hit us on the palm of our hands and on the back of our hand. We then marched in twos to breakfast. I remember we had oatmeal and toast, an apple or orange. Do the same for noon meal, basically the same routine. Hell, you get into that drill, it's still in your head because it's daily. If you got demerits you got punished and couldn't go to town. You had to take a brush and scrub the floors. It was a little scrub brush, round; scrubbed on your hands and knees. I know I had to do my share of that. I'd get punished because I didn't listen or follow instructions. Then they told me, "Take a pail of water and go do the floors and when you get done there you go do the steps outside the building."

If anyone wet the bed, they got a spanking from the night matron. She would check our beds and if you peed the bed you had to take off your bedding and get punished. She used a wooden paddle. They got hit so hard they couldn't sit down. I never peed the bed.

I used to like spelling, which was my best subject. I had a first-grade teacher that was nice. In second grade, I saw a teacher hit students' palms until they were red. I do remember several teachers that were nice. There was a matron that was pretty good; I could confide in her. I didn't really tell her too much; I told her little bits. For fun, they let us play outside the building. We had swings, a merry-go-round, and [a] teeter-totter. I had a best friend; we were always together, inseparable, could say we were buddies. I've lost touch with my friends from Wahpeton.

For meals the older girls brought pitchers of milk to [the] table. We couldn't eat unless a prayer was said. Whoever sat at the end had to say grace. Then we had to eat in a fashionable manner, had to have manners. We had to say, "Please pass the milk, please pass the bread," and so on. We ate in silence. If someone didn't have any manners, they had to leave the table and wouldn't get to eat.

We went to bed around 8:00 p.m. We had to say our prayers kneeling at the right side of the bed, then go to bed. We had to pick a church to go to. They made me go to the Catholic Church, because I couldn't remember which one we belonged to.

I learned to speak my language from my grandmother after I returned home from boarding school. She had kept the language and she taught me. I still speak it to this day. At school we were not allowed to do any tribal artwork or dancing. My grandmother told me, "Keep your traditions when you're away to school, but you need to hide it or they will take it away from you." So I told her, "OK, I won't tell them what I do." I kept my traditions secret, kept them hidden. She went to boarding school at Pipestone, Minnesota. My biggest regret is that I didn't get to see Grandmother more. When she died I really took it hard. The school wouldn't let me go home for her funeral.

Every year when school started I always ran a high fever, and I never could figure out why. I'd be so sick I'd be in that infirmary. Usually I was there for a week with a temperature of 103. It wouldn't come down, so the school nurse had to come give me a shot, and then come back and check to see if I had improved. It has to do with all that stress from that school. I remember a favorite time at boarding school was taking trips in the spring to the zoo or other outings like movies.

The school, before they changed it now, had these old buildings. There was the basement where the showers were. In the summertime, when I would be down there, I could hear these spirits, restless spirits from these other kids, and there were some things they didn't like. I don't know if someone did something in there. I sometimes can see and hear things other people can't. Some say it is a gift.

I had wanted to go to boarding school because my grandfather was sexually molesting me when I was three years old. But at boarding school an older girl began molesting me when I was about seven years old. This went on every week, almost every day during the day. She would take me up to these old fire escapes. I didn't dare tell, she threatened me. I thought she was going to stab me or something. I kept it quiet; I never told anybody after all these years.

My mother abandoned us, and everyone thought she was dead. The sheriff and the FBI even went to the ravine to look for her. Here she was up in Moorhead [Minnesota] all that time. When I was fourteen years old, I went to Pierre Indian School for seventh and eighth grade. It was like all the other schools. I had kitchen duty, peeling the eyes out of the potatoes, [making] toast, making sure the butter was run through that thing to make little square pats.

I graduated from eighth grade and went to Flandreau High School. It was kind of harsh there, too. They put you on restrictions; we couldn't do anything, had to stay and do the floors. There was this one matron there; she was really hard to get along with. She made all my work impossible. She kept nagging me and said I wasn't doing it right. I said I did that all the right way. Well, she made me angry so I picked up my bucket and I dumped it right on her head, and I said, "Now you can clean it up!"

A matron came to my rescue. I would help her; she had a little sewing room, and I also helped her with the laundry. When I got done she gave me a reward.

I was at Flandreau for one year; then I ran away with two other friends. They were just too strict. We saved up our candy and what we had for supper. We went through by the golf course and hid in the shadows, went all the way through Brookings [South Dakota]. We walked all the way back, we slept walking, we didn't [stop to] sleep, we stayed awake, and we were trying to get as far away as we could. Someone gave us a ride part way, dropped us off at our yard. The school officials came and took us back. That's when I started rebelling. I refused to do what was asked of me, and I just kept it up and finally I got expelled. I got kicked out of there and they said, "Don't you ever come back here." I said, "Don't worry; I won't be coming back here!"

I was a sophomore at the time, and I was determined to get my diploma. I wanted that diploma, so I went back and got it. I went through the graduation ceremony. I was kind of shy. I never seen so much people; the halls were just full of people. It was really something, and I felt proud. I then moved to Chicago and took a job with the Naval Ordnance Station, where the navy brought stuff that had to be repaired.

Then my father was robbed and stabbed, so I had to return home. I learned through the Bureau of Indian Affairs about the Relocation program. I went to New Mexico to a baking school where I learned how to bake pies and cakes. I returned home and began working at a goose plant, processing geese. It's seasonal. I start in the summer and go until fall. I've been there for thirty-one years.

I don't participate in community doings. You know, being in a boarding school probably had some effect on that. I kind of isolated myself. I have no sense of belonging. I had problems with alcohol. I don't drink anymore. I quit. One day I started looking at my life, and I asked myself, "Do I want to keep doing this?" I've got to make some changes. I don't want to be like the rest of them in my family. I want to keep my family together. I haven't had a drop since 1989. I don't smoke either. I am having some health issues with my heart.

The teachers made me feel ashamed of being Indian and that is still with me to this day.

What would help me heal is if I could see beyond me being an Indian and just make contact with the white people. Right now I only see one color, my own; it's kind of racial in a way. I'd like to mingle with other people, and once I do that maybe I wouldn't be so isolated. I could get out and talk to people. My boarding school experiences make me feel like I don't appreciate myself. I'm always kind of looking down on myself. To make myself feel better I just push thoughts of it off and start working from there. I have told my kids and my husband.

I was strict with my kids, but I never sent them to boarding school. I never spanked my kids, because I think that is abuse. I'm close to my sister, though I never told her about my boarding school experiences. Looking back at my boarding school experiences kind of makes me feel lost.

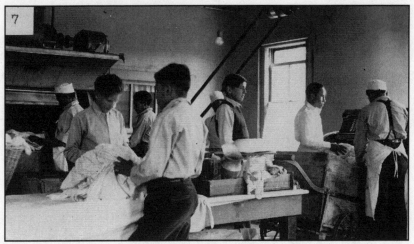

Doing the laundry, Flandreau Indian School, SD.

National Archives at Kansas City.

Making knitting needles for the Red Cross, St. Francis, SD.

Bureau of Catholic Indian Missions.

ROOM NINETEEN

Dennis Decoteau (b. 1953) was born and raised on the Turtle Mountain Band of Chippewa in Belcourt, North Dakota. He is the principal of Dunseith High School, Dunseith, North Dakota. Dennis got in touch with me through the National Boarding School Healing Project, stating that he wished to be interviewed. He did not wish to remain anonymous, stating that he wanted the world to know what happened to him at Wahpeton Indian Boarding School. Both of his parents are Chippewa from Turtle Mountain. He received his Associate of Arts degree from North Dakota State University—Bottineau Branch, his Bachelor's degree from Mayville State College in Mayville, North Dakota, and a Master's degree in Educational Administration from the University of Mary, Bismarck, North Dakota.

My dad died in '92, and my mother just turned eighty years old. My dad had an eleventh-grade education and my mother got her GED, then going on to get her four-year degree from [The University of North Dakota]. I stayed with my parents off and on, and also my grandparents. They lived over by Belcourt Lake. I grew up in Belcourt. At that time, my parents were uneducated and poor. We moved around a lot. We didn't have our own home, so we had to rent, or we stayed at our grandparents'. We lived in a log cabin where we didn't have running water or electricity. When I was young, we would go out to the Red River Valley and hoe beets and pick potatoes. I didn't do that, but I would go out there with them. At one point we even stayed in a bus that we fixed up. There was no running water or electricity. We had to haul our own water and use kerosene lanterns. I was pretty young, but I still remember the bus. It was a bus that was junked out by my grandparents' house, and they really didn't have any room for us because they had eighteen kids of their own—one of the largest families in Belcourt. They didn't have any room for us because they lived in a three-room shack, and so we fixed up the bus and we stayed in there for a summer.

We moved around a lot. We had moved to Minot for a while, and my grandparents, on the Decoteau side, had brothers that lived over in Minot, so we lived out there for a while and then we moved back.

Life was so simple back then. We were happy to get an orange and an apple and a few peanuts and a couple of candies or a pair of gloves for Christmas. Now things are so complicated. Christmas is so commercialized. For New Year's, we didn't have a lot of food, so we used to hunt rabbits with my dad. A lot of people ate rabbits—that's where the Chippewa got the nickname "rabbit chokers" from. That was a happier time in my life. I still hunt quite a bit.

I started school in Belcourt at the elementary school, the government school. I was pretty young when I started school. My birthday was December 30, so I was only five years old when I started school. I went there my first six years. I went to Wahpeton Indian Boarding School for my seventh grade. It wasn't really something that we decided on. It was out of necessity because my parents really had a tough time supporting all seven kids, so we were court-ordered to go to the boarding school. I attended boarding school in Wahpeton for seventh and eighth grade.

Leaving my parents was really traumatic. I didn't understand why I was leaving. It was traumatic because we were court-ordered, so the police came and picked us up. I think we were court-ordered because my dad drank a lot. I don't know if he was an alcoholic, but he drank a lot. They were unemployed and the home environment wasn't really that stable. The police came to get us. My brother was also supposed to go, but he made off like he was fainting or something, so they left him. I ended up going the first year by myself. I didn't even get a chance to say goodbye to them. That was really traumatic. My mother was crying and the kids were crying. I can't remember if I even cried, because I really didn't understand what was going on. The police took me to the Bureau of Indian Affairs agency in Belcourt. The bus was waiting there. I was put on the bus and I didn't even know where Wahpeton was. I never heard of Wahpeton. We never traveled outside of the reservation too much except for when we'd go to the Red River Valley. The bus ride was a long ride to Wahpeton, maybe five, six, seven hours. A lot of kids were crying. We left in August and little did we know that we weren't coming back until the end of May. We wouldn't see our parents for a whole year. I stayed in the boarding school during the holidays. Parents were allowed to come visit but at that time our parents were poor. Their transportation wasn't that good. They couldn't send us any money. We didn't have very good clothes. You very seldom saw parents around there visiting. They would write to us, but all of our letters were censored. They would open them up and check for money and read the letters to make sure that we weren't telling them something that we weren't supposed to tell or just to find out what they were writing to us from back home. When we sent out letters, they read them, too. I received letters from my parents once in a while, but they were opened.

When we got off the bus, they lined us all up and they were cutting all the hair off these kids. Then we got doused down with this powder for fleas. I don't know exactly what they were putting on us, but we were getting powdered up on the head. It was to kill lice, but I didn't know that then. I had short hair. I was trying to grow it out because that was back in the time when the Beatles were popular and they had long hair. Well, everybody wanted to have hair like that, but some of the traditional Native American children that came from traditional homes had longer hair. They weren't allowed to keep that. That was pretty tough, I mean, stressful, because we had to go through that.

I stayed in what was called the Big Boys' dorm. I was on the seventh- and eighth-grade wing, and there was another wing that was for the fifth and sixth grade. There were boys there that were a lot older than I was. I was twelve years old going on thirteen, but there were boys there who were sixteen, seventeen, and eighteen years old. They were staying in the dorm. It was really difficult, in that respect, to live with these older boys because there were certain activities, like sports, that we wanted to be recognized for, but I couldn't compete against those kids because they were five, six years older than me. The dorm rooms had bunk bed sets and there were four boys per room. I ended up with some boys that had spent maybe seven, eight years at the dorm or at the school and never went home. First night in the dorm there was a lot of crying going on. I was terribly lonesome. I didn't know what I was getting into. I didn't know whether or not I'd ever go back home.

We had to get up at six in the morning because we had chores that we had to do called detail. We had to go to our jobs until around eight o'clock, and then we'd have to go back to the dorm and straighten up our room, fix our beds. We'd go have breakfast and then we'd have to go to class. We'd stay in class until three-thirty, and then go back to the dorm. The rest of the evening was spent in the dorm. Lights out about eight-thirty at night, nine o'clock at the latest. We were assigned different details every quarter.[36] As an example, I remember working in the bakery; they baked their own bread and rolls. I spent a whole quarter in the bakery. I spent some time in the kitchen too, washed dishes, empty garbage, and mop floors. We didn't do any actual cooking. Washing dishes, I hated that. We didn't have very many clothes. The clothes that we wore were either from donations or else they would make us sign up for Christian Children's Fund. We'd have to send them pictures and write them letters. We were required to do that. I don't remember who my sponsor was, but I did have a sponsor and I was a member of CCF.

The matrons were pretty strict. They tried to keep an eye on all the kids. Some of the kids did manage to get out of the buildings. The windows would open up, and they would run away. The first week I was at the dorm some kids ran away. They didn't want to be there. That morning we went for breakfast and went into the cafeteria. As soon as I walked in the cafeteria, I saw these kids, boys and girls that were standing up. There was about six or eight students around the cafeteria, and they all had green dresses on. So they made them wear these green dresses. They also cut their hair off. Some of them had long hair, but they got their hair cut off and they were wearing these green dresses. They didn't get to sit down. They had to eat their meals without utensils. That was part of their punishment. Everyone had to watch them. Well, everybody saw them when they came through the cafeteria to eat. I didn't try to run away when I was in Wahpeton.

For breakfast we usually had cold cereal or oatmeal. They had this meal that they called "SOS," and you know what that is? We'd get a lot of that. That was one of our jokes that we used to talk about that all the time. "SOS," I thought, "What the hell is SOS?" It was "shit on a shingle." It was hamburger gravy on toast. The food really wasn't that great. As far as I was concerned, the amount of food was inadequate. Kids were always hungry and we weren't allowed to take food out of the kitchen. If we did bring that back to the dorm, we were going to be in trouble. I was tempted to put something in my pockets when I worked in the kitchen, but I was so afraid because I didn't want to take the punishment.

Over the years, this has been forty years now, and maybe about ten years ago, I was thinking about the green dress situation. I wrote a short story about the green dresses and I sent it down to *The Fargo Forum*. I

[36] Because boarding schools were based on Richard Pratt's military model, "detail" here means students assigned to a particular duty. Students were detailed to the kitchen, barns, laundry, bakery, etc.

wanted the public to know that this was going on just a few miles from their area. They refused to publish it, so they sent it back. It probably wasn't that well written because I get emotional when I think about some of this stuff. It's some of the stuff that I tried to block out of my mind because it was painful. I was thinking about it this morning. After forty years, I'm still thinking about this stuff. How come I'm still thinking about this? I have an uncanny ability to block things out of my mind, but when I think about this stuff it's painful.

When I was in high school at Flandreau, we tried to find jobs. They allowed you to leave campus. The dorm was located outside of town maybe a quarter or half mile. I worked in a bowling alley and I set pins for ten cents a game. At the time, I would have to stand in the back where they would throw the bowling balls. Those pins would just explode! They would fly all over the place. We'd get all banged up, bruised up. To me—I was a kid—it was fun. I never got knocked out or anything. Then we'd have to pick these pins up and set them up on this machine, set them up on this rack.

I wanted to mention that the boarding schools, like the Wahpeton School and the Flandreau School, they considered Native Americans as not intelligent. They forced us to take shop classes like Wood Shop, Metal Shop, and Electrical Shop, and Masonry, and Mechanical Drafting. I wasn't very good with my hands. I was young in comparison to kids that were sixteen, seventeen, or eighteen years old. Some of them were a lot more skilled than I was. I thought, "Why are they making us take all these stupid shop classes?" I hated them. But that was part of their philosophy. They didn't think that we were smart enough to be educated, so they thought we're going to be carpenters, we're going to be brick layers, welders. We had to take Welding Shop. I hated welding. We were forced to take all those shop classes.

When I got to Flandreau, I ran away the second year I was there, my sophomore year. I think I spent about a half a year there. I just had enough of it so I ran away. I came back home. Belcourt was trying to send me back and I said, "I'm not going back there." I wasn't going back there because I saw a lot of kids that were involved in alcohol; some of them would drink shaving lotion. Aqua Velva was the preferred drink if they couldn't get alcohol. When I got back to Belcourt, I tried to enroll in school to finish my sophomore year, but they wouldn't accept me because I had run away from Flandreau. That was kind of a traumatic experience, too, because all of the kids that were my friends were in their sophomore year in high school.

They were going to finish school before I was going to finish school. My high school career was five years because they would not allow me to enroll back in school. I ended up sitting out about a half a year, and then the next year I started. In 1971, when I was supposed to graduate with the kids that were in my class, my grade, I couldn't graduate because I didn't have enough credits, so I had to go back another year. When I got back into high school I lacked skills in a lot of areas, academic areas. I think that because we were forced to take these classes that I really didn't excel in, like shop and welding, and I wasn't really a, well, I was just a young kid; how in the hell was I supposed to excel in those areas? I just couldn't compete against these other kids, and I just didn't have the skills and the coordination you know, I was so much younger, but they took away from my other areas, my academic areas, and so you know, but I did [graduate]; I was persistent. I wouldn't say that I'm stupid or anything like that, I'm just an average intelligence. So I did do my five years in high school and I did graduate because I was determined to graduate. That was in 1972.

I know that some of the other kids at Wahpeton were ridiculed. I saw this video about Andrew Windy Boy on Facebook. I went to school with him. He was in Wahpeton when I was there—it's been forty years. I said, "Hey, I know this guy. I went to school with this guy." I can understand his pain. I'm fair-skinned. I really felt for these other Native American kids that were a little darker skinned and had long dark hair. They weren't allowed to speak their Native language. They weren't allowed to practice their culture. The school wanted to move them to be "Americanized," if that's what the term is, or "assimilated." They wanted them to be white people; "You're going to speak English and you're going to go to church." They made us check out every Sunday. We had to go to church. I went to the Catholic Church, which was located close to the river. It was at least a mile away from the dorm. Every Sunday we had to check out and go to church. Sometimes we'd get so cold that we'd duck into the college to warm up on the way down there. We'd have to walk in the wintertime. We had to go down to church and walk all the way back and when we got back we'd have to check back in. I'm a Catholic; I don't practice it regularly, but I'm a Catholic.

We never got paid for our chores. We'd get back to the dorm and have to wash our own clothes. They used to give us lye soap. It used to come in these big square pieces of soap. It was pretty harsh stuff. They had washboards down in the laundry room. We'd have to go down there and wash our own clothes. We'd scrub our jeans. They'd dry them for us, and we'd pick them up in the morning. That was difficult too, because we were missing clothes all the time. There, kids that were really poor didn't have a lot of clothes and so sometimes they would take other children's clothes. That was part of our daily routine. We didn't have that many clothes so we'd have to wash quite a bit. I learned how to sew. If there was something wrong, like a button was off, I'd have to sew my own button. I learned how to press clothes and I still do that to this day.

I still remember this dorm attendant. He died maybe about ten years ago. He enjoyed punishing kids. He was Native American. There was this old room; it was an equipment room, and we called it Room Nineteen. The reason we called it Room Nineteen was because these rooms were numbered in the hallway from one all the way to eighteen. The next door didn't have a number on it so we called it Room Nineteen. It had this little grill at the bottom where we could listen-in to what was going on in there. He would take kids in there if they got into trouble. He would beat them in there until they would start screaming or crying. But I know he enjoyed doing that because his approach would be real calm and subtle and then when he'd get within striking distance he would just haul off and crack these kids and just drop them. He would hit with his hand, with his open fist.

I got into trouble one time for taking a bottle of cherries out of the cafeteria. I stole a jar of cherries. I was hungry all the time. We'd get our three meals, but we'd have to go to this building outside of the dorm. It was the cafeteria where we'd have to go to eat breakfast, dinner, and supper. We weren't allowed to bring any food out of there because if you took food out of there you were going to be in trouble if they caught you. I was a little bit intrigued, too, because I really didn't know what they were or how they tasted. But, out of hunger, I think, I took that out of there. I had to kneel first on a broom handle, and then I got my turn in Room Nineteen. My choice for punishment was either a razor strap or a fiberglass fishing pole. He gave me a choice, so I took the fiberglass fishing pole. Pull down your pants and—what happened is these kids would go listen when they knew somebody was going in Room Nineteen. They'd all gather around the corner and listen by this grill to find out how long it would take for you to start screaming your head off.

I read up on this dorm attendant. About fifteen years ago, he was dying of cancer. The first thought that came to my head was, "I hope you suffer a long time because of all the kids that you punished, all the kids that you beat. I hope the son of a bitch suffers because of the way that he tortured kids." When he was dying, I was praying that he would suffer a long time, and I'm sure he did. I never forgot that. It's been forty years.

We couldn't afford toothpaste and stuff so they would give us this Government Issue powdered toothpaste. We'd get shampoo and Government Issue toothbrushes. We had to shower a couple to three times a week and we had to go through inspection. We'd take a shower and come out of the shower stalls wrapped up in towels. Then we had to be inspected from head to toe. They would make us drop our towels and they would inspect us. These female matrons would inspect us. They would check over your hair, your ears, check out your private parts, and make you turn around. They would just look. That in itself when you're a young man is embarrassing. For me it was real embarrassing because there were kids there that were older. We'd have to line up and they would inspect us one at a time, so there's ten, fifteen kids behind you watching, plus this one female on the other side that's inspecting you.

After forty years, this stuff is still with me. I thought maybe by now it would have disappeared, but apparently it didn't. When I start talking about this stuff I'm not only emotional, I'm angry because it's something that the state of North Dakota didn't realize what's going on, this conservative state of North Dakota, that this stuff is going on right within its borders in the mid- to late-sixties, early seventies. I'm telling this story because I want people to know about it. That this was going on, that there is discrimination, and it's still alive in North Dakota. I didn't really appreciate being treated like some kind of animal that was too stupid or too dumb to be educated, you know, so that's why I'm telling you. I've told some other people; I'm comfortable talking about it, and I tell everybody.

I haven't kept in contact with any of the students at Wahpeton or Flandreau. Just my brother went there. We talk about it a little bit, not very much though. My cousin and his brother, we've talked about this, like, we met on Saturday night and we were talking about this situation that I got into when I was in Flandreau. My cousin took some cookies out of this locker, and he put them in mine. I got blamed for taking these cookies that belonged to some other student. These two male attendants busted into my room, dragged me down to this room, and they skinned all my hair off for punishment. Again, that was a time when all the boys wanted to have long hair. That was pretty traumatic for me. I must have been about fourteen years old. Yep, my hair was skinned right to the bone. I sent a letter home to my parents and wanted to go home. They were going to come and get me. This was when I was a freshman. I thought, well, you know, geez, I can't go back home with, looking like this with my hair all shaved off. You can imagine what kind of a situation that would be. So I ended up staying there my freshman year.

After I got older, like twenty years ago, I tried to find out who this guy was, and I called the school one day, Flandreau, to find out who this dorm attendant was. I still see his face. I wanted to tell him I was mad at him. I carried this around for twenty-five years. I was going to threaten them. I was going to sue the school. They wouldn't give me any information when I called over there. I don't know why they didn't want to provide it to me.

I felt sorry for some of the Native American kids that had darker skin, darker hair than I did because it seems like they were the ones that were punished more. I think that they resented the fact that I had lighter skin and lighter hair. They were angry at us because we didn't get the same kind of punishment that they did. It seems like the Sioux Indians and some of the Crow Indians really didn't like us because we were fair-skinned and light hair. Any fight was going to be one-sided. We were going to get beat up because we were dealing with kids that were a lot older than we were. There wasn't much of a chance. We started hanging around in little gangs. We had to do that to survive. I hung around with some boys from Belcourt.

The headmaster at the dorm would grab these young boys, and I was one of them, and he would rub his beard on our face and touch inappropriately. You're the first one I'm telling this to. He had a really rough beard. I remember that, and he used to rub on our faces real hard and then, and I had thought about this the other day, the touch that he gave us was inappropriate. He would touch your buttocks. To me that was inappropriate. I think he's still alive this guy. If I could find an attorney that is knowledgeable in this sort of thing, that would understand which route to take, because I'm not trying to gain any money off them, I don't expect to, that would be OK if I did, but they owe me for three and a half years of torture. The sexual abuse lasted pretty much seventh and eighth grade, my two years there. Nobody knows about this except you; you're the only person that I've ever told this to. I haven't talked to a counselor or therapist. I don't even know how I would approach that. I don't even know like, when I talk about it right now it's pretty emotional for me. When I think about it, I get pretty emotional. I saw a lot of sexual abuse. I saw older boys abusing or assaulting younger boys. I was a victim of that, too. And you're the first person that I told that to also. Some of the older boys were attacking some of the younger boys—that was pretty common. I would see that all the time.

To be honest, I'm a compassionate person. I'm not a violent person. I was thinking about my current health and [how] some of the stuff affected me. Long-term, I had some problems with anxiety I dealt with on my own. It was just like, "I got to gain control of this," and I thought either I'm going to gain control of this or it's going to gain control of me. I don't want to be living if it's going to be controlling me. So I thought one day that this is the end of this and it's not going to happen again, that's not going to gain control of me. So I was glad I was able to overcome that. It was just mind over matter, that's the way that I figured that out. That was the way that I dealt with that. I'm pretty strong-minded.

I started feeling anxious, nervous, felt like my heart was going to pound out of my chest, and like I wanted to pass out. After forty years, I thought it's even stronger now than it's ever been. I thought, well, I'll forget about this stuff, it won't bother me. But it's still there and it doesn't go away. Some of those memories are still there. The one good thing about getting older is that you can tell it the way it is. When I was younger I was a little more conservative, and now I don't care. I'm going to be extremely lucky if I get another twenty years out of life, but it's a privilege. I call it a privilege, because a lot of my friends I went to school with have died. I call it a privilege to be able to live this long. It's kind of the way I approach it.

I stayed away from abusing alcohol and drugs. I observed my father. He drank quite a bit. I became involved in music. I'm still involved in music. I started playing in bands because I needed to earn money and make a living. I made a promise to myself that I would not get involved in alcohol and drugs. All the years I've played, twenty-five years, I never drank or took drugs. A lot of my friends that I played with in the band over the years, a lot of them are dead now because they got involved in alcohol and drugs. I was pretty determined that it wasn't going to control me. I made a promise to myself that I wouldn't get involved in alcohol and I was able to do it. I tell people my story about staying away from alcohol and they are amazed when I tell them that I never got involved in that stuff.

I had some other problems with my anxiety attacks and relationships. I struggle in that—lacked a lot of patience and didn't know how to—I was never a huggy, touchy, or affectionate type of person. I wanted that affection, I needed that, but I didn't get that. And so nowadays when I talk to young parents I tell them there are two things: one, patience; and number two, shower your kids with a lot of love and affection.

My relationship is pretty good with my kids. I have three kids. My two boys live in Grand Forks. They were never beaten; I never hit them. I didn't send them to boarding school. I tried to give them just about everything that they could possibly want, you know, the best of this and the best of that. I worked my butt off to do that. They were never punished, but they understood what work was because I made them work, they had to do things. I wanted them to be able to live on their own, so they understood what work was and they understood going to school was really important to them, and to me of course, so they understood that too. They're able to live on their own. I wanted them to take care of themselves.

Boarding school did teach me some things like responsibility and discipline. It taught me how to work. I didn't like their approach. It was, "You're not smart enough to work on academics, you're going to be taking these shop classes and you're going to be a block layer or you're going to be a carpenter." That was the impression that I got from them.

A lot of the kids that went to Wahpeton made the next step to Flandreau High School boarding school. My parents were still poor and they had a hard time supporting us. We decided that was the next school we were going to go to. It wasn't a choice; it was just automatic. I did come home for the summer. Freshman year in high school I went to Flandreau. The discipline wasn't quite as strict as the Wahpeton school because at the Flandreau School, again, some of the kids were nineteen, twenty, twenty-one years old. Some of the kids used to go down to the bar and get liquor. They'd bring it back to the dorms. We'd have problems with kids that would get drunk and get violent. We had to keep a low profile because being from Belcourt and fair-skinned made it more difficult for us. That's why we hung out in little gangs. We had a nickname for our group. It was called the "gimme gang," because we were always asking for somebody to give us something.

Flandreau School was like Wahpeton school in that the emphasis was on trades. We had to take electrical shop and wood shop and welding. I understood why they made us do that, because they were thinking that we were dumb Indians, that we weren't intelligent enough to educate. I think that affected my skills later on in life. I wanted to go to college and I wanted to make a living. But I didn't have the background, so I really had to work to gain some of those skills that I missed. My grandparents went to Fort Totten. My grandfather went there in 1910, 1911. I went back there to visit with him one time. He took me in the fort and he showed me where his room was at. Told me that he went there and that's how he became a painter, a commercial painter. Back then they were considered to be too dumb to go to college.

I liked reading. I remember reading *Highlight* books and those little magazines. I wasn't really necessarily good in math. Least favorite subject was math and science. I didn't have the background because we weren't forced to take sciences. We had a general science class and that was it.

There was an elderly lady, a female matron at the school, Edna Mc-Cloud. She was from Belcourt. She was one of my favorite matrons. If you ever get to the Dunseith Day School and you walk in the gym, there's a painting, a mural on the wall of a lady with a black dress on with floral designs on the dress. I had that put up there in memory of Edna. There was another lady, this female matron at the school in Wahpeton; I was her pet, I don't know why. She always helped me out. She would give me money, wanted me to do errands for her and work for her and she'd pay me. Those two ladies were really nice to me.

At Wahpeton, they would come around in the morning and they would wake us up and they would turn all the lights on. We had these metal Government Issue garbage cans, and the dorm attendants would take them and throw them on the floor, making all kinds of noise! We'd have to get out of bed, because if you were still in bed when they came back a second time you were coming off the bed with the mattress. They would grab the mattress and pull it right off the bunk bed. If you were on the top bunk, you were in for a long fall. Then they would come around and do inspection. I remember this one male attendant would come around on Saturday before we were allowed to go anyplace. They'd allow us to go to shows or go downtown, give us fifty cents for candy. He would come around and would check the beds to make sure they were fixed right and extremely tight, kind of like you were in the army, in the military. He would walk around with a white glove and check the top of dressers and windowsill. They would come around and inspect the room. I remember kids scrubbing the hallways on their hands and knees sometimes if they got into trouble. The brushes weren't very big. That hallway looked like it went on forever.

I was back to Wahpeton about five years ago. The dorm that I stayed in is gone. I don't know why they tore it down or whatever they did with it. It was kind of an emotional [visit] for me. I went back there by myself.

I didn't want anybody else along with me. I wanted to go through this by myself. I don't want to see anybody along looking at me, witnessing me crying. I didn't cry, but came close. I went to visit Flandreau about ten years ago, and as far as I'm concerned, if I never see those schools again in my lifetime, that would be OK with me.

I had one brother that came to the Wahpeton school with me, my younger brother. I haven't talked to him about all of these things. Nope, we, you know, whenever the topic comes up, the discussion is very short and just maybe joking or teasing about certain situations. That's the extent of it. We don't really sit down and say "Do you remember this?" and "Do you remember that?" We've never done that. I don't think I've ever talked to my brothers and sisters, or my children about some of these things that went on. Some of them are painful.

I'm not involved in a lot of community activities because I consider myself a loner. I avoid social gatherings where there's a lot of people involved. I'm uncomfortable with hugging or shaking hands. I avoid large crowds. I don't go to the casino. I'm against gambling. I've been a professional drummer for nearly thirty years, but I'm just kind of like off in my own little world, avoiding people, large crowds especially. I still play, mostly in bars. That's what I call my "weekly fix." It's kind of like I get off in my own little world. I don't see anybody at all.

Most of my family members are pretty successful, you know, they went on to get educated; they're able to maintain employment. I can't say that they all adjusted well; they had problems. I think that we're not a real close family and—I think changing that would be helpful.

I worked as a laborer for a while. Then I realized that I didn't want to do that kind of stuff the rest of my life. I thought I was capable of doing more and better things. I started taking classes in Bottineau. It used to be the Forestry [school] and was a branch of [North Dakota State University]. I also took classes at the tribal college in Belcourt. I graduated from Bottineau in 1978 with a two-year degree, transferred to Mayville State College, BS degree, and in 1980, I earned a Master's in Educational Administration.

I worked as a principal in four North Dakota schools before returning home. My two boys were going to be graduating, and I wanted to be a little bit closer to home so I could spend some time with them. I wanted to get a little bit closer to God. Spiritually, I consider myself to be religious, but I don't go to church every Sunday. I say my prayers at home. I'm satisfied with that. I've been successful with my education and the positions I've held, but my ego's not satisfied yet. I don't know if I'll ever find that happiness, that contentment. Some people do and some people don't. I'm still searching for mine.

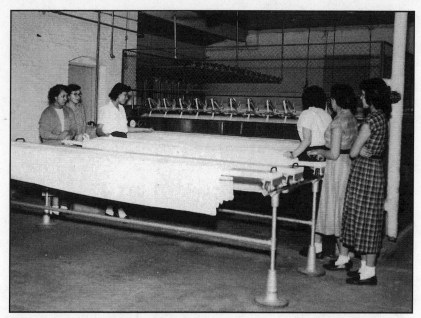

Handling the mangles, Flandreau Indian Boarding School, SD.
National Archives at Kansas City.

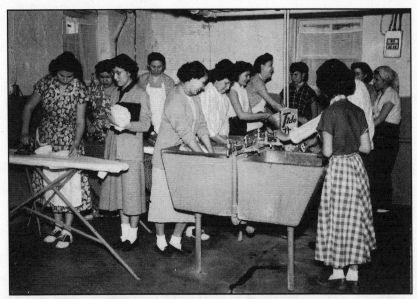

Laundry day, Flandreau Indian Boarding School, SD.
National Archives at Kansas City.

STUDENT OF THE YEAR

I traveled to north of Dunseith in the Turtle Mountains to interview Mary (b. 1941, pseudonym). A narrow gravel road wound by the decaying, ghostly remains of the San Haven tuberculosis sanitarium. We sat in Mary's son's home, surrounded by birch, fir, and aspen trees, with sunlight flowing through east-facing windows. Below the house is Mary's renowned garden, overflowing with fruit and vegetables. On a second visit, perfectly coifed, slender, but wiry, Mary met me at the door of her home. Sitting around a new dining table in her immaculate house, we caught up on her family and tribal news over a large cup of coffee. Mary is quick to laugh uproariously at her tales.

My name is Mary Weston, and I am just seventy-six years old. When growing up I lived north of San Haven. . . . My grandparents had little houses all around, and they rented them out. In the summertime, I would spend time here. . . . I grew up in a log cabin. It was built from little logs that were made from the trees around here. Our house had three great big rooms; we had big bedrooms, big living room, and a big kitchen. My grandpa was a wealthy man when he came here, and he was a white man . . . He ended up in this area, married my grandma. So I'm related to all [my grandmother's people] up here . . . my grandmother's half-brothers.

We'd get up in the morning in the summertime, and we'd run around the bush. I mean it was thick woods; there would be little houses here, and the rest would be all woods, but I mean there were *many* houses here close together. There were a lot of little kids to play with in the summertime. We had nothing to play with. We didn't have bikes or nothing at that time. I remember when my dad came; while he was in the war, my mother built a little playhouse for us, out of oak trees, but then when my dad came back, he took it down [laughter]. He used it for wood in the winter [laughter]. So there went the playhouse. But we did have swings out of rope; we had two swings. There was no electricity, so you know, when it started getting dark everybody was in the house. But I remember in the summertime when we'd come home from Wahpeton there was all these people that were still around here, and as young teenagers we used to run around, all us kids would run around, all the relatives, all the cousins and all the other ones that were around here.

We didn't have running water. For laundry, Mother would haul water from the lake. See, there was a big lake down here; there still is a lake there, but it's not like it used to be. They'd haul water, and in the wintertime they would melt the snow. She'd give us that big tub — that she'd wash clothes in — she would fill that and give us a bath, and she'd put one [of us] in, and she didn't change water; we'd all take turns [laughter].

There were nine of us kids. We all had beds. Like I said, we didn't hurt for anything, because my grandpa was wealthy and he only had three kids. My grandma used to have gardens all over here, too. She had three huge gardens. Not like the garden that I have; my grandma had *fields*. She did all this stuff herself. Us kids would be out there playing. She'd put sunflowers all around her garden. It was just pretty. In fact, one of her gardens was just right down here, one of the big long ones. She planted everything, and she would harvest all that stuff herself. She had a great big house, and she had a big cellar underneath. So she did a lot of canning. I remember Phillip [pseudonym] canned deer meat in those days because they didn't have freezers. Even though they were wealthy, they didn't have freezers. But she had a great big house and [when] the cellar was full . . . she'd get big bins of everything [in] the fall of the year, and then she'd can, pick berries, do all that canning, plus she bought at the store — like peaches — and she'd can those. Plums, peaches, and then in the wintertime she'd go — all these people that rented from her — she would go and give [the canned food] to them.

My grandpa worked at San Haven; he was a painter. My grandma, she just re-did her homes and houses when somebody'd move out, and in the inside of those houses she would put cardboard boxes, real even-like, all over, and then my grandma would wallpaper those. She'd make them just nice, re-paint.

My dad went to work on the Garrison Dam. He worked that fall, and then that fall he bought us our first bikes. We never got bikes until we were about thirteen. We used kerosene lamps, and didn't have running water. I don't remember when the electricity came in, but I remember when they brought in the water. It was just amazing because with all the pipes, and then they turned that faucet on, it was actually, you know, water coming out. I went to school in Wahpeton and we had running water, but here we didn't have that.

The outhouse! Oh my God! [laughter]. But you know, we always had a slop pail inside, they called it a slop pail, so we always used that at night, but in the daytime we had to go outside. Every year, every fall, my dad would have to dig a new toilet. For toilet paper, there was Sears [catalog pages], and there was National Balas Hess—it was a catalog, where you could order a bunch of stuff, just like a Penney's, that was the name of it. And I think there was Montgomery Ward, too, in those times. Oh yeah, that's all we had.

When I was about six years old, I was sent to Wahpeton, me and my sister Deborah [pseudonym]. Actually I don't know why we were sent to boarding school. We spent the first year here in the Dunseith day school, and I have no idea why they sent us out. Because like I said, it wasn't like they couldn't take care of us and feed us and everything because my grandpa was wealthy. He made sure we were taken care of us, his kids and us, so I don't know why. I never did ask my mother why they sent us to Wahpeton. Let's see, I think I was six, maybe I was seven, and Deborah was eight when we went to Wahpeton. We were both in the same grade. See they held her back; they didn't send her to school when she was six, they waited, then they sent the both of us. We ended up in the same grade even though she was a year older than me. So we must have been seven and eight because we went to the Dunseith Day School the first year, then we went to Wahpeton. Then my other sister, Emily [pseudonym]—the second year we went, my sister came to Wahpeton. As the kids got old enough to go to school, we just all went to Wahpeton, all of us kids, all nine of us. We went by bus. We just went with the clothes we had on, little kids like that, because Wahpeton furnished the G.I. clothes, Government Issue. Well, they had all sizes; they were just little dresses. We always wore dresses. Yeah, yeah, and then they had little shoes, they were high heels. They were the full shoe but they had little high heels about like that [measures with hands], and they were real narrow with lacings or shoestrings.

As we got older, when I was in the sixth grade, I still went to Wahpeton with just the clothes I had on all those years. My sister was the oldest one, and she had a suitcase. I've got a picture at the house with us washing the head girls' matron Mrs. Martinson's car, and I had these G.I. clothes on. They're just regular G.I. clothes.

I was lonesome, but there was nothing you could do. You'd get a let-ter—my mother would write, but that wasn't that often—and we'd write back. We didn't go home for Christmas, not in those days. They never start-ed bringing us home at Christmas time. We came home at Easter, I think, the last year at Wahpeton.

I got presents from my family. If the parents didn't send presents the week of Christmas, the Wahpeton Indian School people would go out and they would solicit the people for gifts for "a girl this age" or something, you know. I remember, I don't know why, one year I didn't get a present from home, so the next morning they gave me this little present, and it was the cutest little purse [laughter]. It was just neat. It was nice. But most of the time, most of the parents sent Christmas presents. But it was a long time to be away from home, from the end of August till the end of May.

In the dorm, we had nice little beds; we had each our own bed. There were big long rows, two rows. They had the second, third graders, and fourth in one dorm, then the other one would be the fifth and sixth and then the seventh and eighth. They didn't have them all—they separated them by age—but we had little beds; it was nice. We had lockers against the wall; our little beds and then the locker would be there for each student.

Oh, yes, we had matrons. They didn't sleep with us; they were awake all the time, going around and around. They had night people that watched all the students. I got up at 6:00 a.m., then we went to the dining room. Now this is when we were small—of course it never changed—we got up at 6:00, got dressed, had to make our bed, go wash up, go brush our teeth, always had to brush our teeth all the time. We didn't have toothpaste; I think it was [baking] soda we had. Then we had to go downstairs in the recreation room there, or whatever it was, and we'd all wait. Everybody was down there, then we'd go across. Our dining room wasn't in the same building they had the girls' dorm in. It was the girls' dorm, then the dining room, and then the boys' dorm. So when everybody was ready, they'd take us to the dining room to go eat. For breakfast I know we had oatmeal, and I know we had cockroaches [laughter]. You'd see them once in a while, not in the food, but around the building. It was an old building.

After breakfast, when we were small, we'd go back to the girls' build-ing, and then after so long then they would take us over to the school. From school we'd go back to the dining room and eat dinner. Then we'd play outside for a while, and then we'd have to go back to the school for the afternoon and then we'd come back, and then we'd have to wait for suppertime. There was people and things constantly, all the time, but then there was a lot of people that were lonesome. I'm sure we were lonesome, too. I'm sure we cried at first, but then you'd get used to that. When I would leave there, I'd get lonesome, but I'd be happy to get back home. Because, see, at that time they had good people over there, all of those people. I can't remember anybody actually really being mean to anybody. If you, like the one time when I told you when the eighth-graders had gotten in trouble, but getting a spanking like that with a belt wasn't going to hurt anybody, their feelings you know, sting a little bit. But all the years I went there, nobody, I never seen them to be vicious or mean with anybody.

What happened was the eighth-grade girls had left the school during the night, and they met with some science school kids from Belcourt. Must have been relations, so they went out and partied, they drank and partied. Well, during the night towards morning, when they snuck back into the building, the staff was waiting for them when they came in. [The staff] ran them through the line to get a licking so, that's what they did. Actually, that was the only cruel thing that I ever knew anybody did down there. They had to stand in line there, then all the staff people—all the men and all the matrons—were down there and even the superintendent of the school. The staff would hit them with a belt. But they said they got hit on the legs, and then after they got a good licking from all the faculty, then each one of them would get a toothbrush, and for the rest of the night, on their hands and knees would have to scrub the floor, the cement floor. The next day [the staff] sent them all home to Belcourt, they were all Belcourt students.

When I was older, I think sixth grade on up, I had duties. In the morning, set the tables up when the kids ate—we would set out the sugar and that stuff on all the tables and there were certain things we would have to put on the tables—and then the kids would come in line, just like they have to do in Belcourt, get in line and go through. After they were done, we would have to wipe up all the tables, pick up everything, and then we would have to sweep and mop the floor. Then we would go to school, yeah, and that was all three times a day. There was a girl [laughter], she liked olives, so we were in the dining room doing all of our work and we were putting stuff in the pantry, so she stuck her hand in this gallon jar of olives, and when she turned around—this is Cynthia [pseudonym] who is stealing the olives—and Mrs. Solin Hill was the dining room person. She caught her, and she said, "Cynthia! How dare you stick your hands in that jar, your germy hands in that jar!" So Cynthia had to clean that pantry out for her punishment [laughter]. Made her wipe up the pantry, where they keep all the food, and you know pantries are big. She had to wipe everything, and wipe up the floor.

We didn't get allowance for our work, no, no. Well, you see, that was a boarding school. They'd use so many of us at one time, and I suppose three months down the road you'd change to a different job, but I don't think that they ever used all of us, because there were different places to work. But Wahpeton was a place of learning; they taught us many things down there that we still use today. I worked in the laundry, and they did all of our clothes, all of our bedding was done right there, our own laundry, and all of us were assigned to laundry. They had what they called big mangles where the sheets would go through. [The sheets would] come out of the washing machine, then you'd take them and put them on that mangle. It was rollers, and the sheet would go through and it would come out the other end and it was dry, it was just nice. So I was there.

Our dresses, government clothes, we had to iron. I worked in the laundry twice and Crumpert, in the class, she taught us how to embroider dishtowels. I still embroider today.

At one point they had us paint on the dishcloths; instead of the paint I used the thread, and I sew. You know, I learned to darn. When I went over to the boys' building, one of the matrons there, she showed me, I had to do that. So I just learned from her, watching her do it. So that was another duty I had to do. I did this in the evening. Rather than go play or walk up and down—after supper we got to walk up and down, visit with the boys—instead, I was over at the boys' building darning socks [laughter].

All the years I went to Wahpeton, when the Belcourt bus unloaded in Wahpeton, the first thing they did was, you went in there and they checked you for nits or bugs. Then they had these DDT cans, like when you spray for bugs [laughter], that powder, it's amazing they never killed anybody because they sprayed us, you couldn't hardly breathe, they sprayed everybody. Then what they did if they found out you had bugs, they just chopped, they just went with a scissors like this, they just chopped their hair off. I mean a lot of those kids had long hair, they just took the braid up and cut it right across. It was to get rid of bugs . . . but we never had bugs going down there, but there was a lot.

My mother always permed our hair real tight. She cut it real short and she'd permed it just tight for us. We used rags to curl our hair [laughter]. When we were young, people made them . . . I don't know what they called them, I suppose just curlers. But what they did, they cut tobacco cans, the Prince Albert cans, they'd cut those in small pieces, strips, and then they'd wrap that with paper. You'd take your hair, then wind, then clamp. That's what we had here, but a lot of people used . . . a piece of rag. Then they did it the same way, just tie it . . . your hair would be just kinky, kinky [laughter], well it was—we thought we were cute though [laughter]. Oh yeah, we couldn't afford, I suppose they had bobby pins in those days and stuff, but yeah we used those tins, brought them from home. I bet the sharp edges cut our hair a lot.

Oh, yes, when I was in the eighth grade, I had this teacher, and his name was Mr. Anderson. I was always a shy kid, and I never knew if I had the right answers; I was always a shy kid. So he'd give us our assignment and we'd start to do [it], and then he'd start asking what do you have down for your answer? I was shy and everything, and he'd be looking around the room to call on somebody. Boy, I'd put my head down and you know, he never, never called on me.

The teachers and all the staff were good; they treated me really good. I worked for a lot of them . . . Mrs. Horn was one of the teachers and I worked for her. Cleaned house, but when I worked for them, they paid us. We got fifteen cents an hour [laughter]. Mrs. Horn's house was uptown in Wahpeton, so we walked from the school to her house and then walked back when we were done. Mrs. Selkirk, I ironed clothes for her; she was right on campus, and she was a schoolteacher too. For Mrs. Horn, we vacuumed, we swept, and we mopped, we cleaned the bathroom, the shower, we dusted everything. She had a big home, American Beauty, so there was a lot of dusting after we vacuumed. We never got tired because there was two of us. It was fun. We got paid for it and we got to eat [laughter]. Oh, yeah [laughter], she had all kinds of luncheon meat, she had ice cream. As soon as she'd leave, boy, we'd be eating and then we'd start our work, then dinner time we'd eat again. We'd put lots of chocolate on our—all kinds of chocolate and strawberry, caramel—she'd tell us whatever you guys want in the fridge, and the ice cream is in the freezer, so we'd fill up good, but mostly we had chocolate; we both liked chocolate. But eventually it got to the point, after eating all of that, I don't like ice cream that much anymore. Well, I was 5'2" in the seventh grade and I weighed 142 pounds [laughter], so I ate well. Fed us well.

There was very few that got to go work for staff people. For Mrs. Selkirk I would go and iron in the evenings after school, after supper, I would go iron for her. Mrs. Mortenson, she was the head one for the girls' dorm and I worked for her too. I would go and clean, but she had an apartment above the dining room. So I would go and clean once a week for her too, that was at night. As I got into the higher grades like sixth, seventh, or eighth grade, I was always out there working.

With my money I would go to the show or buy things when we'd go to town. My mother had a bad habit: she'd send me a dollar and she'd send my sister Deborah ten dollars. I don't know why, because we were in the same grade. She should have never done that. A lot of parents are like that, to this day, they have a favorite kid and they will give them more than the rest. It's wrong, but I learned to outgrow that; it got to the point where I almost got expelled in the seventh grade, because I wanted to borrow one of her skirts. I had to wear the government, the G.I. clothes, and at that, getting to be a big girl, you want to look nice. So, I asked her if I could borrow it for the next day and she told me, "No, I'm going to wear that!" Well, then the next day she didn't have that outfit on, so then that night we were arguing. I was arguing with her because we were in the same dorm; couldn't remember if I hit her, but anyways, I got called in. They'd called the principal on me and they had a meeting that night; because of my atti- tude, they were trying to send me home. You see, they had been working on me for many years; that's what it was, they were going to send me home. They said, "Well in the morning we'll see about sending you home." I was just hurt, but then Mrs. Renville's daughter, her name I think was Doreen . . . came in, and I was crying on my bed . . . so she came and got me and took me into the office and she started asking me what happened. After I got done telling her everything, the next morning before she left—she was off duty—she called and met with the ones that met that night. She must have explained to them what happened, and so then they just let it go. Right then and there I decided that I'm not going to get into trouble because of my sister, so right then and there I made up my mind that I was going to let that go.

Well, when I went back in the eighth grade I had the clothes I had on and plus I had one outfit, one extra outfit. That year I did really good. In Wahpeton, they would have Outstanding Girl of the Year [and] Outstand- ing Boy of the Year awards. See, I had worked for all these staff people and I got along good with all the staff and the matrons wherever I was placed. It was the staff that nominated certain ones in the eighth grade, a boy and a girl. So, then, we were all in the gymnasium, this was at the end of the year there, it had to be in the first part of May, so everybody was in the auditorium. So they announced the winners for Outstanding Girl of the Year, and all of a sudden they said, "Mary Weston!" [gasp!], and everybody started hollering! It was just like I was in the mountains, you know, the echo; I was way out there [laughter]. So after we were dismissed and we were all going out, everybody was so excited, and my sister Deborah comes up to me and says, "They made a mistake, that was supposed to be me!" [laughter] You know what made it worse for her? Her boyfriend was the one that was picked for Outstanding Boy of the Year [laughter]. But then, that must have been right in April though because in May, May Day, May first, we all had big doings at the school. When I won, it must have been in April because then I had to sit, just like the king and queen up there, and I had to wear a formal. Well, where does a kid get a formal? But here this Mrs. Renville, she said, "Don't worry; my girl Doreen has lots of formals. Now after school, you run over to the house"—they had a house right in the back of the school too—"You come over to the house and we'll try on those formals." Sure enough, I did fit one. I wore a bright yellow one. I sat up there, and then they took pictures of us; every time there was something going on, they took pictures. Then they made that into a movie . . . I didn't know that at the time, but when my kids got old enough and they went to Wahpeton, they seen that and they said, "Ma! You were in the movie!" [laughter] Oh, for dumb; I should have tried to get ahold of that because there was lots of things on there.

All those that came in to Wahpeton, nobody ever spoke any of their language but English. They came from South Dakota, Montana, Minnesota. Everybody spoke English.

When we got older, when we went to church, we had to walk uptown to the churches, no matter what church we went to, whether it was Catholic or Lutheran or whatever. So we walked. This one time, I think it was around Christmas, they had some things going on at the churches; they allowed some students, the bigger ones to go down there. Coming back there was some girls—we weren't all together, we were kind of lagging—and they were smoking, I don't know how they got the cigarettes but when they got to school they said it was butts that they had picked up, but where did they get the matches, too? I don't know, but there was a few of them and somebody had told on them. The matron knew who they were as they came in. The punishment was they just had to sit inside. A lot of the times the punishment was you had to pick the nits off the other kids heads. If you got detention, that's mostly what you had to do. You had to sit, like on the weekend, in the afternoons, instead of going to the show, you had to sit there and pick nits. I never did that. My sister Deborah was always picking nits [laughter]. And I was a Girl Scout, for three years. I had ALL the badges. I wish I would have kept them.

I don't *ever* remember a teacher screaming in the classroom. I don't ever remember anything, no hollering. The kids were well behaved in the classrooms. I mean, in the dorm, the older kids, like Vickie [pseudonym], was down there and she was older than me. I might have been a fifth-grader and Vickie may have been an eighth-grader. She was a mean person. Of course the one she fought might have been mean too, but Vickie took that Sioux girl and she put her upside down in one of these trash cans. And she was just beating her. I can't remember if she was sent home too. See, they really didn't tolerate vicious behavior.

There were railroad tracks right behind the school, but you still had to go wherever the depot was, I don't know, but yeah, the trains run right in the back of us. And that's probably how they sent a lot of those kids home, I don't know. A lot of kids, they were so lonesome that they'd run away. Lots of kids ran away, and sometimes it was so cold. But some-how they managed—they must have had people out there watching for them—runaways from Wahpeton school, because they always brought them back. There would be one or two that would try. They were from Bel-court; how did they think they were going to get from Wahpeton all the way to Belcourt? But then, these were older kids, too, they were seventh- and eighth-graders. A few girls ran away, but mostly those boys.

Oh yeah! I had a lot of friends and a lot of them were Sioux from South Dakota. Then I had, when I was in the seventh grade, Sarah [pseudonym]. She and I were good friends [laughing]. Oh yeah, in seventh grade her and I were real good friends. Cynthia, my first cousin, we were friends all the way through, we were always good friends. Then I had a girl from South Dakota—her name was Jackie [pseudonym], from Sisseton—her and I were real good friends.

Evenings I would listen to the radio; we had a big old-fashioned ra-dio. There was downstairs where you go and do things, then upstairs there was living rooms where you could do things too. Country western music. Sitting by the radio—what's that singer? Hank Williams—I remember sitting, listening to the radio when he came on. I mostly just, like I said, when I got older, in the upper grades, I was doing a lot of work, evening work. About once a month we had a dance. It was not for the little ones; I think it was the sixth-, seventh-, and eighth-graders. Gene Thomas would get the guitar and sing [laughter]. When it was nice we would walk around; we could walk around the school — Wahpeton Indian School — you could always walk around, but there was always matrons, somebody watching out for all the kids.

Yeah, Gene Thomas [laughter]. But you know, it was like a friend, a boyfriend. It was so funny, you know. When the Garrison Dam went through and those Indians over there got all that money. Sanish, those people got all this money and a lot of those kids were in Wahpeton, and this guy, Mathew Foolish Bear his name was, his dad came down there with a big fancy car and lots of money, and they'd come give their kids money. Because they got their pay-off from the government [laughter]. So Gene and I were sitting on the Home Ec. steps, and he always tells me, "Boy that was dirty of you, you traded me in for Mathew Foolish Bear just because he has lots of money!" [laughter] Oh yeah, I started being friends with him [laughter]. But see, when you got money from your parents, it was fifteen cents for the show, twenty cents for candy or whatever. The most they gave us was a dollar, out of our accounts. But I mean, you got to go to the show and get candy. If there was money left over, like my money when I used to work, I would turn it in and it would go into my account.

Many years later, Gene Thomas was selling trailer houses so I called him up. He came up here to see me. Then we were kind of driving around and we were talking about when he told me that it was a dirty shame you traded me in. I worked with him in Belcourt. Oh God I used to tease. I don't know if he's still here.

I graduated from Wahpeton in the eighth grade, and that was another thing, that year in the eighth grade, I think there was eighty-six of us that graduated. Every one of us girls had to make our graduation dress. Every one of us, from our Home Ec. class. Mine had a low neck, short sleeves, then it was tight and it had a flared skirt, and American Beauty Rose was the color of it. Then I wore three-inch high-heel baby doll shoes. They're round, just round-like.

I came back here when we left Wahpeton. We were admitted to Flandreau for high school. So when we got back here we were all ready to go to Flandreau that fall for high school; then my mother and dad got a letter saying that we couldn't go. What happened there was Carrie Mills [pseudonym] was the boss over here and her two sisters were sent instead, she let them bump us off the list.

The Belcourt bus came right up here, so we could have gotten on that bus, the Belcourt bus, over here by Barbara Azure's corner. Well! We were *not* going to school in Belcourt! Dad and them should have did whatever they needed to do to get us in to Flandreau. Dunseith was a white-kids-only school back then.

So then we started running around, both my sister Deborah and I. Deborah got married—let's see, we come out of Wahpeton 1955—in 1957 my sister Deborah got married; then 1958 I got married and had three kids. I went all over, worked in a nursing home in Fargo. California, I worked out there with my husband. My kids went out there, Pat and Kelly [pseudonyms] went to school out there for one year. Then we came back to North Dakota. In 1965 I went to school. My husband was in the state farm, Mandan or Bismarck, got a year, and so the state forced me to go to school here in order to receive welfare benefits. They were forcing me to go to school for my GED. We went to school in Rolla; there were fifteen of us. The principal or whatever he was over there, he taught us, all fifteen of us. Then there was a couple others too that taught us, but then after they forced us to take our GED. We went to school for five months, just in the mornings, and then they said, "Oh, you're ready to take your GED." So nine of us showed up and out of the nine, six of us passed. I was one of them. I didn't go through the ninth and tenth grade, I just took my GED. But see, I guessed through the math and sciences, I didn't know anything about those subjects. I hit all the right answers [laughter], enough to get me through.

I was told, "Mary, you should go to school to be a LPN."

"No, no, I'm sick and tired of school. I don't want to go to school, I want to work."

"Well, where do you want to work?"

I said, "San Haven." Well I could just walk there. So in about three days I had a job. I started working there with the mentally handicapped. Then I quit one day and I stayed home for one year. The next year I put in for this position in Belcourt, a teacher's aide. I've been there for forty-two years. You know something, I can't remember being in Mr. Erdrich's class, I had to be but [laughter], well, I could remember that red hair, just like a carrot [laughter]. But he liked Deborah because she was such a noisy kid, even in school. She hasn't changed; if she has something to say she's going to say it [laughter].

The only thing I could say, the only reason I sent my kids there was because I had a good experience there. They were good to us. Again, by the time I had left, by the time my kids went there, things had already changed, and I think that a lot of the people that were down there after were people who just didn't care about the kids; they just cared about the kind of money they were making.

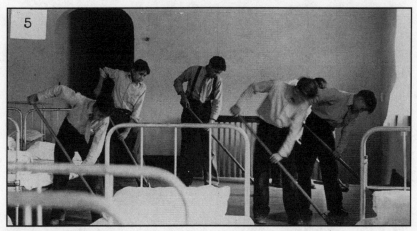

Cleaning detail, Pierre Indian Learning Center, SD.
National Archives at Kansas City.

Sewing class, Pierre Indian Learning Center, SD.
National Archives at Kansas City.

HIDDEN SHEETS

At fifty-five years old, Kathryn (b. 1955, pseudonym) was one of the
youngest survivor interviewees. She is Yankton Sioux. Kathryn was living
in Bloomington, Minnesota, at the time of this interview. Her parents were
Yankton and Oglala. Kathryn believes, after seeing a large picture of one
of her uncles wearing a uniform, that he, too, went to boarding school.
She could tell that he was only perhaps fifteen years old. Her mother
attended Holy Rosary Mission (now called Red Cloud Indian School)
boarding school located at Pine Ridge Indian Reservation in South
Dakota. Kathryn has eight brothers and sisters. She attended St. Paul's
Indian Mission (later renamed Marty Indian School) in Marty, South
Dakota, for nine years.

I was born in 1955. I didn't ever live on the reservation because my family
relocated to Indiana. My father was sent to Marty Indian boarding school
in South Dakota, but he was expelled in eighth grade. He didn't get along
with one of the priests there. Even though he had a bad experience, he still
sent us to Marty. He wanted us to be good Catholics. He wanted to be assimilated. I remember my dad saying that he would get mad at Grandma if
she was speaking Dakota at home. My parents were divorced when I was
in the second grade. [Mom] left when I was eight and I didn't see her again
until I was sixteen. My dad was physically abusive to my mother, beat her.
They both drank. Mom went to Holy Rosary in Pine Ridge. My brother and
sisters were all small when Mom moved back to the reservation.

My dad worked construction and then trained as a welder. He was having a hard time managing with five small kids and working. That's when he
sent us to boarding school. I was ten years old. My dad drove us to Marty
Indian boarding school in South Dakota, and came and got us at the end
of the school year. Sometimes we took the bus from Marty to Chicago and
back at Christmas. I was in boarding schools from fourth grade through
high school. I graduated in 1974. Had I not gone there I probably would
have gotten a better education. There came a time when my father was
making good money and we could have stayed home, my brother, sister,

and me, but he continued to send us there, and just basically made good money but kept it for himself. He never sent us money when we were at Marty.

My first experience at Marty was overwhelming; even if we didn't have lice, they put DDT in our hair, the powder stuff. In the dormitories, I could hear kids crying all night. There was the lack of privacy; bright lights were turned on in the morning. We could hardly talk to our own siblings. We had to put our name on all belongings. We had uniforms off and on. A navy blue jumper. When you knelt down the hem of the jumper had to touch the floor.

I'd never even seen a nun before! We didn't have any background about being Indian. We recognized that we were darker but had no real concepts, didn't have a clue. Dad never told us anything. It was a rude awakening when we got to the boarding school and all the kids were from different reservations. It was easier for me because I was so smart. The nuns seemed to like me because school was easy for me and because I liked school.

It was lights-out at a certain time, and I could hear kids crying. I mean, there were little kids from all over different reservations from way up in Belcourt, North Dakota, and Crow Agency, Montana. It was surprising how all these kids were from so far away, like college, except they were little kids in boarding school away from parents.

The Bishop came around that first year I was there, and we were all confirmed. My sister was only in the second grade, my brother in third grade. Everyone was confirmed from first grade all the way to high school; they got them all.

There were boundaries, certain areas that were out of bounds. It was very religious — Mass, vespers, benediction — we were like whoa! It was very segregated. You could hardly talk to your own siblings. Priests and brothers and nuns and Mother Superior, it was just overwhelming, a total change of what I knew.

To get up in the morning, the nun turned on the light. We had to make our bed, wash up, get dressed, and had to go to a different building for breakfast. We were lined-up by height and grade to go to breakfast. I was never hungry. Our utensils were metal, like army trays with the indentation, metal cups. When I first got there, it was hot cereal, oatmeal, or cornmeal mush, and a sweet roll or some kind of coffee cake they made in the great big full sheets, and milk. I don't recall we ever got juice or fruit, but I don't think anyone ever went hungry unless they were punished and didn't get to go to supper.

My sister was sexually molested by a priest there. I knew that he was considered kind of a, you know, a Chester Molester, but I didn't realize that my sister had been molested. She's only admitted to me within the last five years that she was molested by him.[37]

The nun in charge of the little girls' dorm had a tiny room and her own private bathroom facilities. Someone must have wet the bed and took their sheets and stuffed them in a closet, and they were found by the nun. She was just infuriated. She told us if someone didn't confess, we were all in trouble. She got input from some girls that were in seventh and eighth grade to decide what they should do to all of us, since no one would confess to these sheets. They decided that they would pee in this bowl and they would put our nose in this pee. We all had to get in line and well, geez, they just slammed those girls' whole face right in this bowl. This is other girls! The nun allowed it! That same nun got into a fight with an eighth-grade girl. The girl pulled off the sister's veil, punching away! [The girl] got expelled.

High school girls had to do the dishes at lunch; different ones did breakfast, lunch, and supper. Someone had to do the silverware, cups, and put stuff in this big thing, a restaurant type of thing. Stack the stuff and run it through. Someone had to take it off, people had to dry it, and you had to wipe off all the tables, sweep and mop the floor every day, and help the cooks.

I really enjoyed meeting kids from far away tribes that I would never have met otherwise. We got to watch movies in the gym, and during Lent they had lots of religious movies about the Apostles and stuff. There was a playroom where there was a TV, some games, and books. As I got older I resented leaving my friends at home in Indiana and being in two different worlds. I didn't have a difficult time fitting back in at home when I returned from boarding school; it was a small town, and we just picked up where we left off. I still maintain friendship with one of my fifth-grade classmates.

We were allowed to make a beaded headband and beaded daisy chains; someone came in from the community to show us how. Native people in charge of the dorms would take us to pow wows. I remember Crow students that came in with English as second language, but I don't recall them ever getting in trouble for speaking their language among themselves.

---

[37] "Chester Molester" is a slang name for a child molester. Originally prison slang, its usage is now more widespread.

My grandfather wanted his kids to be good Catholics and would get mad at my grandmother if she spoke Dakota at home. He believed in total assimilation into the white world. My grandfather even named my father after a priest, Father Ignacious. My grandmother had balked repeatedly telling him, "No!"

Math was my favorite subject, but I don't recall ever having to work very hard in high school. The principal at Marty told people that I was probably the smartest student that she had ever seen go through the school. I was in a trigonometry class and the teacher thought I was just extraordinary when I really wasn't. I got good grades, but we weren't challenged. I was very ill-prepared when I got to college. I didn't know how to write a paper and had no speaking skills. It was hard, because I was smart and got to college and then it was, "Oh, I don't know anywhere near what I thought I did!" When I look back, it was really a detriment being smart because I was never challenged. It was a huge transition to go from boarding school and not have the skills, not have any self-confidence, a total lack of self-esteem. I remember going into the small off-reservation drugstore and knowing that the white people are watching because you're a little Indian kid. We were the only people of color in the town.

I had a favorite teacher during my junior and senior year. The English teacher would write these goofy plays, and it was fun. He didn't stay at the school for long, moved on after several years. I was in choir my freshman year, and then they didn't have it anymore.

In high school, there were more things to do. They had pool tables and things like that. In grade school, they would have movies sometimes in the gym. During Lent, they had lots of religious movies. I didn't realize they had all these movies about the Apostles. They had a bakery on campus, and after school you got to have a roll.

I remember getting pretty sick when I was probably about in fifth grade. They had a little infirmary. The nun was pretty nice; some nuns were nicer than others, but then the nuns had their favorites. When I was a senior in high school, there was an outbreak of hepatitis. I got hepatitis and was in isolation for three weeks. They vaccinated all of us. I can remember getting the smallpox vaccination when I was in seventh grade. All of us got whatever shots from a nurse from Public Health Hospital in Wagner. Every year, whatever shot or vaccinations, they would take you by grade and we'd all go in and get whatever it was. They also took us to the dentist.

My favorite subject was math; I was really into it. It made sense to me. Looking back, we weren't challenged, so it was easy to be lazy. I don't recall ever having to work very hard in high school. In my senior year, I took Auto Mechanics. We overhauled [an] engine [belonging to] the instructor; it was his truck. I had no speaking skills. Even now to this day it can be difficult. I just took a Dale Carnegie seminar. I have to find another job. I don't have a degree, although I have a lot of experience with the same company for twenty-two years. My lack of self-esteem and self-confidence didn't necessarily come from my boarding school experience. It was more from going out into Wagner, going into a drugstore and knowing the white people are watching you because you are a little Indian kid. The school would sometimes take us into town for movies, but you knew that we were being watched by the white town folks.

During my senior year, someone from Concordia came and talked to us. They said they had a lot of help for Indian students with financial aid, so I applied there. Concordia accepted me before Christmas and that really impressed me. I did really well the first semester. It was really strict and kind of snooty. I transferred to [Minnesota State University] Moorhead, dropped out, got a job, and just never went back. I have worked as a temporary, then at Scheels. Then General Motors Acceptance Corporation as a switchboard operator, then into accounting, wholesale, lease administration, and Commercial Lending until the office closed at the end of 2008 and I was laid off.

I haven't had any problems with alcohol or drugs. I was the oldest in the family when my mother left. I was eight years old. Because of my dad's immaturity, drinking, and partying, I had to turn into a mini-mom. I was the boss. I grew up being more of a bossy control freak. Not that I didn't go out and drink; that was the thing to do, especially my senior year. It was easy to get booze on the rez, put our money together and someone would go and get whiskey. But like I said, I'm a control freak and did not want to lose control.

I'm still a "recovering Catholic." I heard that term somewhere and I just love it. I didn't practice an organized religion. I just felt if I lived a good life, believed in God, I didn't need to be part of an organized religion to be a good person. I've started going down more of a metaphysical spiritual path, and that's where I'm at now.

I think the Catholic Church should apologize for what I saw that a lot of other people went through. I saw a priest just slam a boy's head against the wall, and then a third-grader, the same priest just slammed him in the head, I mean whiplash, just slapped that kid in the face. I saw kids having to hold their hands out palms up and get hit with a rubber thing that was like the size of a ruler but thicker and wider. Their hands would be red. *Red*. We're talking little kid hands. That would have been the school year 1964 or '65. There weren't any nuns or priests that were mean to me, but I witnessed a lot of stuff.

Kids on lawn at Preventorium, Fort Totten Indian Boarding School, ND. *National Archives at Kansas City.*

Cleaning duty, Pierre Indian Learning Center, SD.
National Archives at Kansas City.

NUMBER 76

I interviewed my auntie Annie Plante (b. 1922) in the tidy kitchen of her small, cozy home in Sandy, Oregon. A tiny lady, she has sparkling eyes, with a hint of shy flirtation. Auntie Annie does prolific and gorgeous beadwork. She and Uncle gather her work and hit the pow wow circuit throughout the United States in their RV.

I'm eighty-seven years old. My birthday is on February 10. I was born in Belcourt, North Dakota. My parents were Eliza and Ezear Grandbois. Growing up in Belcourt I didn't do nothing. We never went nowhere, we just stayed home. I didn't go no place. My parents had a sleigh. A lot of years ago they used to run around in a sleigh. We played lots outside in the snow, made tunnels all day long. Didn't mind the cold. A lot of snow in those days; yeah, the snow was way up to the roof of the house. I don't remember if we lived in a log house.

We had chores. We used to help Mom wash dishes, stand on a stool, yeah, used to help, all us kids were helpers. We had to haul water from the, I don't know where they got it, but they had to haul water. We didn't have no inside plumbing or nothing. Yeah, a wood burning stove, an oven you know, a well, and they'd pour water in there to heat it up and we washed up.

When my mom and them went to Minnesota in a covered wagon, I was, let's say, eleven years old when we went over there. I never was in school yet. Then when we come back, I got on the, what was that, yeah, that big truck there I was telling you about, they had a truck and I got on that truck with them, I think it was in Bismarck, I can't remember. No, not Bismarck, I mean Grand Forks or some place, and I went to Marty [Indian School]. I was twelve years old then.

Yeah, it was a truck, it was the back of it you know, it was two like this and then you'd get here and some kids would ride in the back and here was the end, and up here they had a thing in the middle. Lot of kids in there. Yeah! We were all cramped up in there, all sitting in bunches. They were all Indian kids. From all over; from Belcourt, most of them.

They cut our hair right away, but lots of kids had lice in their hair and they used to comb them with kerosene. Yeah, I had long hair, lots of hair. If you didn't have any lice, well then you'd get it from somebody else.

I was in the first grade and then they promoted me to the third grade. Then I went to school there for two years. That was 1932 or 1933, I think. Then I come home, stayed home for two years; my mom was sick so I stayed home, but I went to school in Belcourt. I went to the government school and I also went to the hill over there, the St. Ann's [Catholic School].

At Marty, we used to get up pretty early. We'd go to school half a day and we worked half a day. I worked at the kitchen, at the dining room. Oh, one day, I was pulling the table apart, and there were dishes piled in the middle, and they all fell—not all of them, some of them—fell on the floor and they broke. And I was going to be on the honor roll that month, and they took me off the honor roll because I broke those dishes.

Didn't have to wear uniforms; we got numbers on our clothes and my number was seventy-six. Everybody wore dresses and, yeah, we didn't wear jeans or nothing. So they'd go off to the laundry and they'd bring them back—I don't remember [who]—but then you'd go take a shower and then your clothes were all bundled up with your number on them.

Sister Peter Julian—she was, she was a tough one. She used to get, when we'd get up [too early] in the morning, she'd get up and holler at us kids, "Go to bed, go to bed, go to bed!" and she'd poke you on the back with her finger like that. She never poked me, but she used to do that to all the kids. My niece, she used to sleep with me, and she'd wet the bed and she'd wet all over me. Then, you know what they used to do when they'd wet the bed? The sister used to make them kneel down, they'd put that wet sheet over their head, over their face. That Sister Peter Julian. I don't know how long they'd make them kneel, but then I remember that Nora used to have to kneel down there and put that sheet over her head. And of course she'd wet all over me. There weren't enough beds, but she was my niece so [I] had to share the bed with her. And our beds were not very big, they were just single beds. Lots of beds.

St. Ann's in Belcourt was OK. Wasn't a boarding school; you got to come home every night there. Didn't have to do any work there. I don't remember. Used to work at home [laughter]. Momma was sick, work at home.

Oh yeah, for New Year's Day, Momma used to make pies. Big stacks of them. Raisin pies. They'd stack on top of each other. They wouldn't break, no, no [laughter]! Yeah, she'd stack them way up, then she'd make bullets in the wash boiler.[38] Where'd they boil clothes in there, clean all that up and make bullets in there, that thing would be full. Everybody used to come over on New Year's, eat bullets. And of course, gallette. Make that, too.

People would come in sleighs. Oh yeah, jingle bells on their sleighs. Ben and Adele used to come at four o'clock in the morning [laughter]. My brother Albert played the fiddle. Albert also played accordion. And my brother Bill played organ. "Willy" they used to call him. I never jigged.[39] I never learned how. My niece JoAnn was a jigger. So many people used to jig over there. I don't remember none of us in the family have ever done any jigging.

My dad would give us a blessing on New Year's Day. Yeah, he'd go like this with his hand and he'd bless [us] in the morning when everybody would come. They'd kneel down in front of him, and he'd give them his blessing. Yeah, they don't do anything like that no more. Yeah. We'd celebrate from New Year's Day till the seventh of January. We'd go down to Uncle Dave's place, that was his birthday. And we'd celebrate his birthday on the seventh.

Oh yeah, we used to have gardens. Momma used to make gardens; of course, Papa helped I suppose, I don't remember, but we had a big garden. Carrots, cucumbers, and I don't remember, they used to call aen souchem, or rutabaga. Corn, yeah, different things.

I remember when we were in Minnesota, went to Red Lake. My brothers used to fish over there. Yeah, we lived there over a year. Got there in a covered wagon! My mom had some relatives over there. I didn't go to school there, but they used to have pow wows and I used to go dancing in the pow wows. We lived in the country, by a river . . . must have been Red Lake, I suppose, Red River or, I don't remember. I don't remember all them things. I remember one time my sister Alice and I, we were home alone—Mom and them went some place—and there was a fire. Forest fire like, oh my God everything was burning . . . and there was cows inside the barn and Alice and I—she went in there—was pulling them out. Boards were falling down already in the barn, but we got some of [the cows] out of there. Mom and them got home, and the fire was across the road. The house didn't burn or nothing, but there used to be a little pond there and we used

[38] "Bullets" are meatballs served in a broth; a "gallette" is a kind of biscuit.
[39] "Jigging" is a type of dancing, particularly a traditional dance of the Canadian Métis.

to see a bunch of turtles on the shore, you know, turtles. And we moved over there and then we came back; that's when, on our way back, I got the bus to go to Marty. I was twelve years old when I went there.

I was married at age twenty-one, 1942, December 8, 1942. Got married in Rolla [ND] the first time. Been married going on sixty-six years. For our wedding day we didn't do nothing. No dance, no cake, no nothing. When we left there, we went back to Grafton [ND], that's where Uncle was working. Yeah, married by the justice of the peace, the first time, then later, about six months, we got married in Belcourt, by the Church, St. Ann's. Then we went back again over there where he was working.

We decided to move out to Oregon, to Portland; we just decided to come over here. It was 1950. We never got nothing from the tribe. We used to pick potatoes; we'd pick potatoes and save our money. That's what we came out here with. We picked potatoes over there where we lived in North Dakota. Put a bag on your back—Uncle used to carry the bags on his back, and then I'd hold up the sack and he'd poured the potatoes in there—and [we] picked potatoes together. We each had a bucket. Oh, of course we'd have to bend over to fill the bucket! And then when we'd get our buckets full . . . I'd hold the sack and he'd put the potatoes in there. Four hundred pounds sometimes, a day, we'd pick; we were good pickers.

I don't remember how long we lived there [in Portland]—after we lost all our babies [in North Dakota]. My niece was babysitting and I was baking bread, and she let the fire go out—she was listening to the radio, the old-timers were playing, were fiddling—and she went to, there were still little coals in fire, and she poured some kerosene in there and it exploded. That was April 1. April Fool's Day. We lost two little girls and a boy in that terrible fire. We had three more, three more girls. Two born in North Dakota and one was born in Oregon. Henry was a mechanic. He was a painter. He painted cars and all, mostly mechanic all the time. Well, he retired at seventy. Then he went back to work at eighty [laughter]. Then he worked like, four years, I think . . . he was eighty—three, four years—but he's retired now, again. But he still works all over the house, all the time, he's always working.

I used to cook. I used to be a cook when I'd work. I never worked while the girls were little. Oh, I did once. I worked, washed dishes in Portland, when they were little and somebody used to babysit them, I don't remember. I used to go off to work on the bus. On 92nd and Division, go downtown. Ida used to work there too.

I remember your grandmother Josephine Plante used to always play with cards and she wore all the faces off those cards. I remember that.

That's enough!

Preventorium students at Fort Totten Indian Boarding School, ND. *National Archives at Kansas City.*

Weaving and embroidering, Flandreau Indian Boarding School, SD. *National Archives at Kansas City.*

THE BIG GREEN BUS

As I drove up to Ramona (b. 1948) Klein's lake home on a late spring day, she was in her large front yard checking on winter damage to newly planted rows of trees and bushes. She waved and met me at the door. We sat in comfortable recliners overlooking the lake, watching pelicans drift by in large groups. Earlier, I'd had the privilege of attending one of her workshops. She is a highly animated speaker, lively, funny, and demonstrative. During the interview, Ramona was thoughtful, even pensive, and there were often long pauses and tears. Ramona, a high school dropout, got her GED and went on to college. She has a doctorate in Educational Leadership, and currently owns her own consultant company in school curriculum and instruction, traveling to all fifty states. Her mother had a fourth-grade education, and her father attended Wahpeton Indian Boarding School in North Dakota until eighth grade. She grew up on the Turtle Mountain Indian Reservation in Belcourt, North Dakota.

I'm the fifth child of my full brothers and sisters, or the sixth child, because of my half-brother. The first four years of my life we moved a lot within the reservation, so we didn't have a stable home. We lived someplace in the bush by a lake until my older brother was hurt in school. He broke his arm falling down the steps, and he was permanently disabled from that arm because he had surgery by probably a very incompetent doctor at the Indian Health Service Hospital. He had seven scars on his shoulder, so he couldn't raise his arm above his hip. He had limited use of his arm. At that time, I remember my parents growing flax, because I remember the beautiful blue field. There were also cattle. My mother had a large garden. My dad took my brother out of the hospital and had an ambulance take him to a hospital in another town. [My mom] then had to sell the cattle to pay for the hospital bill, because of course, we didn't have insurance.

During that time, we were left alone a lot because my parents were at the hospital. I think they probably lost everything that they owned because of that. They had to sell the cattle, and then we moved close to town by a different lake. We lived in a log cabin with no running water, and that's where I started school. I went to something called "Beginners." It wasn't kindergarten. It was equivalent maybe to kindergarten, but it was called Beginners. It was at the Government School, as it was called then, so we rode the bus. The other thing I remember about that time is spring. I think of all of the rushing water in the ditches. I don't know who, probably my dad, made a bridge to cross to the road so we could get to the school bus. I remember being very afraid of the water that was rushing. I'm still afraid of water. I like looking at water, but I don't like being in water. I don't even like a tub bath.

Then we moved again, to my uncle's house at the foothills on the western side of the reservation, where I spent a lot more of my childhood years. We lived in a three-room house with one of the rooms used for a kitchen during the summer but not during the winter. There was a little room that was big enough to hold my parents' bed and a makeshift closet. All of us then slept in the other room. There was the kitchen, my parents' room, and the "everything room." We didn't have running water.

One of the happiest early memories I have is the first time having popcorn. My dad made popcorn on the wood stove in the kitchen, and we had to sit in the other room. I remember hearing that popcorn made in a cast iron pan.

My mom may have gone to school part time on the reservation. My mother's family traveled some; they went from the reservation up to Canada through Montana. They were gone for seven years, traveling with a wagon. They carried their chickens and a cow with them. She talked about having a makeshift kind of a crate under the wagon, and they'd keep the chickens there. They had fresh eggs most days. They lived in a tent and used a galvanized washtub for heating [water] and for a stove during the winter. I did not know my grandpa. He died before my parents were married. He would work on farms or do some [other] work. They'd get enough money and then they would travel. I'm not sure why they went up to Canada and back again, but they did. My mother said that Grandpa spoke seven Native languages.

I was around six when I went to Fort Totten. I was there for four years. I'm not really sure why I was sent away to boarding school. I think it was so that we would have an education and we lived way out in the bush. There just weren't any resources to take care of us. I think that's what people did then. I think that's what they did because there were five of us. Five of us went first, and my oldest two brothers ran away from school. My oldest brother didn't go to Fort Totten for very long; he ran away. I know my brother Dan ran away, but they took [him] back to boarding school. Then my oldest brother and my oldest sister went to Flandreau High School for only one semester, because my dad died in January. My mom became widowed with eight kids under sixteen years of age. My youngest sister was seventeen months old, and my oldest brother was sixteen. They did not go back to Flandreau but stayed home with Mom. My older brother, a younger brother, and I went back to Fort Totten after Dad died, and [we] stayed until that spring.

I remember leaving on the bus from in front of the school. A green bus, kind of a really dark green bus. I still have the image in my mind of my mom standing on the sidewalk. I was sitting on the side of the bus, closest to where my mom was standing. I think she had my little sister or my little brother by the hand, standing there, and I—my mom had a crooked nose because she had a broken nose, and she would take her hand, I know she was wiping away tears, but she held her hand on her nose—and I often wondered what she was thinking. I often wonder what it must be like for a mother to see her children leaving, knowing that she may not see them for a while, and knowing that she had to struggle even to feed us. So, the decision, if it was partly hers, my parents' decision, for us to go to school, they probably had to make the decision for the kids to be educated and fed and sheltered, or stay home, possibly freeze, absolutely, or being hungry. I don't get hungry now, not hungry like I was hungry when my mom had to pick up food from the dump ground. She talked about the store and a man who worked at that store who used to save soup bones, sometimes old wieners on the side. But she fed us from the dumping ground. So, to make that decision to either let your kids go knowing that they might be hurt and lonely, well, she was too.

One of the first things that happened when we got to the school was I got a haircut. I had long hair. I had head lice, and to this day [I have a scar], right at the top, this part, the crown of my head, there were scabs there and there were lice underneath. We were fine-combed. They had black fine combs dipped in kerosene. In the sewing room, they had long tables covered with white sheets, and we'd see the lice on the sheets. I don't remember how often that happened, but it seems like it was a lot. We'd get fine-combed with kerosene, and we had some kind of a shampoo that had a really strong odor to it. I don't think I'd call it a fragrance; it was an odor.

We were de-loused and the kerosene burned my scalp. To this day, every once in a while, when I'm brushing my hair or combing my hair, I sense the scabs and the head lice that were, right here, this part of my head right here. Our skin was also very *very* dry, and for a long time I only knew the homemade kind of soap; it was whitish-yellow and had cracks in it and it was always dirty.

We got assigned to a room. I remember that room seemed to me to be very big. If I remember, there were eight of us to a room, but I think there were more than that. We had bunk beds. There was a sewing room. There was an apartment where one of the matrons lived. There was an office, and then upstairs on the second level is where the big girls lived. There were little girls and then big girls, and I think seventh grade up, because there were some high school girls there. My sister was upstairs, and I was on the main floor. We weren't allowed to go upstairs. But, everything, *everything* was strange and cold. The other thing I remember was the sheets seemed like they were starched stiff. The blanket must have been a woolen blanket; it was itchy.

Walking in a line, having girls who were strangers in the same room, walking from the dormitory to the dining room was unusual, strange, unfamiliar, and very different from home. We did not wear uniforms. I think I kept my clothes from home because the benefactors used to send us stuff. I have no idea who the benefactors were. There was one teacher who used to get boxes of clothes from somebody, benefactors, and I didn't have any idea what a benefactor was, but we'd write thank you notes — "Dear Benefactor." I do remember getting some clothing, some dresses, and a couple of dresses from one of those boxes from a teacher.

The school was operated by the Bureau of Indian Affairs, but on Thursdays nuns came. They wore habits. Every Thursday afternoon there was religious instruction. Most kids went to religious instruction with the Catholic nuns, but I could not go to the religious instruction with the Catholic nuns. I had to go with the missionaries because I was not baptized Catholic at that time. I was baptized in Fort Totten so I could be a part of the religious instruction and be included in that group. Father Tim baptized me. One of the girls from high school was my Godmother. I'm still in touch with her.

My parents worked in the valley picking potatoes. I do remember them coming one time during October, very likely after they finished picking potatoes, because they had money to come and see us and take us to Devils Lake. We got new jeans and I got a haircut too. My dad took me to a barbershop. I don't know if they came any other time. We went home for Christmas, took the bus. We went home during summers, too.

I stole soap. I did. I walked to the little store. I snuck away. I was probably about seven years old. As a child it seemed like that store was a long way; in reality, it wasn't. There was a post office, and then the general store. I stole a bar of pink Camay soap. I hid that soap. I'd use it to bathe with and then I'd take a brown paper towel, wrap it and tuck it underneath my mattress. I *did* steal. As an adult, I went back to pay for the soap but the store was no longer there. It bothered me that I had stolen something. I remember seeing a boy's hands. He was close to my age. I have an image of his hands that were so chapped they looked scaly and were bleeding. That's when I stole the soap. I didn't want skin that way—I remember his hands.

We got up about six o'clock and made our beds. We had details before we went to breakfast. Details consisted of cleaning bathrooms, cleaning hallways, either dusting with a dust mop—oil rags, oil mops I think they were called. The broom closet was right across from the bedroom that I slept in. We had to clean our dorm room and clean that broom closet. We then walked in line to breakfast. The girls ate on one side of the dining room and the boys ate on the other side of the dining room. Boys and girls could not talk to each other. I seldom saw my brothers. I seldom saw my older sister, because the little girls weren't allowed to go upstairs. Sometimes we had burnt toast. I know they didn't make it on purpose, but what they would say was that if you ate that burnt toast you'd be a good singer. I remember a girl who ate that toast because she wanted to be a good singer. That just sticks in my mind. We had a lot of mush, a lot of cornmeal kind of stuff. We rarely had cornflakes. That was a big treat when we had cornflakes. We had milk. I don't remember ever having fresh fruit. For lunch, I remember soup, a barley soup or something. We ate a lot of beans, a lot of bean soup. I remember wanting to have something to eat before I went to bed or as soon as I woke up. I still like to eat as soon as I wake up. I did take some milk from the kitchen and I managed to get some sugar out of there, too. I didn't think of it as stealing, not like the soap. The soap I stole. The milk and the sugar I just took. We had storm windows in our dorm room. I'd open the window and put the carton of milk between the two window panes. We went to bed very early at around 6:30 p.m. The little girls went to bed very early. I still don't require much sleep. I didn't require much sleep then. After things got quiet, I would open that window, take the milk, and put the sugar in it, because by that time it had frozen, it had crystalized. Shake that up and that was my first homemade ice cream. I'd wake other kids up so I could share it.

When I was between six and eight years old, I was pretty little. I was always the littlest one in class as well. We would line up by height, and I was always the shortest one. I got into some trouble in the dorm. I would not say that I was a bad kid, and I don't think I'm being biased. I think I was doing things because I couldn't sleep. I was doing things to be entertained and [to] entertain. I would wake up other kids after it was quiet, and we'd take those army blankets, put one kid on the blanket and have two of us pull it. We would go down the hallway and back up, and then we'd get shocked—like electrical shock—so it was kind of little sparkies. That was fun, because we didn't have toys. I don't ever remember playing with a toy of any kind. And then, that wasn't enough. Going upstairs was a no-no, so we took the mattress off the bed, took it up to [the] second floor and [rode] that mattress down, turn it around on the landing, and go down the next flight. The matrons lived in the dorm, and one in particular, would take out the "board of education," a green board. The board seemed very big to me, but I was a little person, and it had holes on one end and it was green. It was a paddle. She'd have me get out of bed, because I'd run to get into bed and cover up since I knew she was coming. I had to get out of bed, kneel on a broomstick or a mop handle with my arms stretched out, and I would get paddled. I had bruises from that, but I would not cry. I remember thinking, I will not cry. It was a decision that I made. I would not cry. I got up and she told me to get in bed. My hands were together and I had my face resting on my hands, looking at her, probably staring at her, probably glaring at her, and she said to me, "Face the wall!" And I said, "Mrs. Gadess, I am facing the wall, there are four walls in here!" I was real wise even then you see? I thought I was pretty—you know—challenge me! So then I had to get out of bed and I'd get hit again, because then I was sassing. I got hit again, but I still would not cry. Not crying impacted me for a very, very long time. I would not cry until I probably was forty-five years old, because I thought, "No one is going to get the best of me. I will not let you get the best of me." Tears at that time I think were viewed maybe as a sign of weakness or giving in or something, but I would not let that happen. I cried myself to sleep and so did other kids from loneliness. At that point I would not cry when I was hit, and even afterwards, it was like we had to be tough. I was beaten up by other girls. There was a group of girls, a family really, who, and I think to this day are still just very mean people, very abusive people, and in today's world, I think I was bullied. That day we didn't have that term, you know, that terminology, not that I knew of it anyway. They were from the same tribe as me, but they beat me up pretty badly. My brother got ahold of one behind the flower house and took her across the square away from me.

We made our own beds. One matron in particular used to flip a coin. The sheets had to be tight. I think [the coin] had to bounce; the sheets had to be tight enough. I can still see her flipping that coin every morning. We'd change sheets on Tuesdays.

There was one woman I would call a mentor, Miss Daggs. She was a first-grade teacher, but not my teacher. Thelma Daggs was an African American woman; she wore brown loafers, brown skirt, yellow cap-sleeve blouse. She took me under her wing. I don't know if she took other kids, but I learned many things from that woman. I learned to work. I learned that if I worked, I got paid. I would take a brush and a dustpan and clean the steps. I would do errands. I learned the word "errands" from her. I love that word, because I didn't know what an errand was, but she'd have me do errands. There were two little stores in that community, and she had me go get things, Hydrox cookies, or Oreo cookies I think. If there is any teacher I would like to say thank you to it would be to Miss Daggs. If I worked, I got paid. I learned that if I made a mistake it was OK. Every time after I'd work, usually on Saturdays, she would keep Premium Saltine Crackers on the radiator, and after I'd finished working I would get a snack. It was warm Premium crackers and peanut butter, like a little peanut butter sandwich, and milk. She would also take a group of us to the pow wow that was across from Johnson's store, and she encouraged us to dance, but someone pulled me out, didn't want me to dance. I don't remember who that was, but I liked, wanted to dance. I always like to dance. She would give us either ice cream bars or Popsicles, Push-ups. She'd treat us when she was there.

I saved my money that I earned from Miss Daggs, and every once in a while we'd be able to get on the bus on a Saturday and go to Devils Lake. I remember buying my mom a handkerchief, my dad a white plastic cigarette holder that had two parts, and my little sister a brush and comb for Christmas. I was able to bring presents home for Christmas. I remember going back after Christmas telling lies. I would lie about what we got for Christmas, because we didn't get Christmas presents. My mom always tried to make it a point that we'd hang up our stockings. Sometimes we got an apple, an orange, some candy, some nuts, but never got toys. I would lie when we'd get back to school and I would say, "I always wanted a pink hair brush with a mirror." I would say I had one but I had to leave it home. I made believe that I got it, but really I was lying. I didn't get any presents at all other than maybe candy and nuts. Mariel Miller was a fourth-grade teacher. She always had a thermos of coffee, and she had sugar and cream in her coffee. I remember the smell of it. She'd open the thermos of coffee on her desk and pour that coffee. I think of her when I smell it. My father-in-law likes sugar and cream with his coffee, and when I prepare him a cup of coffee I think of her when I smell that.

I don't recall ever being sick at boarding school. The clinic was next door and every once in a while I would pretend that I had a sore throat and then go over to the clinic and get these little wafers. It was kind of gray, taupe they might call it today, but it was like a little lozenge. I'd suck on those because that was the closest thing to candy. I don't remember a playground, not at all. I don't remember toys at all. Miss Daggs brought me twenty jacks and two balls. It was a big set. I could then play jacks with whoever was playing jacks. Other than that, I don't remember a toy at all. I don't remember swings or outdoor kinds of equipment.

We did go to movies occasionally at the square. At Fort Totten it's where classrooms were, the dining room was there, it was the old military square. I don't remember what the movies were but I do remember we had to pay. You had to have a dime to go, so if you didn't have money you didn't go. I never ever got money from home. Sometimes kids would get food packages, sometimes clothes. I got shoes once from my mom. I got a pair of saddle shoes.

I think back at that time and—it was such a weird time. I can't say that I had friends, not people I'm in contact with or were afterwards, you know. I don't know how to explain—it was like I was not connected to anyone. I was almost eleven years old when I left Fort Totten. We finished school the end of May, and I went back to the reservation. That was the spring after my dad died. At that time, St. Ann's Catholic Mission School would run from Easter Monday to Christmas, all summer and fall. I'd finish school in Fort Totten maybe Friday, and then start at St. Ann's on Monday, so we went to school during the summer until the next December.

I spoke English. My parents would speak their tribal language at home, but they would talk to each other. There were kids in Fort Totten who didn't speak any English when they came to school. They had to go out and learn how to speak English. There was punishment linked with that. I don't re-member what the punishment was, but it was almost like you didn't want to speak that language, your Native language, your Indian language as it was called then, because it was punitive and almost shamed for having to speak that language. There was a time when I think there was a lot of denial in the culture, not only in the culture, but denial. A deeper feeling was a denial of who I am as a person. We did absolutely no cultural activities at all. I don't ever remember seeing anything other than that community pow wow, but it wasn't school sponsored. I don't remember reading about or studying anything on culture. I heard remarks, "dumb Indians, you're never going to get it." I remember feeling very, very dumb and, for a very, very long time, not giving myself credit for what I know and how I think. Thinking that I didn't have anything to offer, thinking that I could not speak intellectually, and so much of it was kind of like a feeling imposed on us. I'm not sure how to explain that, but way back from the very early schools, it was like I was not a smart person. But talk to me now!

One thing I remember was not having any decent clean underwear. I remember having very dirty underwear, and having to have the matron sew my underwear, the elastic on my panties. At that time they were called bloomers. I wasn't the only one. There was a girl, it was windy and her skirt blew up and she didn't have any underwear on. There was a male teacher, and he either gave her money or something, to get underwear. It was those kinds of experiences—I was so little, not knowing that I could, well, even wash it—not having those kinds of emotional connections with anyone.

When I think of that boarding school experience, it was those kinds of things, or lack of, that had the biggest impact on me, especially not having that emotional connection. I think as a young little girl that was probably the deepest scar. The bruises healed, but I think of that when I'm either exercising or use my knees and my knees hurt. I think of kneeling on that broom handle, but it's not the same scar as not having that emotional connection.

Because it was a government school, the sisters and the priest were there only occasionally, so there wasn't that relationship. There were two guys who lived in the dorm because there were apartments at the end of one hall. There was an apartment down in the basement. The apartments were for the matrons. There were times, in the middle of the night, when there were unwanted hands under covers—and the fear, the overwhelming fear—waking up to that. I often wonder if that might be a reason I didn't sleep very much. I still cannot to this day sleep without being covered. I don't care how hot it is. I have to have a cover on of some kind. Um — the fear of — because there wasn't that emotional connection, who do you tell? If you did, they were connected, they lived there. And already having been hit with the board of education, or being yanked a lot — one does not tell. There are certain smells to this day that will trigger those emotions. It's almost like a breath, somebody's breath sometimes, and I feel myself re-acting. I wonder how someone could not have known. The unwanted hands were older high school boys, big boys, and big people. They didn't work there, they lived with their parents. Also a girl older than me. She was abus-ing other girls. I wonder what happened to her. I wonder how many people she hurt. I wonder what happened to those two guys.

I never used alcohol to cope. The way I coped was to stay focused. I worked. Focused my energy on work. I'd set goals and I knew that I had to do something to change the life cycle for my children because I was then in a marriage with my children's father who was very controlling. I'd gotten married when I was seventeen. He was older than me. He didn't allow me to spend money. He would count the loads of laundry that I had and then the number of quarters that I got to do laundry.

I decided that things had to be different for my kids, especially after I saw a cycle, it was like, "This is repeating itself." I saw my dad being abusive to us as kids, to my mom. It was happening in my own marriage. I can't let this happen. So I made some sacrifices. I *had* to do something. I had to get out of there. I had to get out of that situation to save my kids. I had to go to school to make things different for my kids. I was working hard at being a mom and trying to do what was right, probably made a lot of mistakes, took some risks, but I wanted it to be different, it had to be different. I did not want my kids to grow up seeing me abused, them being abused. I put my energy into purposefully trying to do something different. Oftentimes I was lonely, very lonely.

Self-esteem-wise, I'm in good shape today. I'm in a good place. I got to this place slowly. First I went to individual counseling. Then after my kids were young adults I started taking care of myself. The counselor I was seeing suggested that I do group counseling, and I did that.

I think after my kids were gone I sort of slowed down a little bit. Be-cause I wasn't parenting, I had time to think. I know I went through the Employee Assistance Program. I had to talk to someone. Beginning Ex-perience is a group for separated, divorced, and widowed [people], and

I helped bring that to North Dakota. I was one of the first twelve people who did that and I worked a lot of retreats. I got in touch with many things during that time. After the girls were gone I worked more on those personal issues because through Beginning Experience I was able to work on the marriage part. But I knew there was something else that was there gnawing. I knew it all the time, but I wouldn't verbalize it because I didn't think anyone would understand. No one in any of the groups had any kind of similar experience that I had. I wasn't in a good place yet. I was very busy for a long time. I was busy probably to cover up those feelings. When I got to group therapy, that's where I broke, even though other people were not the same, I was just at a different place. I remember turning in a chair and just losing it, just hitting it and hitting it and hitting it. I was angry. I was angry for the things that happened and using language that's not a part of the normal way that I talk. I was totally exhausted. I was so exhausted. I went home and I took a bath. I drank some orange juice. I put flannel sheets on the bed, and sprinkled it with baby powder. It was just like I needed some nurturing, and I didn't have anyone else to do it, so I had to do it. Those are the kinds of things I mean when I say I do things on purpose and I do things in a cognitive way to get to my emotions.

I've become stronger as a person, as a woman, feeling more confident. But each of those instances I'd try to look at it and say, "How could I look at this situation and make the best of it?" I'd go back to that little girl kneeling on that stick and I'd think, "I'm not going to let you get the best of me." There are times in my life I know I did that, and I know what went on in my head when I did that. The overall impact allowed me to be determined. Somebody said, "You survived." I said, "No, I conquered." I conquered it. I survived it for a long time, but I learned to conquer. I am a Native woman. I am who I am, with scars.

I'm very much a spiritual person. Religion is meaning less and less to me the older I have become. Currently, I am angry at what the Catholic Church has done to people. I am angry at what the Catholic Church has done to children. Yet I feel torn because that was such a big part of my life. I feel torn between what goes on. I feel there's so much hypocrisy. This past Easter when I was walking in the forest, I remember thinking I could use all of my senses. I could feel the mist on my face. I could feel the little stones and the pine needles underneath the soles of my feet. I could hear the birds and I could see the deer. I could see the evergreens so tall. That to me is spirituality—there's someone greater than me and it's all around us.

One of the impacts of boarding school is that I see some siblings where they are close no matter what. I don't know if we have that. It's like we weren't allowed to see each other and we're detached. For healing from boarding school abuses, we need a voice, without a doubt. We need to be heard and then to continue speaking in spite of hearing people say, "Enough already of this sob story." It is *not* a sob story. I don't share these experiences because I want pity; please do not pity me. It is part of who I am and how I relate to people today. That voice has to be heard. Healing will not take place in silence. I'm convinced of that. I'd like to see it be acknowledged that boarding school abuses happened. It is a part of history. It amazes me how many people do not know that that has actually taken place in current, contemporary times. We are good people, and people need to know that, and we are so gifted. We are so gifted.

Bismarck Indian Boarding School, ND. *State Historical Society*
North Dakota Heritage Center

Science class, Flandreau Indian Boarding School, SD.
National Archives at Kansas City.

THE ATTIC

I first interviewed Mary Ann Cavanaugh (b. 1933) at the Fort Totten His-
torical Society grounds. Together we looked at what remained of the girls'
dorm. She showed me where the water holding tanks were during the
era of the Fort, with the bathrooms just behind them. The water became
contaminated and the cavalrymen and women became ill. Later we sat
by the Captain's (the School Superintendent's) area on the porch to visit.
The summer day was warm and windy. I later visited Mary Ann at her
lovely home out in the prairie outside of Fort Totten to clarify some parts
of her interview. A granddaughter stopped in with her new baby and took
pictures with Mary Ann, the baby's great-grandmother. Mary Ann was
then fighting cancer, but she was clear-minded and our conversation was
lively. She died shortly after our visit.

I grew up on the Fort Totten reservation. My mom's name is Lillian Lajimodiere; my dad was Daniel Green. There were six boys and myself in our
family. We were raised at the east end of this Devils Lake as children, ended
up in boarding school at St. Michael's until, finished the eighth grade there.
Then came here to Fort Totten, to Cavalry Square; it was called Cavalry
Square even then, when we went to school here, [at] Fort Totten school.

I was about twelve when I come over to this school, and I went to
school a couple years here, freshman and [sophomore]. I went through the
tenth grade and then I went home, because I had a lot of home chores to do
with raising my brothers [and] my mother was in a TB sanitorium.[40] So I
just started taking care of the house instead and staying with Dad. He was
taking care of our family. I worked in the potato field when I couldn't find a
job. There's nothing in Devils Lake, nobody employed anybody, especially
from the reservation. There wasn't much work around, farm labor work
for men once in a while. I guess I just ended up spending more time just

---

[40] Note about San Haven: North Dakota law created the North Dakota Tuberculosis Sanitorium in 1909 to care for
persons afflicted with tuberculosis. In 1911, the governing board chose Dunseith, in Rolette County, as the home
for this facility. Dunseith, on the south slope of the Turtle Mountains, was selected because of its higher altitude,
less snowfall, drier atmosphere, and favorable conditions for patients with tuberculosis. The facility opened to
patients in November of 1912. Eventually the care of those with tuberculosis at San Haven was phased-out, and the
San Haven facility was only to provide custodial care for the developmentally disabled. In December of 1987, San
Haven State Hospital closed.

trying to keep the house up. I did bead work. I did odds-and-ends jobs to get a few dollars here and there wherever I could sell it. I remember trying to find a job at the hospital; I couldn't get one there. Walked all over Devils Lake, couldn't find anything. They wouldn't hire Indians at the hospital at that time. And then there were a couple women that wanted somebody to babysit so I ended up babysitting in the summer time. I spent a couple summers doing that. By seventeen I was engaged to get married, so I ended up working through the season and then got married at the end of August in 1951. Bought all our kitchen stuff at the dime store. Every time I got my fifteen dollar check I went over there and purchased something for my house. Bought my wedding dress—didn't have to pay that much for it—but bought a veil, did the whole thing there. And I convinced my boyfriend he had to wear a suit. It drove him nuts, but he finally acquired one somewhere. Never wore one in his life so he was very uncomfortable.

He was more cowboy. Always horses. Breaking horses, riding horses, rodeos, all the racing and all the stuff related to horses. Cattle, they had cows, but . . . his dad was a horse trader, so he'd go all over [the] middle part of the state here trading with farmers for different stock. The boys, he and his brother Ben . . . they'd have to ride the horses home. So that could be Cando, it could be anywhere in the middle of the state most of the times. They'd bring back the stock with them that he traded. Then they'd break it in, get it ready for whatever. Dad would trade it off again, and then they'd have to start the whole thing over again. So they spent a lot of their time supporting whatever Dad was doing for a living because that's how he made his living. He did trade, but made sure he got a few dollars on the side. They had a large family, supported themselves that way. Planted gardens—we all did. We've managed to have a small garden at my place with my dad, but not as big as a lot of other people. . . . He taught me how to bake; a lot of the cooking that I learned was through Dad. He was good at it; he was a good cook. And so, and he helped me learn to sew as well as what I had learned in school. I had my mother's sewing machine; made all my own stuff most of the time.

I was ten years old when my mother went to the [San Haven Sanitorium]. My brothers were all small, in fact one child was born in the San. Bobby was born at the San. They put him here in the hospital at the Fort here. He laid here a couple months before someone finally placed him in a home with a family here, and then Dad went and asked Grandma if she'd take him, too. So he went and brought him over to my grandmother's place where the other two boys were already there, the toddler and then Clarence [who] was by then a toddler almost. So Mom had come home, and then she'd end up getting bronchitis or something and her lungs would break down and she'd have to go back again. So this was part of the upheaval that was going on. We didn't have her long at home, and then, course it was one of these instances she'd got pregnant, then Bobby was born. I went up there [to San Haven] about the time Cap went to Korea; we were married two months and then he ended up in Korea, so the same year we got married.

I was eighteen by that time. I went [to San Haven] until he got out of the service. I worked there a year and a half. Didn't have any nurse's training, not to speak of at that time. It was just something I was learning to do. They were looking for help; my sister-in-law and I both went up there to work because there was no work around here, nothing going on anywhere. And they had rooms where you could stay, nursing units. Maybe six months, maybe a year we were there. They had a beautiful campus for those people, it was gorgeous. I always remember giving this old man his tray and there was a daffodil on it. We always had flowers for those guys. He ate his daffodil and I was thinking, "What am I going to do? He ate that. Well, I can't do nothing now, it's gone."

Then, I went to work at Sioux San in South Dakota, another sanitorium. Then my mom ended up down in that one for a couple years and she ended up back at San Haven again. . . . Everybody was in wards; there's twenty or thirty beds to a ward, big long wards with beds in it. I was working on a men's floor so I'd give them their bath one after another. I was wondering what I was doing there with these men. I was washing one old man up and here he died while I was washing him up and I'd never see anybody do that before . . . let alone in a place like that. And I thought, "What am I going to do now? I was just washing his face." I just called in one of the other nurses, "He died on me; he was an old man." Anyway, that was my first experience with what death was all about. You'd help them wake up, get up. Get them prepared for morning. They had their own thermometer by their bed. And you'd say, "Time," and they'd put their thermometer in their mouth and you stood there and you had a clipboard, and you'd say "Time" again when a minute or two minutes were up, whatever it was for a thermometer to register. They took their own pulse, and then you'd record it by their name for that time of the day. Everybody talks about the privacy act today. Forget it there; everybody'd yell out, "Well mine's ninety-eight, ninety-nine, mine's ninety-seven." It didn't matter, everybody knew what everybody was doing. And then you'd help them wash up because they weren't allowed out of bed. They had to stay in bed. Bring them their basin and water so they could wash themselves, and um, get their hands and face cleaned up at the time, because after breakfast then you went into the routine of um, giving them baths. But this is the same time you brought the bedpans in, too, so if anybody wanted to use them they could. So all you do is take a big gurney in, and put all the bedpans in there, and go in the hallway, bring it in the room because you could push the gurney in the room, in the hall, there was a hall in between the bed big enough to push that through. And then you'd put everybody on the pan, whoever wanted one.

Everything was scheduled. You had to poop on schedule [laughter]. Yeah! Well, that's when you brought the pans for, if they had to go. They could ask for one if they needed one, but everything was mostly routine. There was no toilets for them; you had to put those urinals and stuff all on a cart and go down in the same room and give them their poop pot, and the other pot, and whatever, and then put them back on that gurney, and then take it out and clean it and dump it, wash it up and put it on a shelf until they needed it again. Flushed [the pans] all out, get them all sterilized. They had a sterilized flusher of some kind we used in there. Washed them up and put them back on a gurney for the next go around. They went by every so many hours kind of thing.

Then we'd bring meds over. We had to do all the medications ourselves. They didn't have much of anything for meds. They had some stuff for severe cough that was codeine, give them a shot for that if they were coughing [and] they couldn't stop. And then they had some cough syrups too that they would give out once in a while, but they didn't have much. It was bed rest; just about everything was just plain bed rest. Then they started—at the time I was there they'd been doing it for a while already— Pneumothorax. Was another method of trying to rest your lungs so you didn't use [them] so much and they would heal. That was [the] principle. So they'd fill you full of air from your diaphragm, pushed your lungs way up so you, everybody looked like they were pregnant there all the time, and they'd do that once a week. I suppose, I never paid attention, I never really checked it. They must've deflated, because they'd refill them a week later or something. They'd go upstairs to do that, so you'd be hauling patients around for different kinds of treatments. Then you were busy giving baths, changing linen, once, every so often, I don't remember the number of days. I didn't do it every day. But they changed linen a couple times a week if I remember right. You had so many beds you took care of, and so many patients, changed everything for them. They couldn't get up; they had to be there and roll around on that bed. Many, many, many, many, there were—Mom was there ten years—many were fifteen [years]. They'd tell you, "Oh I've been here sixteen" [or] "I've been here fourteen," and some of them, mostly, it made you kinda sit back and think, "That many years in bed!" So this went on for the time I was there, working. My husband was in Korea, so we didn't have much to do there but visit, work. I learned to find relatives while I was there. Mom lost some of her aunts and uncles while she was there. There wasn't too much you could do there. She couldn't go to any funerals or anything. Streptomycin had become a medication they could use to, uh, help cure TB. And apparently they had tried it somewhere else. I think it became more of an experiment to start with because it was so new, and we ended up twice a day giving them shots. They were two, three CC needles anyway, large syringes with the sticky stuff. And the needles were re-washed and re-sharpened, and the syringe itself was scrubbed out right away, because if you left it for a few minutes it would stick, it would be frozen shut. Then you were responsible because you let it happen. Because there was pans of water in your, on your medicine cart, that you automatically start to push the syringe through right away, soon as you give the shot. You'd go in the room and holler, "Sunny side up," and they'd all turn over and you'd give them a shot in the butt, and then they were done with it until the next go around. But it did help to cure TB. Somehow or another it was doing the thing. They were trying to find a cure for it, and that was one of them. The other one was surgery. Many, many people had lungs removed and ribs taken out to get to the lungs. In fact, the man who ran this kitchen in here, he had no lung on one side and no ribs on his one side while he lived here, while we went to school here. There were a lot of people with part of their lung missing. That surgery was drastic. There were people who went to Minneapolis to have it done and didn't return because it was something they couldn't take or something, it would just kill them. But it was better than laying there for all those years. When I left, there were a number of patients already being discharged because it was helping them.

So I spent my time there until my husband got out of Korea, then I came back home and we bought a small house. Got a little house on the prairie. Yeah, we had a little one-bedroom old house that someone had used to keep his dogs in, he was selling dogs. And then we hauled it home, here, the same spot—there were no trees here; this was all prairie—and got some cement blocks and put them around the corners and that was our first home. We got in there and started to set it up, and I got my first cook stove, which was a propane stove. My, I thought I was the richest woman in the world to have that, because someplace to cook without putting a big stove up and working with that, I had worked with that before so, we had a cook stove to cook on. It was a small house. I don't know if this is part of it anymore or not; I think this might be the first section of it, I don't know.

Did a lot of renovating, working on it, trying to make it comfortable. Harsh winters. Lots of snow. Colder then heck. A big wood stove in the middle of the house, because it was a heating stove for a place to heat us as well. I remember my or Cap's uncle gave Peggy, our oldest daughter, a parakeet. So we had that little thing caged up in the ceiling, and at night when we'd go to our beds, we wouldn't start the stove; we'd let the stove go down, and that little parakeet, we could hear it because he was cold. I'd wrap the blanket around him.

Yeah, you waited up there at Fort Totten to see if you could get some help because you didn't have any money. [Cap's] checks from the government hadn't even started to come in yet, so we didn't have nothing, and no work. There was no work here for Indians, so we sat in that long room at the square to see if you could get, um, I can't remember the name of it—anyway, it was a check or something, I don't remember—and you could get up to twenty dollars or twenty-five dollars at the most and that was, a voucher was given to you, but it was in the name of whatever store you were going to; you didn't get to cash it yourself. You had to bring it to the store. So we used to take ours to Tokio store because we lived in that area, and pick up whatever you were going to buy, and then put it on a slip. We did, everybody else did too, but you sat there for hours and hours. The people that were in charge of that came from Belcourt, and they kept all the books anyway, and that room was full of people waiting to get a check. Something to eat off of. So we did that for a couple years at the most, I don't remember. Nobody had work; there was no employment anywhere. I said, "We've got to do something besides this, we can't do this forever." He found a job then in the summertime to work for a farmer, so he'd be up at 5:00 and take off and be gone all day until evening. He didn't get much, but he got some money anyway.

Well, we're going to be farmers and make our money that way. We're going to make a living there with getting cows. Got something lined up with the government where we could get some milk cows, and we had the

place to put them. The fence and a pasture and a barn and a well. We didn't
have water on the place. We used to have to haul that back and forth from
about eighty acres away with a barrel. We had a team of horses. It was all
prairie so you just drove across trails that were there. But we decided one
time we were going to build our own well since we needed it because we
were going to milk cows. So we're trying to figure out how we're going
to do that. He and I got into an argument; I was in the house, he's standing down there upset, trying to figure out where he's going to put it. [He]
finally start[ed] digging himself a hole there. And, I said well, it didn't
matter to me where he was going to put it, but somehow or another we got
into an argument. Anyway, we got a team of horses — we needed only one
horse but we borrowed our father-in-law's team — and we found an old-
time well-digging outfit of some kind. It was a big auger; it looked like the
size of a barrel or a garbage-can size, big, bigger than that. And that was
on a pole, and it had gears at the top and there was another rod or piece of
metal that went across to another set of gears on another pole, and that one
was hitched to horses, so you went around and around with this horse, in
this circle. And the gears went around, and it created a motion for the auger
to turn. So you start digging with that, and there were at least, it had to be,
it was good size, good thirty to forty inches across anyway, it was probably
a fifty-gallon barrel deep or something that would fill up with dirt. The
horse, we'd have to take the horse off of that gear, hook it onto something
else so we could pull up the bucket, dump the bucket, bring it, put it all
back together, and put it down in there again. And this went on most of the
day, and finally about thirty feet down, we hit shale, which was gray metal,
almost makes me think of the shale you see on the roads. It's chipped up; it
breaks up but it's hard to cut. So he decided to go down in the bucket with a
hammer and a chisel and stuff to break this up so we could get under it, see
where the water was. In the meantime, I'm still manning the horse and he's
got the bucket and going down in the bucket, and the horse run away with
me and he was spinning around down there [laughter]. Man, he thought I
did it on purpose. I got it stopped, but it got the chips out and we got the
well finished anyway. Got the water, hardest water in Fort Totten, so hard
you could walk on it. But we got our well dug [laughter]. We put culverts,
metal culverts, around the sides so the well wouldn't fall in. And that made
it even harder I suppose because it's metal, too. We put a big board across
the top of it and put a pump on it and pumped it by hand for a long time.

Then we eventually found a trough of some kind, got that set up when we were getting the cows.

Oh, at St. Michael's school you were there nine months of the year. You went in early September maybe, yeah, first part of September, and you were there until the end of May. You got to go home, I think it was a week, maybe it was a week at Christmas. You could spend a day on Easter and Thanksgiving, but you were back to school right away the next day. So most parents didn't have the transportation to pick up their kids unless they lived nearby. Many of us spent the holidays there except for Christmas. Most people got away for Christmas, except those permanent boarders who were orphans and stuff like that. They stayed there; they were always there. Sometimes we would bring one home with us if they would give us permission and stuff like that. But, there's fourteen sisters taking care of about four hundred kids. So the kids, just like in the history of all these boarding schools, kids did the work. They almost had to, I suppose, in order to survive as a group. And you were assigned duties for a month at a time. Even as little ones you had the same jobs as the bigger ones. We had the little girl side and the big girl side. Big boy side and the little boy side. Boarding school in Fort Totten was the same way. They were divided in that way.

Your routine in the morning was get up by 6:00, get your shower—no, you didn't have showers [every day], you did that once a week. You get yourself washed up and brushed up; you had lavatories in long lines of sinks and toilets; they were all in a long building out, room by themselves, and you went through that. Oh yeah, in the shower we wore a long, they looked like long night gowns or something. You took showers in that. You couldn't go in there with clothes on, you had to use that. And they were kind of a handicap, when trying to take that wet thing off and dry off, and all that whole bit. It was a skirt, just pulled it on and it was knit, kind of like an underwear material? It was kinda stretchy, and then after we got under the shower, the thing stretched even longer if it got wet. So there you are all draped in this thing, trying to take a shower; that's the way it was. You had to do it that way. And I don't really remember much about the toothbrushes; we had them, but I don't know if everybody used them [laughter]. They had a lot of soap and all that stuff.

So you'd go wash up, get yourself cleaned up, get your bed made—that had to be perfectly made. And then you said your prayers. I think we said our prayers first, I don't remember. You knelt, every time you prayed you knelt. And when you got done, you had to go downstairs. By that time, it's seven o'clock or so, and you're lined up to go to church. You went to Mass every morning, so you were there an hour. You all stood in line . . . it'd be cold in the winter, warm in summer, it didn't matter, but you all lined up. You had your partner you lined up with most of the time, same people. You had your own section in your pews, the little [kids] in the front, and the big ones in the back. And then those, most of the time it's high school kids that were in the choir part, they did all the singing because they had full singing at every Mass. They'd have hymns, and the Mass was usually something where they did a lot of singing in it. Then you'd get done with Mass, you filed out again, file back to the . . . playroom, because you were done in your bedroom, so you went to your playroom—big girl playroom, little girl playroom. There was a certain age level that you broke off between both of them. It was a big long room in the whole building, but it had folding doors between it so you're on one section and they were on another. You had two matrons for each section. One would be there one day and then the other one would be in the evening or something, they'd split up. So each section, or room, had two matrons. And then from there you went to breakfast. Always in file. There was a bell that hung on the wall that had different bell rings for different things. And then, for the kids to go to meals they had a big long-ringing bell with a big handle on, and they would ring that, just like you'd do on a farm or whatever. Almost a school bell thing. They'd ring that, and you'd line up, and go to dining room again. You'd get to the dining room, all the tables, all in round circles, you had round tables, six or eight to a table. You had your milk on the table, and I think that was it, it was a pitcher of milk on the table all the time. Aluminum pitcher, I always remember those. You'd sit at the same place all the time; you didn't move around to any specific place. You were assigned seats, and that's where you were all the time. The tables were made by hand by the brother that worked there; he did all the carpentry work on the place. He built the chairs and tables and all that stuff. And then there was almost cafeteria style, you got your dish, you went up and got your oatmeal and your toast or whatever you're going to eat, you brought it back, and you ate in silence until they told you not to. But before you ate you had to stand there and say your prayers. You had to say your breakfast prayers or . . . whatever prayer they wanted you to say before you started. Then you got your food and you ate. You had a half hour maybe before you're done with that. Assignments to the kitchen went to the kitchen, the rest went to do their chores, and then they were in a classroom. So, by nine o'clock everyone was in a classroom wherever they were assigned to.

Grade school, high school — most of the time they were double — there were first and second together, and third and fourth, fifth and sixth, seventh and eighth. I was pushed from second grade, no, third grade to fourth grade, and then from sixth grade to seventh grade when I was there. They moved me up but I, it didn't matter to me, they were the ones telling me I had to do it. Because sixth grade was decimals and fractions, and I was strong in those subjects, and the fifth-graders were all standing in line doing something for the teacher and standing up and had to do some reports or talk about something, and I was coaching them in the back. So they caught me at that and they put me in another grade. So I don't know if it was to punish me or just to tell me to keep my nose out of their business, I don't know. Anyway, I was there; I had less time there as far as school goes because of that. So I graduated from eighth grade there; then I came to Fort Totten. It was still a boarding school with weekend passes. You could go home on the weekend. So that was a little different again.

At St. Michael's, oh gosh, we did everything. We ended up in the laundry room for a month and we did those once a week. Monday, the whole day you're in the laundry room. I don't remember where we got the classroom time in there in those days! I don't remember. They were so specific about schooling though, I'm surprised, I can remember being in that laundry on Monday though. So we must've did something. I don't remember that quite well; maybe somebody else can remember.

Oh, mangles. You had to have mangles. You mangled all the sheets, the pillow cases, the flat stuff you mangled dry. Because they went through agitators, and they got all the water out of them and you mangled them through. You didn't have driers like we do now; that's the only way they dried them. And then, what did we do with them? We had to have driers, I can't remember that though. We did a lot of ironing.

Some of us got assigned to the rectory to do the priests' rooms and stuff, spent a month there. And then sometimes we were in the kitchen, we were there a month. Most of the time in the fall they had to can and, you, we had a huge garden back of the hill, that was forty acres large. And we had every kind of vegetable in the book out there. Some ways it was nice cause we always had a snack at three o'clock when we went out for that fifteen-minute break at recess time. That's how I learned to like raw vegetables. Because they'd cut up a bunch of turnips or they'd bring out a bucket of tomatoes or something like that. In the fall you got vegetables or carrots. You got all the fruit or whatever was put out there. They brought it to the kitchen and everything was redistributed when it was snack time or lunch time for the kids, which was good. We'd all get those for a snack. If we didn't have vegetables they'd bring out a piece of bread; it was dry, but we ate a piece of bread. The milk was from the kitchen, and that was dispensed because of the barn, they had a big barn, a big farm. The boys worked in the dairy, and they worked where the chickens were because they had eggs galore, and they had beef cattle and sheep, so the boys took care of a lot of that as well as their chores. Yeah, they had a big barn and they milked cows, so those poor boys, they'd be up at 5:00 in the morning going to the barn and milking cows and bring those cream cans back to the kitchen. Milk cans, I slept above on the second floor above the door that went to the kitchen, and in the morning I could hear them with their cans; I could hear them getting them in and out of the cart, so I'd look out the window to see who was doing what, [out of] curiosity, and then I'd go back to bed again because we had to be up at 6:00, went to church by 7:00 and back to eat breakfast by 8:00, and in the classroom then by nine o'clock. There was a routine that went along with it. They did the same routine, cleaning the bedrooms and playrooms and everything like that, too.

I guess I learned about social activities that you have when you have holidays, because many of us at home didn't have the means or the time to put decorations up at Christmas, probably no money for it, or [a] variety of [reasons]. But they made it important enough where we'd put curtains up on the window, special; of course it was always to impress whoever the dignitaries were coming, because they had these people who were benefactors and many times they came through during the holidays. We'd all get some little package at school. For Christmas they'd have a boy, girl thing or something. That's the only time we got anything for gifts. But they thought of it to do that.

At St. Michael's you were disciplined if you needed it or whatever they thought was needing it and um, but there was no physical, nothing physical. It was just like any school; you just stood in the corner or you had to do extra work or something. My memories of that was it was OK; you're just lonesome for home, for your folks. And I don't think we got anything there that wasn't needed. Oh, you got knelt in the corner! Or, you got slapped with the ruler. I guess the boys had some different things that they complained about, but the girls' side, we never had anything. My brothers remember something that was always disturbing to them and their part. The matrons there, if two boys got in a fight out in the yard, they brought them *all* in and *all* the kids sat around because it was always in a square where you sat, you sat around that square room, and they'd make that boy get up, the one that won the fight, make him get up and fight another boy. Another boy would get up and fight with him. And then whoever won that one, somebody else got up and fought with him. And, I don't know, that one sister that would do that. They were all, after you been in school you'd be like brothers and sisters with all of you, no matter if you fight, and whatever, and to them it was shameful, especially boys. It was shameful for the person who lost, and it was shameful to be made to get up and fight with somebody. So there [were] some hard feelings over their period of being in school. I know couple [of] my brothers talked about that. Otherwise they had a couple of nuns that were there, and they'd go play with them on the slides and everything, and you'd see them running around trying to slide down those toboggan slides, their skirts flying in the air, and they didn't care; they were playing with the kids. So there was a variety of things that went on. Some of it good and bad. And a lot of it was the discipline. They didn't like the way it was approached and the sensitivity they didn't have for the student. And the kids were lonesome; they lived there, but they'd rather have been home. Everyone who's in a boarding school feels that way for a long time. And with us I guess most of it was being ashamed of having to stand up in public among your peers and say something. I remember one gal that raised her fist to a sister [hit the back of her hand in the palm of the other] and then walked away, ran away from the school. She was hot-headed; she was a sixth-, seventh-grader already. And the next day the mother brought that girl back and we *all* had to line up in our square again. We were all standing there and here comes Marie with her mother, and her mother says, "You kneel down and apologize to that sister," in front of all of us kids. And that was hard for that girl as well; they accepted her back of course, because that mother was sanctioning, you know, was disciplining her in front of all of us. And it made you feel bad when people were disciplined in that fashion, but the mother was the one who was doing that one. So a lot of times the parents supported what was going on and you didn't have a choice; you couldn't go for relief to anybody, because you'd beg your parents to get outta there [laughter], you'd do anything. I got a kick outta my one brother that went to the service. I had three of them in there for their career: "Not hard to go into the service. We went to St. Michael's, and we went to boarding school. You learn to march, you learn to do what they told you to do, so there's *no* problem going to the service, you already did that before!" [laughter] So I guess it has its place, I don't know.

Oh! Yeah, we didn't have to bring any clothes to school. There was, well, didn't have much anyway. You went there, they brought you to a clothing room; you looked through the closet where all the clothes, the dresses, were hanging, and you tried them on, found two that could fit you, and you had found one for Sunday. Then you were assigned a locker [where] you put . . . one; you wore one for a whole week. You got some brown stockings, cotton stockings; you had put them on, too. You got into a room that had a bunch of shoes in it, and you tried shoes on until you found a pair that fit you. And then that's what you had; if you liked them and they were big, too bad, you chose whatever you wanted, so there you wore them for all year cause that's the only pair you've got. Then they gave you underclothes, and that was the old cotton bloomers and some kind of a little t-shirt, sweatshirt thing that you pulled on; you could wear that. It was interesting when we got to the bra stage, because they were trying to figure out how to handle that after a while, too, cause some of us got a little bigger than others [laughter] at our age, and, so you'd take off those clothes when you had your shower on Friday. They all went to the laundry, got all washed up on Monday and they had them back in your closet again for the next week, so you were traded off every week a different dress, and you wore that all week. In the winter they had coats; you had to pick a coat that you could fit, and then they did have snow pants because we'd go play outside and slide down stuff, and we got heavier clothes to play in. That was when we were getting closer to high school; grade school we didn't go out that much, and we just went with what we had on and played outside in those.

They had a big mop, a big long mop that you'd just, you know—a string kind of mop—you'd push that down the hall, and depending on what you were washing, in the playroom part where the kids could play later on, we'd have to polish the floor there. . . . They were all cement; there was no carpet down or no linoleum, it was all just plain cement, but very shiny because you know they kept it shiny, washing it and sweeping it and the big mop. So when the sisters weren't around, we'd sit on the mop and go to beat heck up and down. You'd push the mop, and [the kids would] sit in front of it, and you'd go up and down the hall and shine the floor with it that way. We'd be kids and do things like that, too. Well, they wanted to make sure it was clean enough you know because they'd spill on it and different things like that. They were shiny for sure. [laughter]

You know, we'd used to have to wash the floors in the building, and we used a great big old tub that we used to use scrubbing clothes with way back then. I can't believe how we'd haul those tubs around up those stairs! There are four flights of stairs on both directions all the time, and all these kids would be, they'd do the work! You know? They'd do it, anyway, pull that tub in there, scrub up the floor, and they'd take that all the way outside. We didn't have to; that could have been dumped someplace else, but we made an ice slide outside because it was near a hill where we could. We thought it would be more fun to do that. So we'd take that water all the way out there and dump it on that hill. So, next one washed, they'd put it out there, too. It was an ice skating thing rather than a slide, but you sure could go down that hill. And everybody had paper, pieces of paper cartons, and they'd go flying down that thing, and they had fun though, and they'd play like that. It was fun. Then you'd have to do your chores—those were the ones who didn't have chores got to do that—then the next time, the month was over, somebody else did it and you had to, you could do other things.

I like to read so they used to kick me outside. I'd find books, and I could sit in the corner and forget everybody was there, and I'd read all the time, and then the sisters would come and kick me out during play time because they made you play out for a certain amount of time after school. We had to be outside for an hour or so, and then, supper, you went through the supper thing. You had to get in your room, your playroom, and around the walls were benches that had covers that lifted and your materials were in there. So there's your . . . gloves and your papers, everything that is yours is in there, and then you'd sit on that bench when it's closed. And then we'd get in there, we'd have to have our prayers and all that kinda stuff. Then we'd go down and the bell would ring—we'd have bells for everything. Go downstairs and we'd eat our supper, and then we'd have to go to benediction because the sisters all went, everybody went. And so we were there by seven o'clock, and that took a good half hour or better. Then we were back to our playroom. We could spend a little time reading, playing, or whatever. Then they'd start playing ring-around-the-rosy if they were the younger group, or the other ones would sit in the corners and visit and stuff. I'd grab my book and go sit somewhere again until it was time to get ready for bed. Then we'd go back upstairs; we'd file upstairs, say our prayers again, get ready for bed. We'd be in bed by eight o'clock.

Still daylight. Yup! Nice outside! See the little ones had to do that when they were younger. The older ones got to stay until nine o'clock, so you'd hear them playing outside. They'd be raising a ruckus outside. It made you feel, "Gee, I wish I was out there too," that sort of thing. But if you had that routine of getting up that early I suppose it was a schedule! It was totally scheduled. And to this day I schedule. I've learned to use that in just about everything in my life [laughter], I guess. Then, being a nurse, I'm scheduling anyway, so, everything, I'm thinking schedule all the time for different things, looking at time.

We'd wash the floors. Everybody would line up across the room with their brush or their scrubber, or whatever they had, rags. We all went up, all the way across the floor, washing and wiping, washing and wiping. Then we got to wax; did the same thing. We found rags again, because the sec-ond-hand store had lots of rags. We'd get somebody to sit on one end of the shirt or whatever we had, most of the time was old skirts and stuff. We liked the wool ones 'cause that way we could really slide. We'd swing around and pull everybody around till we got the floor polished. Sometimes we'd swing 'em around and let 'em go [laughter]; they'd bump into each other like golf balls or something [laughter]. That was the fun part of it!

Yeah, we had to wash floors on our hands and knees. We didn't have nothing; if you found a rag to put under knees, but most of us didn't even bother with it. We just got on our knees to do it, just cement, and it was colored. So it was kind of a red color. So we'd scrub those floors and polish them up; the hallways the same way. All the sewing rooms—all the rooms, we'd have to do that. Kitchen help had to scrub them—all the kitchen floors, dining room floors—so they all had chores. Boys' side, same way, they had to do their chores on their side. We were not allowed to talk to the boys; we're not allowed to go on that side, so I never got to see my brothers much when we were there. Unless they would come outside; we would get together outside on the playground.

We [boys and girls] couldn't eat in the same place; we were divided. It was an invisible wall; the boys were on one side of the room and you were on the other kind of thing. We were all in the same dining room, but they were off to one side and we were on the other side, so you got to see each other, but you didn't know, you know, you didn't talk to each other much, and there was a couple of nuns walking the floor while you're doing all this eating and stuff, so they were supervising no matter what. And you brought your trays or your food, plates, or whatever back to the table where they served it, and then somebody washed dishes. So, kind of where that was at. You didn't throw anything away to speak of because that was just not accepted.

Every month you went through the hair combing situation. Yeah, that was a routine. They lined you up one day, usually a Saturday. They'd comb your hair, and everybody had to do it. They used vinegar and kerosene and a nit comb. Some of the staff, the kids had to do it for each other, but they'd have these towels, and then you sat there and you got your hair soaking wet with this stuff, and you're all excited when they'd find a bug and that person had to get some kind of powder put in their hair, and their hair was wrapped for the rest of the night. That was usually before your shower, so it had to be a Friday or a Saturday. Saturday is when we had our shower—I don't remember for sure—but anyway, that would be once a month we'd do that. Oh we hated it because when we got to be the bigger girls, we wanted your hair curled, you didn't want to go around with a sopping wet head, but we had to! Then we'd put our little paper curlers and curling irons up, or whatever we had. Beautified ourselves again [laughter] after we got out the shower. Oh! We used rags. We used to do that for the long-haired people that wanted the ringlets. And you could use it for long hair and just comb it out too, because you could put it higher; strips of rags, usually about, oh, ten inches long maybe, at least, and then you took the lower half of it, you divided it in half, folded it in half and you take half of it, the lower half of it, wrapped your hair around that, and you left a little tail on the bottom of it so your hair was wrapped snug around this rag. Then you took the other side of the rag, took it from the top of your curl you're making, and you wrapped it and folded it around just like a bandage—bandage goes all the way down to the bottom. Then you tied the bottom end of that curl with the two pieces that were on the end, made a knot in it so you had, then you slept with that. Then you took it out in the morning. It made a soft curl. Most of them, just about everybody, used cans, and sisters used to let us use scissors to cut those. Cut them sharper then heck, because you'd cut them on a coffee can or something, a metal can, because we'd get them out of the kitchen, because everything was in gallons when you cooked down there, and you had these cans you'd cut up and make rollers out of. Cut strips about two inches wide and maybe three inches, four inches long depending on how big a curler you wanted. Then you'd wrap newspaper or paper, brown paper bag or something, around it to cover the edges of the metal. You made your rollers that way. And in order to keep the paper in place until you used it, you folded it over. You'd wrap your hair in it just like you would a regular curling thing they have nowadays, but you'd put both ends across the hair so it held it in place. So you had these little knots all over your head when you went to bed. And you took them out in the morning, real fast during that period of time when you were supposed to get dressed and polished up for church and whatever, and everybody learned to go fast. The ones that didn't, used to have problems.

I used to feel sorry for those that wet the bed, because they were disciplined and that was not, they didn't look at it, course, in those days, they didn't look at it that way anyway. They had rubber sheets under their beds, which is, you know, for them, but we had a couple girls that were obstinate as heck over it. They didn't want to be—they didn't want to get out of bed, and of course everybody's getting up, except these two. So then the sisters they're pulling on the sheet, and they're pulling on the sheet, and they're fighting with them. They'd have to wash their sheets, and get them all aired out, and used to hang them out the window for a while and all that kind of stuff. So it had to be hard for them because they couldn't help what was going on. But that was the time; [the staff] thought discipline was what they needed, and I'd heard horror stories of different ones, especially on the boys' side: they'd make them put the sheet over their head and all that kind of stuff, but I don't know how true that was. The boys never wanted to talk much about what went on their side. This is just pretty much where I was at. So I was different.

Then you'd get sick. If you caught, oh, chicken pox, the whole place had chicken pox, everybody was down. For a while you'd think it was fun, but you were sicker than a dog . . . all in dorms together. And they'd take care of you; the kids would have to bring the soup up, and whatever, and you ate right there. We had a case of mumps one time and all the little girls, big girls, everybody, the place was full of it. And, you just went through it; you waited till it was over with. Everybody was running around trying to find the pickles to see if they had mumps, because you'd chew a pickle and then your mouth would hurt so [laughter].

You couldn't talk your own language; it was *all* English. Some of the girls wanted to talk, or they did it automatically because they were so used to doing it, and they were censored for it. You learned to talk English and only English so that you learned when you'd see someone disciplined, you learned not to do the same thing, or not get caught at it, so that would put a stop to a lot of it, just being that way. And they were French nuns;

they'd talk French all the time. Those old gals be rattling away while you were sitting there, listening to it, not understanding a thing they said. But, otherwise it was strictly English, and I learned grammar like you wouldn't believe. I enjoyed it for a long time. If you had a teacher that was good and could explain it well, you were all right.

I had, well, one that was the strictest turned out to be the best person I liked afterwards, but, at the time, boy she was a disciplinarian and a half. If you said something wrong, she'd slap you right there. I had a favorite nun who was a matron, Sister Parrin was her name. In fact, she would kind of advise me about boyfriends and stuff like that, so, because I didn't have a mother since she was in the San, I didn't really have anybody to visit with on things. And we never did get close as far as talking to sisters about anything. We just avoided them and played together most of the time. We didn't pay attention to those things, until one time, I think I did sit down and unload with Sister [unintelligible]. I think, she of all people . . . about [the] time I left school almost is when I did that.

I did a lot of beading there. I beaded and beaded and beaded all the time. Every day and the last year I was there, I'd bead billfolds and belts, and coin purses; loom beading, most of it was loom beading we did, but we were making gifts for the priests and that was that God-awful Greek key on black, white Greek key on black. I thought I'd never get over seeing those things in front of my eyes after we did that. Coin purses, yeah. They used them for gifts I suppose, or something, I don't know. Yeah, beaded a lot of that stuff. But they got all their beads by mail from Czechoslovakia. It was all good glass; you could tell that yourself when you were handling it. They knew where to buy it; it was better quality.

Then when the priests—we had Father Julius and Father Cleatis come there, they were young, yeah, they were both in their twenties when they first came to St. Michael's—they were just like fresh air because they were young and they wanted to play ball with you and do all kinds of things with the kids. About after the first year or two, they wanted the kids to have sports, and they were out playing kickball with them and they were out, baseball and whatever, and then they'd have teams, table teams, that was fun. They'd have contests; there were six, there had to be six to a table because that's what we'd play. They'd draw names and then you had to play against each other for basketball. It was a big contest in that little tiny church, that was our gym, little tiny building. And we played, and we'd play our little heart out; it was funny. And then they'd con the sisters into letting us wear pants, 'cause before that we were jumping around with these skirts on and our bloomers were showing and our stockings were falling! Oh my, they must have felt sorry for us because they told Sister, "We don't want to see their bloomers anymore." Oh my, my, my!! Give them some pants! So the second-hand store here we come. We all got jeans; boy we were really proud of ourselves then. We got to wear them to play basketball. So that was kind of fun. We did that for a long time.

Even here in Fort Totten we had an ice rink going. Made our own. They used it for both ice skating and roller skating. The kids helped make that when those priests came, those two that were young. And the kids, they all helped build the cement slabs and stuff like that. The priests put them to work.

Yeah, St. Michael's, it was a beautiful building. They'd send us out to the garden to pick a lot of the vegetables and stuff and we had to send it to the kitchen so they could can it. We did a lot of canning there. We learned how to can easy. You spent a month in each department . . . in the kitchen you helped can, and they used half gallon jugs, those great big two-quart canning jars, and I don't remember, they just sealed them I think, I don't remember, they didn't put them in the oven or anything. They had a potato peeler, which I liked because you can't peel by hand, and then I'd work that kitchen area at different times. You had to get up early because you had to do this before Mass, get the breakfast started and put the coffee on. That's the first time I'd even seen people put eggs in the coffee grounds. They smashed a raw egg and they mixed it in with your grounds, and you put it in your coffee with water. Because all the grounds stuck together afterwards, you didn't have to have, well, what it did I don't know, I didn't drink coffee. But we had that for all of the employees and sisters, or whoever wanted coffee, for them. Kids never got it; we got milk.

Yeah, and I remember Dad coming to get me for Easter break or something. Anyway, he had, of course we used buggies and horses then and he was wanting to take me home. So I was sitting beside him, and then here comes the priest. He was the old man that originally took care of the place way back. He was a businessman and he kept the place going. He brought a couple old people from New York with him. They were walking with him, and I was sitting by Dad, and we were about ready to leave . . . Father asked me if I would consider going to school for music in New York. This old couple wanted me to go, and they were going to let me train in Juilliard School of Music for singing, and, oh! I'm not going nowhere.

I'm going home! That's more important because Dad just turned around and said, "Well, it's up to her." He said, "She can make up her own mind what she wants to do." I said, "No, I'm going home." I was just a kid you know, I didn't know any better. Yeah, I sang for all the plays and sang for the church in the morning sometimes. I had a soprano voice. Yeah, I sang, and then they'd put on big plays and stuff, you know, for the community and stuff like that, and I'd sing too. "La Paloma" is the one I'd sing a lot of times alone. Then I'd sing in the choir alone sometimes. I also remember the family saying, "Mary Ann, when I die I want you to sing for me." I was just a kid then, you know. I just shook my head yes, but I didn't know what that was all about. I sang soprano for years.

Father Ildaphonse. Yeah, he was a business man more or less; he ran the place. He had about a half dozen priests with him, and then all those sisters from Canada were here, too. And then he used to make me go sit in the parlor. There was an Indian parlor and a white parlor. Well, the white parlor had a piano in it, so I'd have to go sit over there and practice singing, and they were teaching me how to use the piano, too, but I never did do much with that.

When you first went into the school, you went up the stairs and the Indian parlor was the first large room on one side where people would come and [see] their kids or whatever they wanted to do. Across from that was the office that they had hired a couple of people to be in charge of, oh, greeting people and writing stuff down and keeping track of the kids' numbers and stuff like that. There was the Indian parlor across from that, and then down the hall about, oh, I don't know, about a block or something down the hall—it was a big school building—and that was the white parlor. Nobody went in there very often unless somebody came that was going to do something special or wanted to donate to the church or something like that, so they'd go in there. I was using that piano; I was learning to play a little bit. They wanted me to learn how to play piano, but there was nobody to instruct you, you know? They'd give you some lessons to work with on the piano, but you were on your own. Well, you didn't take to it after a while, you know, kids. Anyway, that was the two parlors and the office. They were on both sides of the hallway, and on the left side was the boys' playroom and rec center and that big room where they all gathered together. On the right side was the girls'. Then you walked up the stairs to the second floor for dorms. The young kids, the little ones, the girls were on one side and the boys were on the other side, and then third floor, the sisters stayed up there, and there was still another floor for the older kids, older teenagers. They weren't as big, but they had that for the older girls and the boys on the other side. Yeah, there was, one, two, three, at least three levels of floors there, as well as the big dining room downstairs, and there was a big kitchen where they cooked the food and they got it all lined up and ready to set out so they can all walk by and get their food.

Originally I started going to school here because my dad was a policeman here. He was the only one who was on the police force. What they had was the night watchman and one policeman that worked all, the whole area, the big old stone jail over here somewhere. And I went to kindergarten, first grade, down in the building over there. Ms. Fink was our teacher, and there were, I suppose, twenty, thirty kids in that classroom. My brother went, before I had started school they had picked him up; the two boys went to the Preventorium, the days when they were trying to prevent the TB epidemic from getting out of hand. So that was in the top part of this building over here where the girls' building was. At that time, they had, it was like a kindergarten type of thing, where they had them there. They had to take naps, and [the staff] took care of them. [The staff] came around and picked them up in a little bus that they made out of a van, an old-time van. On the outside it was called, "jumping over the moon" and all kinds of stuff like that for the kids. They had a horse-drawn one, so in the front was a horse and that would come around and pick the kids up in the homes around the square, here on the outside of the square. There were a lot of homes here. We lived in that CC hall, so they'd come and pick up the two boys, and they'd come up here. I didn't know what they were doing, because I wasn't in school yet, but they were . . . taking the little kids in there. And then when I went to school—I was here a year and from there, Dad moved, we moved away from here—I ended up in St. Michael's. I was also back into a kindergarten situation to start with over there. Mrs. Seas was our teacher there.

I always remember when I first went to that school at St. Michael's. I'm going upstairs, because they had play stuff for everybody. There were dolls all over and there were play toys. When I first went to the dorm, to where they would allow kids to play with stuff, I was looking at all the dolls. They had big cupboards where they had the clothing, or the blankets and the sheets and the pillow cases, in great big linen closets. They were all folded up. On the top of there was a huge area were they had all the toys that they let you play with once in a while. . . . I had many dolls. I was the only girl, so I had dolls in a big trunk when I was home. I knew my stuff. I had a little high chair, because I broke the top off, and I looked and told that sister, "That's mine!" Oh, you didn't tell a sister that.

"No, no, no, that's not yours," they'd say.

"And that's my doll!"

"No, no, no."

Mom had given them all my toys [laughter] at the same time that I went. . . . I never got them back, but she didn't say anything, she didn't get too harsh [with] me, but I was sure determined to get my stuff back. But I didn't see Ma for almost a year [laughter].

But anyways, the classroom was fine; we got along good. She wasn't a nun. She was [a] lay person who took care of the kids at that age. You learned to do your reading and writing and stuff. When we were over here at Ms. [unintelligible] place, she had a big playhouse at the back end of the classroom, so when you were done with the class—it was all inside—you could go in and open the door and go through and play in there. She'd let you go and play in there, so we'd play house.

At St. Michael's, when we played house—we had all this recreation or whatever we were doing—we'd create playhouses under the trees. We used to bank up the dirt and bank up the leaves and make rooms and all that good stuff, so we'd play that way, too. So we used our imagination when we played, no matter, someone would think of something and then everybody else would jump in. But up here, by the time we came back, it was high school time and I was in day school situation or boarding during the week and home on the weekends, because I was still kind of half-way helping Dad. But we had to walk two miles to the road to catch the bus, and that was a son-of-a-gun in the wintertime, because the snow was so deep and you had to plow your way in to get there. There were no roads to the house.

I always remember bringing my dirty clothes—why did I bring them home? I don't know, but I had a suitcase with me and I was going home, and I fell in the snow because the snow was so deep. I went down, and I was chest deep in the snow. My suitcase opened up, and my clothes had blown all over that snow, and I'm trying to plow through it [laughter] to pick it up. I thought, "There's something better I can take home besides this!" So I was thinking of that when I was fourteen at least. But you had to be down that road—you could hear the bus coming down—you had to kind of judge what time you had to get on the highway. You had to be down there in order to catch it. They didn't drive to your yard, nowhere; you went to the bus. So those were things we all had to do when we got into that situation. St. Michael's—we were stuck there all year, and we got home when your parents picked you up.

We'd kind of have to dust the playroom off, and that kind of stuff, and those were the ones that were boarding here. The other kids got on the buses and went home. Most of them did; there weren't that many that stayed here. We bused them in; we stayed here all week and then went home on weekends. So Friday we went home, and we went back here on Monday again, and we spent the week.

I told you the story about the hairpiece, didn't I? When I was at Fort Totten we were . . . I think we were in high school then; we were boarders there, too. Ten or twelve years old maybe, older than that maybe, because we used to ride the bus home on weekends. I remember one time there were three of us, four of us, and we had bunk beds, two to a bunk bed, and there was four of us in one room, and one of the girls was messing around and was digging around up in the attic. Because it was a bunk bed . . . you could reach the attic, and there were little blocks of material that would close off the attic from the room, and this one girl, she was pushing on them and fooling around in our room, and she'd dig and push and she wanted to see what was inside of there. So she was reaching around inside of one of those blocks, and here she pulled this thing out. And we thought it was a tail—it looked like a squirrel tail or something, long hair on it—and she pulled it out and then they started playing with it. They ran up and down the hallway with it and put it behind them like they were horses. I wasn't doing it, they were, but that was all right. And they shoved it back up in there when they got done with all that good stuff.

That night, I was sleeping on a lower bunk, and the two girls were on the top bunk and there was one down with me but I don't remember how we arranged that, but we were all together, and here this Indian man come along. You could smell the buckskin on him, and he was wearing buckskin, and he was looking at us, and I could feel his breath when he'd look over at me. And I'd kind of open one eye to see what it was all about, and he didn't say nothing. He was just looking at us, looking around us and over our heads and stuff. Then, in the top bunk, he did the same thing there. I could smell him, the hide that he was wearing, and I thought well, what's that all about?

Then, one of the girls—after that was over with he disappeared, he left after a while, he wasn't there anymore—we were telling her aunt about it.

[Her aunt] had gone to school there when it first opened for a school. She said, "You girls know what you were doing?" We said, "No, we were just messing around with this, there was something above the ceiling in there."

"Well," she said "don't you know that the soldiers used to scalp the Indians and sell the scalps to people in New York?" So she says, "That's what that was. That was an Indian scalp that somebody had put up there to take and send to New York." And I thought "Well, I didn't know, we didn't know, we were just playing."

So I often wonder what happened, because we moved out of there shortly after that. I often wonder what happened to it. Soldiers did that to Indians all the time; when they killed them they took the scalp and they shipped it off to the East Coast to sell. We didn't know any better. We were just playing with these hair pieces, they looked like a squirrel tail or whatever, so I never did try to dig up there anymore. We left it alone.

It was close to the end of the year, and we were able to go home then. We stayed [at the school] during the week, and then, on the bus, we'd go home for the weekend. It wasn't long after that, that they tore the building down, so when they did that anything like [the scalp] was missing. I don't know whatever happened there and I often thought of it. I thought, "I wonder, I should go back and look." Well, I didn't have a chance; the building went down. And of course somebody, I don't remember who, I was telling the story to somebody, and they said, "Well, don't you remember they had a prison down on the boys' side?" The basement, or the lower part of it, was a prison. A lot of people were put in prison there, Indians too. Anyway . . . I was done; I didn't have to go back there anymore to school. I don't remember, but that was interesting to know.

Oh, we did have chores, that's right, because we ended up working in the kitchen. I always would tell everybody how . . . John was a baker; he'd bake all the bread for every meal. And in the morning he'd bake cinnamon rolls; we got those. He loved to bake. And if we worked there, he'd save us a pan of cinnamon rolls and a big old bucket of butter, and we'd eat all that up [laughter] before we got started with the day. So during that time, it wasn't as strict or anything. It was just regular school; it's just that we were boarding here. We had to go help cook and put [away] dishes and stuff. We washed dishes and cleaned the house.

What I didn't like to do was go down in the root cellar underneath the building to get food out. It was underneath the kitchen. Yeah, you had to go down there and bring up potatoes and odds and ends and stuff, and under that whole place there was a bunch of, oh I don't know if you'd call them tunnels . . . what they are, you could walk through the whole place if you wanted to. I never did, but I mean, I knew they were there. All we did was go get those potatoes out and get the heck out of there.

I didn't feel that the teachers were really, I want to say supportive, but really expecting you to do much. They said, "Well, you'll learn if you want to." So you kind of lack direction, because when we came from a strict education environment at St. Michael's, we expected you had to do things, but not here. And it was a lot of play, but there was a lot of horsing around, too. Yeah, we had to go into assemblies. We had general assemblies in that, the big place, where they have their place now, where all the people got all the kids. But we had high school assemblies upstairs above the auditorium . . . once a week we'd go in there and we'd sit there. You couldn't hear yourself think, because they wouldn't listen and the teacher would be trying to talk and it was a wood floor and [the students] were bouncing around. And then you were getting your assignments for what was going to happen for the week or something. One day you just lost that time, because you couldn't hear what they were talking about half the time. A lot of the staff wanted to be friends with the kids, so they'd let the kids get away with this stuff, too, so that didn't help any. Then we had teachers that were in love with each other and all that good stuff. We watched these romances as we went along, and oh my goodness! At the time we were here it was a little different, as far as that stuff went [laughter]. So we got to see what was going on, how it developed anyway, and it was nice.

We had bad timing for our biology, and when we had to do lab work and stuff, and science was just before dinner, and that was awful because all you smelled, you could even smell the formaldehyde on your skin when you got done, dissecting all the junk. You could hardly swallow food when you got in there. It was poor timing for that.

But we'd put on plays here, too. We had some for our assemblies, and they did a lot of contest types of things for the kids. But my enjoyment here was the basketball. We had a girls' team, and that was fantastic. I enjoyed it. So we'd play, and then the boys' team went to state, and they just fight their way through over there because it was just so anti-Indian, as far as that goes. But we had one of the best gyms in the country here. It was [a] beautiful, great big thing, and you learned to play hard, and we played boys' rules until after a while they pushed it to the girl's rules and that wasn't fun anymore. You'd just go half court and you shot. Oh, running across the floor, it was a lot of fun. We went and played Belcourt, like I told you, then we got into a big egg fight afterwards when we won [laughter]. But we had a heck of a time winning. There was a few of us walking over their lines and we were in trouble all the time! But we won.

Nuns with little boys, reading under the eagle and flag, St. Bernard's, Fort Yates, ND. *Marquette Archives.*

Stoking the coal fire, Flandreau Indian Boarding School, SD.
National Archives at Kansas City.

S'TER

I interviewed Demus McDonald (b. 1944), along with his friend Eugene Hale, in a friend's office on the Fort Totten reservation. I offered water and sandwiches along with traditional gifts of tobacco, blankets, and cloth. Earlier, we had taken a tour of the historic Fort Totten boarding school. As we sat resting in the superintendent's house, Demus told a story of living with his grandparents as a young boy and having a little bed by the wall. The spirit of his great-grandmother would come around midnight and hit the outside of the house four times. In Dakota, his grandfather would say, "Come in!" Demus would then jump onto the sofa bed between his grandparents, as the long-handled dipper in a tall pail would rattle.

Upstairs in the little boys' dorm at the fort, there is a rusting wood stove stamped Warm Morning. Demus stood by the stove and explained to me how his grandmother would scoop out the ashes and put in rocks to heat. She then took the rocks and put them in a pan. Putting a blanket over his head, she would light a root and have him sniff the smoke through his nose. He said he never had a cold. She would also heat the old flat irons on the wood stove, and then iron around the bottom of the doors and window frames of their house that were thick with ice.

My name is Demus McDonald. My Indian name is Makah Wamni Omni, like kahomine dance. It means Dust Whirlwind. I was given that name by my grandma. I was raised by her. I was born August 14, 1944. When my mother brought me home from the hospital she brought me to my grandma's log house, and more or less gave me to her, told her to raise me, so I was raised by Grandma. The first language I knew was Dakota. My grandma didn't speak English.

I was dropped off at St. Michael's Indian Mission boarding school in 1950. I turned six on August 14, and two weeks later I was out at my grandpa John Sherman's, riding horseback, and I noticed a glint, like a window you know, in the sun. I was just riding around in the trees, so I rode the horse back up to the house, and one of my aunts was in the house and

I heard her say in Indian, "She came after the little boy to take him to St. Michael's." She said her friend—that was my mother—asked her to bring me and drop me off there, so that's where I ended up. First I took off in the trees. I didn't want to go. I went to hide, but my grandpa had a dog that was my friend. The dog's name was Jack. So the dog—they knew where I was at when they seen the dog. Eventually they loaded me up and dropped me off at St. Michael's. That's it, the start of my boarding school days.

Yeah, it was a three-story brick building and first thing we had, when I got there, we had supper and then, well, no, we went to benediction first, then we ate supper. And then we played outside, and then we had to go to bed. There was one large room; you could see all the beds. You could see all the little boys all in that room. They had a big nun, Sister Forest, tall sister, mean [laughter]. Coming down the line, she would point to the floor and say, "Pray." So the little boys would get on their knees, and they would pray. And when she came to me, because I could barely speak English that first day of school, I didn't know Hail Mary or Our Father and all that, so I started praying in Dakota, the way I'd hear my grandma pray. When I started praying in Dakota, that sister grabbed my ear and twisted it, stood me up. And Father had an office up there; she marched me to him, said, "He's not speaking English." Anyway, they put a ruler on the floor in the corner, and that's where I had to kneel on the ruler, straight up like that with my hands in front of my face. Yeah, when I tried to lean back and sit on my ankles, Father would come and grab my hair and hold it straight up. That went on for I don't know how long. Finally they sent me back to bed. I still speak Dakota at home, but to this day when I'm asked to pray in public I say no. Too many painful memories of the priest grabbing my hair and neck.

In 1997, my oldest sister passed away, Adeline White Thunder Trottier . . . I was sitting at the wake at St. Michael's Tech Center building, and the door opened and I noticed, I seen this priest come in—he was an older priest—[and I noticed] the way he walked fast. I was watching, and it looked like Father Julius, so I was watching and he went in the back; he was shaking hands with Wayne and everybody, so I went in the bathroom and washed my hands. When I came out, he came around the corner. He was going to use the bathroom too, and he stopped right in front of me and he pointed at my face and said, "I know that face, I know that face. I cannot remember the name that goes with that face." So I made off I was mad at him. I pointed at my face and said, "You should know this face,

Father, you made me kneel on a ruler many times; my knees are soft." He turned around and walked real fast around the corner. I should have made off trying to choke him.

Back to the boarding school, those nights . . . Brother Vital . . . was a carpenter or, he used to make desks, tables, little wooden guns for boys to play with. Yeah, he was the house barber. He would put a bowl on our heads and trim all around. I think he was the only brother that I remember. But he was the barber and everything. They had, what do you call those, clippers, they clipped everything off. I didn't have braids, but anyway, I was bald after that [laughter]. Then they washed our hair with kerosene.

We had to get up around 6:00 a.m. We'd look out the window and we could see Father Julius; he was walking around outside. He'd have a big long rosary around his—he'd be wearing this big long rosary—and he'd be walking, and he'd have one bead—he used to walk real fast, that's how I remembered that walk—then he'd go to the next bead. He'd be saying his rosary. Then we'd go to church; after that we'd go eat cornmeal mush. You had to eat it, too. If you didn't want to eat it, they'd put your face in it. You couldn't get up from the table until we ate everything. They used to use the milk from the—they had a dairy barn there, and it wasn't good pasteurized milk—it was milk from the dairy farm there; it didn't taste too good. But that's what we had to drink. They would come around to us during the day [and] they'd ask us to drink that milk again.

Then I remember getting punished for talking Indian. We had to go work in that—I think it was like three big barns where they used to run those thousands of black and white cows—had to go right in the stalls. Back then they didn't have that electricity thing; you had to sit down and milk the cows. So when the cow raised [her] tail, I'd slide back when [she] moved that tail. The cow would poop like that; [she would] stand there with the tail, and then we had to use a long brush to wash the cow manure. After we washed it out, we'd sit back down and continue. But that's the milk we had to drink. It didn't taste too good. I don't remember eggs; we had mostly boxed stuff, sometimes oatmeal, but most of the time it was cornmeal mush. For supper, I remember, yeah, well, they used to eat, they had potatoes. There was a dungeon, like a room, on the east side. When you'd come in, there's the kitchen; right across, there's a cellar; it looked like a dungeon. If you were out in the playground and you'd be starting a fight with a little boy, the next morning they'd bring the two of you in there to peel potatoes, and they'd be standing right there in case you tried to stab each other. That was our punishment.

There was a lot of little boys crying. I cried too. We didn't go home every night although my parents lived close by, about ten miles from here. My grandma is the one that I really missed. I didn't, I wasn't, I wasn't lonesome or anything for my mom and dad. I hated them because they're the ones that put me in that place. Grandma said, "You already have your dad's name; take your mom's name, White Thunder. But I didn't want to change it. I said, "No I don't want to; they put me in that place. I don't want nothing to do with them." I don't know if they were threatened with jail or what. I heard they were threatening parents that they would go to jail if they didn't put us in school.

Yeah, ran away many times. There was no fence, but we'd take off on a Saturday, or they let us go out. There's an area now where some people live, but nobody lived there back then. We used to go in there and make hideouts. We'd call them "hideouts," but that's where we used to be. We could hear the bell ringing for dinnertime or whatever, and we'd take off back. But one time we took off, we were coming through the trees by Mission Hill. We came over that hill and we came to [another] hill, and there was a lot of trees, and we came to a hill that's in an area right now where Oliver Jette used to live—Bill King lives there now—but we came to a hill, and one of the older boys said, "Look at that log home. That's Mushy Albert's log home."

"Well, let's go!" We took off walking around the trees again, [and] we came to a hill again, and the same boy said, "Look, there's Mushy's place again!" We walked around in a circle [laughter]. Anyway, we made it home the next day. My dad brought me right back over there.

Yeah, went home for the summer. That's where my ma would come get me and bring me to my grandpa John Sherman, because he didn't speak English . . . brought me to Ziebach's Pass and dumped me off. So all summer I was with Grandpa John Sherman. He never spoke a word of English.

Just a bell woke us up in the morning. We had to fix our own beds and then we went to church. They had, they used to call it low Mass and high Mass, but they had low Mass early in the morning. Then we went to eat breakfast. Then we were in the classroom by 8:30. Later on we found out they were only supposed to do one hour of catechism, but here at St. Michael's there was catechism pretty much—we had math and everything—but catechism every day, mostly Bible and stuff. I remember, I think in fifth grade, I was going to make my confirmation. Anyway, we had to do the lesson; the fifth-grade teacher, Sister Chevette, had a picture. She showed a picture of a long line of people standing on the shore of the lake, and John the Baptist was baptizing Jesus, so Sister Chevette showed that, and I raised my hand and I said, "S'ter, where, if that's Jesus getting baptized, where is his godmother and his godfather?" She got mad at me. I said, well we had to have godmother and godfather. "You think you're smart, aye?" she said. Yeah, she couldn't answer that. But her method of being mean wasn't beating; it was the mental thing. She would [assign] the first desk . . . for the smartest person, the next smartest down the line, and then the last desk was for the—she used to call it the dummy seat—one that didn't know too much . . . It was always her favorite white girl that was in that smartest seat, so one day I asked her, I said, "S'ter, I'm as smart as Juanita. I get A's. How come I don't get a chance to sit there?" Well, after I asked that question, the next thing I know is she did put me there. It wasn't very long, then she put that girl back in there again. She was a white girl. Her parents lived there. I think they worked there someplace. Juanita Abadeya, that was her name, so they would always have the smart seat.

Yeah, they showed us how to make the bed. It had to be tight, but I don't remember them flipping a quarter on it or anything. They just came and checked it. They checked the crease under the pillow; that had to be perfect.

We just went to eat after Mass . . . Then these big boys—they were in eighth or ninth grade—they were kind of naughty. They would come in—there was two sides to that building, there again, one was the girls' side and one was the boys' side; when we went to church, one side was the boys' side one was the girls' side—but those big boys would come in. They'd be laughing, coming up, and they would come behind us and they would look at our table because we had a little square of butter on our cart, [and] then they would reach over and steal our butter. So when we hear them boys coming, they'd be coming toward our table, I would take my butter—I'd be licking the butter so they wouldn't take it. They didn't want our germs.

We [were] always hungry, lonesome; at night you could hear it. You could hear the little boys kind of sniffing and they're trying not to cry loud because you'd get punished for that, too, but yeah, I was one of them . . . so hungry. One night, one [boy]—he wasn't hungry; he was scared of the dark—you could hear, he was from Belcourt, and you could hear a little boy crying, trying to sneak crying, but we could hear him sniffing. Pretty soon the big sister came to the door. Sister would tell a boy, "On your knees and pray!" She asked a boy, "Why are you crying?" The boy said, "S'ter"—we didn't say "Sister," we said "S'ter"—"I'm afraid of the dark." She made him go to a dark tunnel and she shut the lights off. Wasn't very long we could see him in the doorway, the light behind him. The nun asked, "What for you back here?" They spoke French. He said, "Sister Laverne brought me back."

"Bah!" Sister said. We found out later that Sister Laverne had died there years before.

There was a lot of kids there that, we all had to do things, we were the janitors; we used to clean our classes, the erasers. There were no janitors there, so we were the janitors. I don't remember being sick. We had to drink cod liver oil and skunk oil as prevention. Them nuns learned that from the Indians and where they come from . . . In the spring, that nurse, that sister, had a long cane . . . with a curve, and then—where Sy Arnhardt lives on the railroad tracks, that's where I said we used to make hideouts and stuff—we used to go in there with the nun, and she would pull them branches down with that cane, and we'd have to haul pussy willows and put [them] in a little pail. The whole class, ten or twelve of us. Just the little buds. Used to boil for medicine. For colds and stuff, drink a tea. Learned from Indians in Canada. Every now and then I'll remember the name of that berry; I should write it down, but I can't remember it right now, but we used to pick [them], fill up the pail, and then they'll take them and they'll boil them and then they'll use that for medicine, cold medicine or something. In the spring, around May or so. Then that's what they'd give to the ones that got sick; they would take that. But I don't remember ever being sick where I had to stay in the room or anything. [Interviewee told story of using skunk scent for asthma; said—in Dakota language—that a four-legged is going to help you, cure you.]

They used to—just the little boys that wet the bed—they'd put them in the room with a bigger boy . . . they'd make them throw you around. I always remember that a bigger boy named Raymond, he was throwing me around because I peed in bed. Just throw—he didn't hit me—he'd just throw me around. Yeah. "You better quit peeing the bed," the nuns said. I must have been about six. That Raymond, he was older than me.

I remember we used to sneak in the trees. Well, in winter, on Saturday, we'd go along the fence at the cemetery, there was a fence, there was a trail, and then we went to the banks where the railroad tracks were. There were some high banks like that, and we would go scoot on our boots. We had to wear sister boots. Laced up shoes. Yeah, they would get them from some place, and sometimes we'd have to go into that second-hand store and make bundles. Bundles. Take a shirt, like four or five, and tie them up with the sleeves and then they sold them. Bundles. That's why we got our shoes—one would be a size six the other one a five—and they'd lace way up here. Not too long ago Alfred Taylor—you know, I would go see my sister Sandra at the Good Samaritan—he was in there and he went around in a wheelchair, motorized wheelchair. He sees me and he would come over, "Still got your sister boots?" [laughter] But anyway, we'd go skiing down the bank; it was all full of snow, lots of snow, so we'd go to that cut-off right there. We'd come running and kind of skiing and go off of that. We had no skates on, just those boots. That snow was pretty deep. One of those little boys, he . . . said, "I'm going to make a new trail." So he made it, and he's using his feet, and he'd go back and forth. First thing you know . . . he went down and he disappeared in the snow. We all panicked and crawled down there. Just his hair was sticking up, lousy barber. We barely dug his face out and he couldn't breathe. Then we told him, "Don't say nothing when we get back." Then he went and squealed.

On the playground there was a swing set. It had about six bars above it like that, and one cable coming down. We used to lock our hands on that bar, and then one of the bigger boys would use a swing and he would go around the pole, he was pulling, so sometimes we would be swinging way out. Sometimes your hands came loose and you'd go bouncing.

I remember once when a movie came out called *The Miracle of Our Lady of Fatima*. I remember that they brought us to a movie on Saturday. Yeah, it was in town. There was two theaters in town back then.

I guess the favorite part of boarding school was the learning part, the subjects. I liked math. Anyway, I got up to sixth grade over there, and then I decided to come here, [to] Fort Totten, for seventh and eighth grade. So I went to school here. In seventh, they were . . . learning about Kit Carson in History. I already knew that back in the fifth grade at St. Michael's. Got a better education at St. Michael's than at the public school.

There is a story I was told about a rock. The white people call it Devil's Tooth. The Dakota people believe that when a person, a woman or a man, considered themselves medicine man, at night, in summer, [they would] stand by there at midnight. If that rock goes and lights up, then that person is a true medicine man or medicine woman. That's the one; the cavalry brought that. They made a stone boat out of logs. They got [the rock] on there, and they used a team of four or six horses and they pulled that rock into Cavalry Square. They unloaded it and set it there. That night everybody could hear buffalo bull howling and hollering and the soldiers and everybody came out, but there was no buffalo bull around there. Then the second night after it got dark again, they could hear that buffalo bull howling, and the soldiers all came out again, walking around. There was no buffalo bull around, so they got scared and the next morning they got their stone boat and loaded that rock back on, and pulled it and set it back over there. They got scared of it.

Another story I was told is about a medicine man. . . . He knew what would kill him. I guess he was wanted by police—he shot somebody or something—anyway, he was hiding out. He was accused of shooting somebody up around Grafton [ND] area. He came back over here, and he was hiding out here someplace in the Ziebach's Pass area. Anyway, they tricked him. They said they wanted all of the men to come to a big meeting at that building there outside of the fort. So, anyway, all the men were invited, were in there, and that guy noticed there were soldiers at all the windows, [so] he got up and took off running. This guy caught him at the door, and, I forgot how that goes, anyway, they locked him in that ammunitions place, but when they looked in there he was gone. They seen him coming down this way. There was a big stone by this church, yeah, this church here, there was a big stone there. I don't know if it's still there, but when that guy was running towards where that soldier's monument is, the flag poles, right about in there, one of the marksman, he put his rifle on the rock and he shot him, picked him off. The medicine man said that when the metal touches stone that is going to be his downfall, that will be bad luck for him. So when the sniper did that, put the barrel on that stone [and] shot him, that was his downfall I guess. He knew that was going to happen.

Grey Nuns, 1949, St. Michael's Mission, ND. *Marquette Archives.*

Pupils of Holy Rosary School, Pine Ridge, SD. *Marquette Archives.*

RUN AWAY

*I interviewed Eugene Hale (b. 1949) along with his longtime friend
Demus McDonald in the office of a friend on the Fort Totten reservation.
I offered water, sandwiches, and traditional gifts of tobacco, blankets,
and cloth. Eugene was soft-spoken, with long pauses before speaking.
He had toured the Fort Totten Boarding School with Demus earlier in
the day. As we stood in the graveled parking lot outside the gates of the
school, we spoke of the spirits of the children that had attended and died
at the school. He said he saw several as we toured the tunnels and one
had followed us out of the girls' dorm. As a Dakota spiritual man,
Eugene has been sober for over thirty years. He said he still needs a lot
of forgiveness.*

My Indian name is Wambdi Nupa, Two Eagle. I was born in 1949, and the
first year I lived with my mom until I was a year old, and then my great
grandmother raised me since then. She spoke Dakota to me all the time;
that's how I learned the language. It was my first language.

My great-grandma was taking care of me, and then they told me I was
supposed to go to school. I didn't go to a boarding school; I went to a day
school, St. Michael's, the same school that Demus was in. Just that, it was
only through the day. Before the year I got there it was only a boarding
school. The French nuns, the Grey Nuns, was there.[41] It was kind of hard
for me. I hardly spoke any English; I spoke Dakota, and I would catch heck
all the time. I was the only person to hate in that area, so I used to try to hide
and get away from school. Back in 1955, I went to school at St. Michael's.
I flunked my first year because I couldn't speak too much English and they
had me do hard work when I was at school, like cleaning things off and
shoveling, sweeping the sidewalks. That was my punishment.

It seemed like I was always wrong. They were too mean to me. I felt
like I was always wrong, anything I would say or do, it was wrong. They
got after me for it, and they would always take ahold of my ear. They would
squeeze my ear with their nails. It bothered me; I got scared of them. I used

---

[41] The Grey Nuns is a community of Roman Catholic religious women. The name originates with The Sisters of
Charity of Montreal, founded in 1737.

to try to run away. I did run away a few times, quite a few times. I always got caught. My grandma would catch me and come. She knew where I was at so she would march me to school. I went to St. Michael's until sixth grade but couldn't get along with the nuns or they couldn't get along with me. I think it was in 1966 I moved away to my mom's in Montana for about six months, and in between that time I had a hard time trying to adjust to the French language. They tried to teach me French. I couldn't hardly speak French but they tried anyway, but between some of the words, I would put an English word in there and that was the hardest part for me, too, because I thought I was saying the right thing but I guess I wasn't. Then I moved to Fort Totten; I went to school at Fort Totten. Then in 1966, I moved back to Montana and lived with my mom. But in the meantime I had a hard time trying to adjust to the French language.

I was really scared because I was catching heck all the time. That was kind of hard on me, but that was back in the 1950s. Sometimes for my punishment, I would have to serve lunch for the whole week or go to the benediction at 6:00 to 7:00 or 8:00. It was kind of hard on that too, because I wanted to go play and have fun with my friends and I couldn't because I had to work benediction and serve Mass. And sometimes I couldn't say those phrases—the Latin—and I would mumble something and I think they knew but they didn't say nothing to me.

But that was the life I lived with in the Catholic school. It was about seven years, I guess, I was there. The last year I couldn't ever do anything right for them. One of them, Sister Marcia, it was like she had eyes behind her head. I couldn't make a face or anything; she'd see everything, maybe she was checking me out from the corner of her eyes or something, but I never was [making a face]. I was always thinking I was always wrong and I was always bad. I wanted to have enjoyed my life better but I didn't know how to up there. They were always kind of hard on me. They had me confused, somehow; they always picked on me all the time. I think about it today when I look back and, boy, it was kind of hard. I appreciated being able to go to school here in Fort Totten with all my friends; they still live around here. Me and my great-grandma, we used to travel around in the wagon. We used to travel from way out east all the way to St. Michael's; that was where we lived and get maybe a pop and candy for hauling water and chopping wood. That meant a lot; I really felt proud of myself. We'd travel from there to here, Fort Totten here, and we'd stay with the Demus family and his grandma. I tried dating Sandra, Demus's sister, but she just pushed me away, I used to tease her a lot. Maybe because I was a boy or something I don't know, but that was, I stayed away from her. I couldn't talk to her because I wasn't a girl.

But anyway, we used to live in a log cabin way up out east here. Me and my grandmother moved out there and we lived out there. Pahsca White Head used to own that place. Sometimes we'd listen to the coyotes and my grandmother would tell stories. She would talk about a long time ago way back as far as she could remember, and she would tell me in them days how strict it was. At a certain age you kind of had to go through a test of going into manhood . . . to learn how to take care of food, water, chop the wood, all that kind of stuff. I did a lot of that. I enjoyed that . . . time for so many years. Then we moved into St. Michael's and I got to go to school.

My great-grandmother's name was Witehi Wi, the hardest month of the year, January. And her English name was Sara White Lawrence. I was adopted by my grandpa, but he took me as his own grandson. He says I'm his first grandson and he gave me that name. I carried that for a lot of years. Two Eagle. I don't know, I guess it had to do with his grandpa. I think that was his [grandpa's] name; he was a warrior or some kind of a chief. I don't know. I didn't quite get what he meant, where that came from, that name and how Grandpa got that name either. I was just told that it belonged to a great-grandpa of his and there was three of us used to carry that name. They came from that same family that my great-grandpa was from, and he adopted . . . my mom, Gladys Lawrence, and my aunt Olivia Lawrence. [Olivia] was called Ebassesah—she had safety pins; she'd find a safety pin and she'd put it on her shirt or dress, and that's how she got that name.

At St. Michael's . . . in the evenings after school, I would go help out in the kitchen, maybe take out some trash or whatever, and bring it. It wasn't a punishment or anything, it was just a regular job. I actually got extra cookies or an apple or something like that at dinner.

I heard Demus talking about some graves outside the cemetery. If you go on the west side of the cemetery, you can find some small graves by the Catholic cemetery, outside the fence, some mounds back in there, really small graves, about so big. Grandma said, "Don't go over there. They will follow you home." And then where that recreation [building is]—now it is a weight lifting building—saw some graves back there, too. You go down just east of there to find some more. What I was told was that some kids got real sick and that they never come out of it and they'd bury them out there. And if you weren't Catholic you were buried outside the fence. So I believe those kids weren't even baptized or anything. Maybe they was going to school there, that boarding school there, because a lot of kids are there. I know they are; you can hardly see them now but if you look around, walk around, you can see the little mounds.

A lot of [the kids] didn't make it home, quite a few of them. And from what I hear from other people . . . they [say] some of these kids were from other places, and they're the ones that didn't make it home so they'd—or they couldn't get a hold of their family either—so they'd bury them there. Kids from Canada, too, that went to school, but . . . a lot of them are people from around here. Had different tribes, got married to different tribes around here, and then a lot of them never went back because I guess they didn't know any of their family back up north in Canada, because probably their parents passed away or something, so they just stayed around here, or they liked it here. But that was a long time ago when they buried those kids out there. No headstones.

We used to walk around back there and look. I was thinking about digging one up, but I got scared. My mom told me, she said some kids were crying and one of them didn't come back, I guess, from wherever they took them to punish them . . . but there was one of them, she didn't say who, but she said it was a little girl that they didn't bring back. I don't know if that child went home or just never came back.

There were tunnels all over the St. Michael's area. There are tunnels from the school to [the] church to [the] bus garage—now it's the recreation building, where the boys slept in the boarding school dorms. There was a tunnel from [the] boys' dorm to [the] priest's house, and from the priest['s] house to the store. A story I was told is that workers found a skeleton of a baby inside the wall of the tunnel to the priest's house, so after that they caved it in. We were going to school there then; I remember when they were doing that.

So these are nuns and priests mostly—well, yeah, both—that, you know, they are all speaking their language, the French language, so you don't know what they're really saying. So me and my friend, one of my relatives actually, we started talking in Dakota, and they'd stop and look at us and point their finger at us, and then pretty soon we were catching heck, "What are you doing?" And they'd put us to work. We wanted to speak our language. A lot of us didn't really know the English language. Myself, I was kind of in between there so I mixed my language up and that's why I was catching heck. But we wanted to speak, but the only time we could speak was when we were away from school, enjoying each other's company . . . talk in our town's language and tell stories to each other. That's how it was back in my day. We were getting pushed around and they make you stick out your hand like this and they'd take a ruler and hit your hands. If caught speaking Dakota the priest also made me kneel on my hands. That was so painful. Yeah, and they'd say, "That's the devil's language. Don't use that language, that's no good." As far as I know, it's good; that was the first language I learned. That's what they'd tell us every time, anybody, not only me but anybody; we'd kind of whisper to each other and then they'd hear that and say, "That's the wrong kind of language" or not the wrong kind—"The devil's language, it's very evil." At that time we started to keep quiet because we didn't want to get in trouble. I was more scared of them than a lot of kids in there. Some kids in there, like Demus was saying, some would cry, and the nuns would blow up, throw things, you know, books, and slam their books on the floor. That scared the heck out of me at a young age. So that was going on a lot of times. The nuns would throw a book or just slam it down, just loud. Everybody had their head down doing work, and she'd throw a book in the air and we'd get scared.

Things like that always happened. I was half-asleep one day and it happened to me, scared the heck out of me. Then for punishment too you had to go and serve Mass for two weeks. It started from tomorrow for two weeks. You want to go play and everything, but you can't because you had to go to serve Mass or go to the benediction. But I was going home, back and forth to school in the morning. That first morning, my grandma marched me over there. The first time she took me back, maybe a couple of times, then the nun would talk to me real nice: "He's a good boy"; all that kind of stuff. They were lying to her. So she was agreeing, she could understand a few words. Yeah, they were lying to her. She'd smile at me, then she would walk out. Sometimes I wanted to go follow her and cry but I didn't. The boys would laugh at me, so I didn't really want to do that, but that was OK. Then other times a semi would pull up, a truck, and then we would unload the truck. The ones that would mess up sometimes had to unload the truck; that was our punishment, but it was good out there. Sometimes they'd give us an apple or something; that was all right, you know? Then there was that one nun, I forget what her name was, Sister Marcia. I didn't really care for her because, to me, she had eyes behind her head, and you couldn't really do anything sneaky behind her, she's watching, she's got some mirrors on her glasses or something. My mom would tell me a lot of kids went to school there, [but] at the end of the school year there weren't that many. She would say she didn't know what happened to them. She would say, you know, she didn't know what happened to them. She was told that their parents come after them and put them in a different school and stuff like that. Then she went to school here in Fort Totten; then she moved over to Montana with her mom.

Recess and after school, friends around at St. Michael's would hang out, hang around and do some of our own things. We did some crazy stuff. In the summer, we'd throw rocks at the [school] window or something. We used to have fun I guess. Demus was talking about that Brother Retau. We'd sneak in his office, the carpenter shop, we'd go down there and he'd cuss us out and we'd run out the door. He was German and he'd cuss us out in German [laughter]. I thought he'd maybe take it to the priest or the nuns or something, but he didn't tell anybody anything. He was always looking at you: "Bad boy!" He really hollers when he gets mad. Face turns just red. I'd make tracks, run away from him. He had canes.

The church had a basement and they used to have a movie projector, and they had like four classes go down there, and then four come down later and see the same movie, and we'd each get a bag of popcorn. John Wayne ones. And then they'd show us people who become saints and stuff like that. On Saturday we'd go to St. Michael's and make bundles, lay a shirt down, put clothes in and tie it up. The only thing that they'd tell us is, "You're going to get a good spanking." That's about it. Which we did. I was one of them all the time. Yeah, because I was kind of a guy that was more like a comic or joker person in the crowd, and they'd catch me laughing and enjoying myself and I'd get in trouble.

Yeah, it was ah, we didn't have breakfast; we just had a glass of milk, maybe a toast and that was about it, before going to class. You're in class, but you wait for [when] the teacher comes over and starts teaching things and then from there we had dinner. It was usually soup; it was a lot of soup. Every once in a while we'd get some applesauce or dessert . . . we had cornbread and syrup. Then we had a meal of mashed potatoes and a small piece of meat or something. Other than that it was pretty good meals. Sometimes I'd get in trouble and I'd have to go wash the dishes. I was always getting myself in trouble. That brings back memories.

Well, one time they took me up to the priest's office and they took a belt, the priest took off his belt, and hit me all over the back. They didn't try to hang on to me so I made a run for it to home to my great-grandma, and she went over there and stayed there. She seen those welts on my back so she was mad. She must have been told something. Anyways, I was bad anyway, something I did wrong and that's why they gave me a spanking. I must have been really bad; I guess that's why I got that spanking. The way she told it to me, she told me to behave myself, "Don't be doing those things." That's what she told me. I had a shirt on. Welts came up on my back.

My great-grandmother she was always telling me you know, "You'll learn this, you'll learn that . . . You will learn to work in business areas." The way she was talking to me . . . but anyway . . . she taught me how to pray. She would pray in Dakota, and I would say the same word that she does and try to remember.

My parents, my mom and dad, I used to hate my parents, both of my parents because they didn't raise me, so I kind of had bad feelings towards them. Later in the years we got to know each other. My mom left me with my great-grandmother when I was a year old, one year old. The reason my mom left [my dad] was because he was abusive. She moved back down here and then she went away. By the time I seen her after that she was drinking all the time, she was drunk. She'll say "I love you very much," all that stuff, but when she's drunk she's saying some other things to me. Today I think it wouldn't hurt my feelings, but I felt hurt at that time. In the summertime I'd go work for the nuns and haul potatoes or carry boxes of apples in, or [do] little things, sweep down the halls, work for a quarter, then it went from a quarter to a dollar. It was all right. During the winter and school hours it was a different story there.

When I ran away I got away from my home, too, because I knew my great-grandma was going to take me back to school. So I would run away and go to some of my friends' houses, or during school I would go visit relatives and stay with them for part of the day. All of a sudden Grandma would hire somebody to look for me and get me to go home. So there I was. I met with many people [unintelligible], but my grandma wanted me to go to school. Sometimes I'd go and sometimes stay one night, and when I'd get home she would get after me all the time telling me, "That's no good" and "Where did you learn that from?" and I would tell her, "I don't know."

She was told that someday I might be some kind of, like a professor or something like that. But I didn't really, I didn't want to go to school until after I went in the service and lost her. Some years later she passed away, but it was kind of hard because she was both my parents, my mom and my dad, and she told me the male and female sides of things, of people. I learned quite a bit from her, like I said . . . Then she would talk to me at night sometimes and she would cry and say, "This is what's going to happen to you in the future" and "Don't be doing this and that, what you're doing today, don't do that," she would say. So I learned a lot from her, more than the schools.

My great-grandma, she taught me how to pray. She told me about the Sun Dance and sweat lodge and she told me at that time, she said, "When you become a man," she said, "you can do that, but," she said, "You've got to do it from your heart." So I did. I had it in my mind when I went to the Catholic school there.

When I—after I got back from the service—all I did was drink. I stayed drunk all the time, and my friends were talking about Sun Dance and stuff and I thought about it and I—my first wife, I was abusive—so she told me, "I can't handle this. I'm going to get a divorce." So that hurt my feelings really bad you know, so that made me drink more. I traveled all over, different places until I came back around here, and then I ran into my wife. She was into the Native American Church. First they took me to sweats and all this was clicking back into my mind, and then a person says, "I'm going to quit drinking and get my kid back."

"Me too," I said. That's where we both started thirty years ago, and ever since then we've been going to sweats. A medicine man, Ambrose, told me, "If you do this and do that it will keep your mind straight." So that helped me along and so did John Chaske at the Sun Dance. My first few years I danced up at John's up here [at] Crow Hill, and it changed my life just completely. I'd be smoking a cigarette [but] I couldn't smoke a cigarette either, because I was told that tobacco was supposed to be very sacred and don't play around with it, all kinds of stuff like that I was told.

So I think about those things, and my mind . . . learned to pray more, because I was used to talking or praying in Dakota, and I'm out there walking around, walking around my place, or I say a prayer in my own language and go to sleep. So I got the notion to keep doing that with my wife here. And my wife, she speaks Sioux real good, she's a good speaker, but she don't talk in public—to me she'll talk. I'll talk to her around people but she'll answer in English, but when she's home with me, and we're home alone, she will talk in Dakota to me. She also went to school at St. Michael's. She said she was there for almost a year when her mother went there and got her out of school here. And it's been that way since. But her and I, we talk. Mine's different from hers, but she knows what I'm saying. And so that's my life. It changed from being an alcoholic to being a sober person thirty years now. I got some people that want me to help them stop their drinking, so I try my best to talk to them and hope they can do what I did and stop.

Yeah, well, [my] first wife and I drank a lot, and my children did that; today my children did that. I buried my son Friday because of alcohol, cirrhosis to the liver, and I kind of blame myself. But again, I shouldn't really because the mom was still drinking so it's kind of hard for me, so I pray. I pray sometimes at night. Ever since I got back from Montana, I've been praying for my son. I hope that he goes in the right direction. He had already done that when he passed away.

[M]y two older daughters, they don't get along, so the oldest one couldn't come to his funeral. She tried to message me, but my phone didn't work. I was in Montana; it was a cell phone. So anyway, after I got back I found out what she sent to me, that she had to go back to South Dakota; she lived in Rapid City or Pine Ridge, she lived down there. But she had a terrible life that woman. When she was in a foster home, eleven years old, she got raped. I felt pretty bad about it too. I didn't find out about it until a year after that happened. I was living in South Dakota. My folks called me up back home in Montana, so I went up there, had a good meal on a Sunday, a big meal, the whole family. Everybody started eating. Her mother said, "I want to talk to you. I want to tell you something." So . . . I thought they were going to tell me something good, maybe tell me to sober up or something, that's what I was thinking anyway, and then they said, "Your daughter got raped . . . We didn't want to tell you right away when it happened; that man he died of a heart attack a few months ago."

That was hard for me for a long time, and it seemed like that got me more into drinking, and so today I am happy she lives here, and they're doing really good. They make me feel proud.

Demus was talking about that place where they would peel potatoes. I was down there once. I can't remember what I did—I think I was playing outside and I got in a fight with a bully—and they put me down there. I had to pick up potatoes, and I had to pile a bunch of them beside me and I was peeling them. There was a nun that was there, and we got dinner ready and they let us go back and then we had to go to church. Sometimes when we'd go to church . . . in the wintertime, we had to go through a tunnel, and then you'd go through the school, the bottom floor; there was steps you'd go down and there was an opening on the bottom there and you'd go through the school.

I used to go hide in there and play hooky until I'd hear them coming back. Then I'd come out and go eat. I got caught once; they kept watching me, they kept a close eye on me, but I enjoyed it for a while. No, not really enjoyed it, I guess. It was more, I hated the school. I used to run away a lot. There was a nun, Sister Gonya, and she was always saying good things to me and making me feel good. She would ask me, "How do you say this word in your language?" Things like that. I would try to teach her and tell her what the word was. She would sneak me an apple sometimes. From there on, she was kind of my friend. The other ones I was scared of; the other ones were always looking at me no matter what. I could just walk by and they'd just look at you sometimes. But there was a regular teacher that came in there, I think it was Mrs. Mahoney. She was from out east some place. She was a good lady; the kids loved her. But what we'd like to see was her when she gets mad. Her face would just turn red. She was nice; she comes over and helps me do my work because some of the words—I could read them, but I didn't understand what it meant—so she'd come over, and she'd tell me what it meant so that I could write the word. But sometimes I'd go out in the hallway.

I didn't worry about the nuns, because it seemed like they were always upstairs in their rooms, second floor, or walking the hallways and praying with their rosaries. Bunch of us would go in the basement and steal apples. Demus was talking about this Brother Retau. He was another one that was scary because he would blow up and scream and say things in German or whatever language he'd use. But that was, I guess, his language, but he'd say all kinds of stuff in German. I think he was OK, and after I could turn my back for a while, but when I first started he was kind of scary. It was kind of hard for me, because I couldn't quite understand what they were saying, what they were asking me to do. I always caught heck for some kind of reason.

Later on my grandma said, "I'm going to take you back to Montana and you're going to go to school up there." So that's how I ended up back in Montana and went to school in a bigger school. Public school, yeah. It was all right. There was a mix of kids there, and they were making fun of me, saying things in their languages and stuff you know? They thought it was funny. Made fun of my words when I spoke my own language. White kids and Indian kids, too. I used to get in fights for a long time. I got kicked out of school one time for two weeks. I kind of liked that because I was out hunting with the older guys. Then I went back to school again, and that's when I was just sitting there—I can't remember what I was doing, arithmetic or something—and I was looking down at my book and I couldn't get that number, I couldn't, it was . . . multiplication. Yeah, and I couldn't get it, and I was sitting on the steps, and soon I felt one of these erasers that you use on the blackboard hit me behind the head and it was that teacher. I didn't even see him; it hit my head and bounced off. He thought I was having problems with nits and stuff on my head because I was scratching. The reason why I scratched all the time was because I was trying to figure out what that problem was. He chased me out and made me kneel down in the principal's office. Yeah, he said there was something wrong with my hair, that I had nits, but I didn't have nits. I had long hair. I had to get a haircut. My grandpa, my mother's uncle, he cut my hair. I got to know my dad and my grandma.

I got a haircut and went back to school, started to go to school. I just walked, it was like a block away, and then my uncle, I grew up with my uncle, he's my mom's baby brother. That one had . . . two brothers and they would do crazy things together. He used to try to speak Dakota and some of the words he wasn't saying correctly, so I would try to correct him. So that was OK because he would do it in a funny way that we would laugh and we would enjoy.

I speak Dakota. I was working at the school here in Windsor. I was one of the school teachers there. I went to school at the college over there, and then [I] went to New Town to work with the professor. A . . . doctor . . . came from Minot college, and [I] worked with them for a few weeks, and then they told me I was going to get a letter from Bismarck. If I get a letter from Bismarck, I'll be a certified schoolteacher, which I did, not quite a month later. Then I went to work at the school teaching the language.

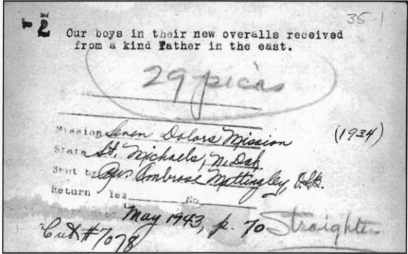

"Our boys in their new overalls received from a kind Father in the east." St. Michael's, ND. *Marquette Archives.*

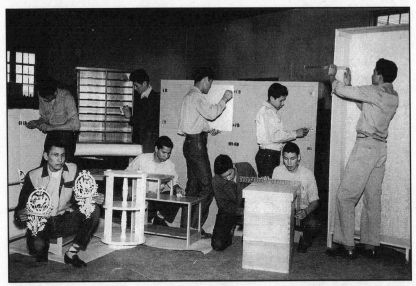

Carpentry class demonstration, Flandreau Indian Boarding School, SD. *National Archives at Kansas City.*

SOLD

I interviewed Phil St. John (b. 1944) at the casino near Ft. Yates, North Dakota, on Standing Rock Indian Reservation. I have known Phil for decades as we were both pow wow people. Phil had recently lost his son, a champion dancer and singer, and was still grieving, as was the pow wow world. Phil is seventy-four years old and very proud of his extended family. He has fifteen siblings, four sons, three daughters, thirty-three grandchildren, and fifteen great-grandchildren. Both his parents are Dakota from Sisseton.

We chatted for a bit about how pow wows, outfits, and dancing styles had changed tremendously over the last four decades or so. Phil attended the Catholic-run Tekakwitha Orphanage in Sisseton, St. Joseph's Indian School in Stephan, St. Peter's Catholic School in Sisseton, and Flandreau Indian Boarding School, all in South Dakota.

According to my uncle Tinah, I was born in a gulch off a little bitty gravel road. The district I come from is Heipa in Sisseton, South Dakota. H-e-i-p-a, alongside the hill or something, and I say that "gulch" because I was born in a house; I wasn't born in a hospital. As a matter of fact, one day I went up to see my dad's grave, and my wife and I, we stopped and just looked at the ground where I was born, I mean that area. There's nothing there anymore; it's a little field, that's where I was born. I know we lived in the country. Close to my grandpas, my uncles.

Then we moved out to, actually, where I was born, we lived there about four years, and I remember being with all my uncles a lot, my grandpas, and as I got older, we moved around after that. Then finally at some point we moved to town, in other words, to Sisseton. And then, but prior to that, we lived at Long Hollow. We kind of made our way back from my district over there, and then we moved up by Long Hollow, which is another district that we moved to. Different houses in Sisseton. My dad never owned a house. We just worked, I mean he did, that's where we lived. I remember us having a dirt floor house. I was pretty darned young. One of my grandpas was sweeping the dirt floor. I don't know how that's possible. I remember that, and I always wondered why they did that.

My parents all went to the orphanage Tekakwitha. My mom went to Wahpeton . . . [She] never did talk too much about her life there other than how mean it was. She thought they were really mean at Wahpeton and Tekakwitha. Wahpeton was a government school; Tekakwitha was parochial, Catholic.

My dad started working when he was about twelve years old, so I don't think his educational level was pretty high. But he's awfully smart and pretty witty. He became a heavy equipment operator, drove gravel trucks, Caterpillars, road graders. He did all of that stuff for about thirty-eight years.

A happy time before boarding school was being with my grandpas, my grandpa Joe and my grandpa Pete. When he lived up by Long Hollow, we lived down below by the church and . . . I used to stay with him. I'd do little things with him. I was just talking about how my grandpa used to let me take a strap of leather and sharpen a knife, and he used to give me a leather and he'd do it too, so I tried. I couldn't do it. He used to whip it back and forth, and I just didn't know how to do that. But I'd get up early in the morning with them. They would sit out in front of the home when the sun was coming up, facing the sun. They'd drink coffee, just sit there, they'd enjoy the sun. I'd go sit by them, and then they were getting ready to go work one time so they were cleaning their shoes, so I would help them with their shoes, clean their shoes off, do little things like that.

They only spoke Dakota, so I had to because that was the only language they had. They'd say something like [speaking Dakota], "now we're going to go," means we're going to go to work, and I'd get to go along with them, Mom would let me go with them. And [speaking Dakota], "Now we're going to leave."

"W-a-n-a," probably "[W-a-n]u-h"—you have to remember that spelling is totally different in every place and [by] every person—"t-'k-e—you put a "y" [insert the "y" sound when indicated by the apostrophe] in between that w-a-n-a and then y-u-n-a then y-a then p-'-t-e that's how we say [speaking Dakota], and it goes together. Maybe that's just something that he said so I'd get ready and go with them then. One time, Grandpa asked me if I had any gloves and I said, "No, I didn't need gloves because it's really hot out." Little did I know what he meant when he said that. We were shocking, we had to shock.[42] Talk about a long time ago, he grabbed these

---

[42] "Shocking" (also called stooking) refers to stacking grain-stalks by hand in the field, getting the stalks ready to be collected for threshing.

shocks and he put them together. This little, what do you call that, sticking out, it would stick in your hands and everything, so then Grandpa put some rags on. I don't know where he got it; he wrapped my hands. So I'm doing that, and if you ever see pictures from a long time ago where the stocks of hay, they sit together like that in the field, that's what shocking was. I remember doing that with them. I don't know if we ever got paid; I never seen any money. I didn't know if Grandpa got any money. They worked for lease; they worked for farmers that were leasing their land, so whatever we got—we'd get eggs and cream, potatoes, and stuff like that—maybe that was our pay, I don't remember. That was really a long time ago.

Tekakwitha was my first school. That's where all of my problems were. The second school from there I went to Wahpeton Government School seventh grade, eighth grade. Couldn't make it there, so I went to St. Peter's, to town school. Lots of racism, lot of prejudice. Got out of ninth grade, went to Flandreau. I tried to go to Sisseton public school, I think it was in ninth grade. So much prejudice, so much things happened. The experience that I had, well I can get into that one later but then from there I went to Flandreau a year and a half, then I went to Stephan and finished up at Stephan, which was Catholic.

My records—see, this is what I was going through with my wife today—I never had a birth certificate, because I was born out in the country. There was nothing in Sisseton for me, they didn't have anything in records up until school. They never did find it. I think I carried the name LeBlanc, my mom's maiden name. I carried her name for about six years until they—finally I think they even made it up—they made up a birth certificate for me. The reason I say that [is] because Mom was telling me one time that when they took me to Tekakwitha you had to be five years old or six years old, for some reason. I don't know if that was a law. I don't know what it was, but, there's this school, and there's this building called Papoose House, and this Papoose House was where all the kids went, the kindergarten kids [and] I think it was the first grade. First grade and kindergarten kids went over there. So I couldn't go there because supposedly I wasn't old enough. My mom said they, I think they moved my birth certificate to 1942, so that made me five years old then, because that's what that paperwork had. Nineteen forty-eight is when I was at the Papoose House. I had to stay in a room with my cousin, in the bed in the dorm, because he was older than me, and I was crying all the time. Because I cried a lot they made me stay with him, so that's why I always say I started school when I was pretty darned young.

As time went on . . . people say, "Why did you go to the boarding school?" I went to the boarding school because my dad said he wanted me to go to school with Indian kids and to be a good Catholic. I succeeded in one area; I was able to stay Indian, but I was not a good Catholic. Talk about being traumatized by what happened. I don't know what happened to me. I don't think anybody hurt me. I don't think anybody abused me, other than beating the hell out of me physically and mentally torturing me. I don't think anybody sexually abused me. I don't even remember, but I can't talk about it, and I don't know why. My daughter asked me one day when they were tearing down that building, she said, "Everybody is criticizing that place, Dad. Can you say something good about the school?" She sat there the same way you are sitting there looking at me, and I looked at her, and for two minutes I couldn't say anything. She said, "You have nothing to say do you?" And I don't. I have talked to three or four or five guys that came from that same era when I was there, [and] they can't think of one thing good about that school. They can't think of one good thing that ever happened to them.

If we did something wrong we were usually punished in a group. I have, I think, six scars on my back. I don't recall where they came from, but I got a good idea where they came from. They used to have a coat room. When you got punished, we'd all have to stand against a wall and grab those hangers and hold them up and stand there while they whipped us. We couldn't cry, and if we cried we got hit again, so we didn't cry.

You can't talk. They had little round rubber hoses, it's not like big water hoses . . . I don't know, small hoses. There were other things they used, too, but I always remember the whip. Then there was another belt thing they used to use. The priests used to use belts on us, but I remember that hose though for some reason, that little rubber hose. Maybe that's the thing that left those scars on my back, I don't know. But we kept going back, and we dreaded it. I did. My dad always taught me I was going to get smart, become a good Catholic, because my dad used to sing in church, hymns and everything, in the church at St. Matthew's. I was an altar boy. I used to think I liked being an altar boy, but as I think back on those days—one of my buddies that grew up the same time as me, Chuck LaRocque, he said, "Any of the priests ever kiss you?"

"No, I don't think so," I said. "How about you Darrel?

"Yeah."

As he was telling me the story about one time at the orphanage he started to cry. My wife and I — my wife didn't even know him — we were standing there getting coffee at the casino at the hotel. This was about seven years ago. He starts telling us this story about Tekakwitha, and he has tears in his eyes. He didn't say why, he didn't tell me why, I didn't know why, but I also had a tear in my eye, as I do right now because I can't remember. I think what hurts me the most was the beating.

They used to cut our hair, shave our heads. Said we had bugs, that we were dirty, [because] we came from the rez. First day of school, that was the routine we all went through, got in line, got our hair shaved off as a joke. The nuns would shave us; the priests and brothers. While they were shaving us little guys, we'd laugh at them, laugh at the guy that was getting his head shaved off, until we got in there, and we got our head shaved off too. But the crazy thing that happened after that was how we got — I can't remember how they washed us if we used, I think we used spray. I don't know if they sprayed us with hose things or what but they washed us, they used lye soap. Mostly nuns. Seemed like the nuns liked giving us baths. All I know is we used to have tubs, galvanized tubs that were stuck into the wall, one, two, then you'd crawl up on a ladder and get in there. My experience in getting in one of them [is that] — because I couldn't get off fast enough one time, and the nun pulled me off of the thing — I fell down and broke my collar bone [and] that's why I've got nerve damage in my left arm right now. Never taken care of. Never sent to a doctor. Never, never. But you wonder what happened then? After they sprayed us and washed us — I can't remember how they did it but I'm pretty sure they did it with scrubbing brushes — this is the craziest thing that happened after that: we're all standing there naked, at least I remember me standing there naked, and they would dump powder all over us. White powder, DDT powder, and we had to stay like that for I don't know how long, fifteen minutes, thirty minutes. I can't remember how long we stayed there, and we stood there, but the purpose of that was to kill every damn bug you ever had in you. If you had any Indian in you that was supposed to come out. That's what I always tell myself. We were talking one time as I got older, remember I have eleven brothers and I have four sisters (five of my brothers have passed away, all four of my sisters are dead). We were sitting in the living room one time as young adults, drinking, watching football, so we started talking. There was about seven of us, "Ever have any of those priests ever," as a joke, you know we joked about it, "Any of those priests ever bother you?"

"Shit, not me, how about you?"

"Hell no."

My brother Ross, he was the roughest in the whole crew, "They bothered me."

"What?"

"Molested me. If I ever seen that guy I'd kill him."

That's what he said. So my mom comes out of the living room where she's sewing, out of the other room and says, "Why didn't you tell us?"

"Mom, you never would have believed us anyway." He says, "You're a Catholic and Catholics don't do that." So all the things that happened to us, the bad things, half of it I think my parents didn't really believe. They didn't think people could be that bad and that mean. But they were.

The thing that bothers me is that I went home when the school year ended in May. A lot of the kids at the orphanage stayed there because they didn't have the home that I had, a lot of us had, a lot of us could go home, Clayton and Darrel and all of us, Randy, everybody would go home, and then we'd come back. And this is the puzzle that happened that I have always asked. I had a friend of mine that stayed there all year, he didn't have no home, he didn't have no parents, never did get what we called "goodies"; he never got nothing, no gifts. His name was Gregory. So he wasn't there when we got there. I was looking all over for him. Every year we'd come back he was there. "Where is he?" we asked. I think it was Sister Cabrini [we asked], "Where's Greg at? "

"Oh, some people went and got him; they took him home."

So I said to myself, "Oh, God, that's good, poor boy, I'm so glad he's got family." That story has stuck in my head now for forty years, fifty years. What the hell happened to Gregory?

Cabrini—I don't remember how you spell it—but you know there was Lucretia, and Sister Katherine, and all kinds of crazy German names. But that's the thing, as I grow older and got involved in ICWA [Indian Child Welfare Act] and working, I got educated. Then I start hearing about people stealing kids, taking kids away. Then I read this thing about Sisseton where a priest was selling our kids for ten dollars. Selling us. Four of my youngest brothers, same issue happened to my four brothers in the '60s. I don't know where we went; we went somewhere and my dad and my mom and us, and my brothers, I think my brother Bob couldn't get back. When we got back to Sisseton, back home, my sister Patty was supposed to be watching [the kids]; they were all gone. Everybody ran away. The house was empty; everybody left. They finally came back, they said, my auntie — that would be Patty — and Ted and all those guys. I said "What happened to them?" They said [the kids] took off [because the] social workers came . . . Roberts County, Mrs. Hosper. I said I'd never forget her name and I haven't. She came and took those four boys. We went to try and find them, my mom tried to find them, and [the social workers] said, "We'll bring them back." Next time Mom heard that they were in Sioux Falls, somewhere in Minnehaha County, and they had court. They got a hearing over there because they were abandoned or something. You don't have to go, Mrs. Hosper says, "You don't have to go, I'll represent whatever is coming." So [Mom] didn't go. Two weeks later, [my parents] asked her what happened: "Oh you didn't show up in court." All four of my brothers got sold. The Geffers family in Brooklyn, New York, and that's where they grew up. Never seen Jack before. Never seen Jeffrey, he passed away. Roger came back. Roger is in Sisseton right now. The fourth, Sandy, passed away, he came back. Sandy came back and Roger, the youngest one came back, but Jack never did come back. Jack's in New York someplace. Jeffrey was working in Albuquerque somewhere; he passed away. He died from cancer. My mom never seen them; she seen Sandy but she never seen Jack.

Roger right now says they were sold for $20,000. Five thousand apiece. Hard to believe that much money, but that's the figures that he had. My brother is really a hostile person though. I mean, he's angry, and I don't blame him for what the hell he was raised on, the way he was raised. So when you talk about losing kids, kids taken away from you, I had that experience with my own family happening. I have a bunch of cousins right now that live in Montana, a lot of them like Ramona and Barbara and a lot of them right in Sisseton that grew up in Tekakwitha. Word is there was a lot of sexual abuse there by the priests. Father Pohlen ran Tekakwitha and he's an alcoholic. P-o-h-l-e-n, Pohlen. He's an alcoholic. We know it because we used to take trash out, and we'd have to pick up trash from the school and drop them off at his house; the trash was nothing but beer bottles and whiskey bottles.

Seems like nobody cares though, nobody's even willing to talk. If somebody feels like I feel about Tekakwitha, I can understand why they're not talking about it . . . some of the stuff we don't remember because you have to remember, we were four or five, six years old. And the things that happened to us, that's why I can't remember. I don't know why this bothers me so much.

I cried a lot. Probably lonesome. Heard the other boys cry. In the dorm, the little boys' one and the big boys' one on that side. The beds were a little bit higher over there. You could lower them. Just like cots. I can't remember exactly what they were like but I remember a boy crying at night. I don't know if it was the beginning of the school year or when it was, but a boy was crying . . . someone tried to make him stop crying, and he wouldn't, so they whipped him.

This was boys — boys were on this side, girls were on the other side, on the other side of the building. You had to be by your section so we were divided. The boy, they made that boy get up and go stand out in the hallway on a tile floor; everything was tile, cold, cold. Made him stand out in the hall until he stopped crying. Mean-ass nuns. They were mean. But to see that, to hear that cry, tears, and as I got older and I think back on those days, god damn people realize that boy is crying for his mom. That's why he was crying.

And a lot of things that went on, like I said, I can't remember any good things. There's one thing that happened to me there, an experience I had there that my grandma — who was a devout Catholic — and my other grandma was another super-devout (all of my family are Wannas, W-a-n-n-a, the whole bunch of them, my mom's on that too, my dad, my grandpa, my dad was on the St. John's side, the Demarises, the Morrises, all of them), but, a priest died one time, and they had to have a funeral, and every one of us there are altar boys. Chuck Peterson, Clayton Adams, Chuck LaRoque, Joe St. John, you guys are going to be the altar boys for that requiem mass. I told that story to my mom and Auntie Alvera and Grandma Grace.

"Oh my God, you should be so proud," my Grandma Grace said.

I thought to myself, "Oh, Grandma, Alvera — my auntie Alvera — do you like the boarding school?" I called [my auntie] Alvera; she's the only one of my aunties I never called "auntie." I just called her Alvera, because that's what she liked to be called. That's my mom's sister, and she said, "I thought it was OK."

"Oh really?" I said, "How about when they cut your hair off?"

"No I didn't care about that."

"How about those shoes they used to make you wear, those funny shoes?"

"Yeah, those were ugly," she'd say.

"How about those dresses you'd wear?"

"Those were ugly too," she says. "Well, I guess I don't like it that much then," she said.

That was her, that was her little . . . what she remembered about, but their experience was a little bit older than mine.

We wore our own clothes. Yep, back then we never had uniforms. See, that comes from the, geez, that's the early 1900s, 1910, '20s and '30s, I think. Some places did have uniforms, but we didn't, we just had our just our regular clothes, and I don't know what the purpose was for that.

We had church in the morning. Church and school. We had to clean. We definitely had chores. We cleaned something that's been cleaned already, it seemed like. Kept cleaning and working until you were done. It was a job. You had to go to sleep at a certain time. Certain hours you could play outside and have fun. That's about it.

Meals were homemade cottage cheese. I can't remember what kind of . . . we had commodity food. I think we had powdered eggs, powdered milk. I can't remember what kind of oatmeal we had, but everything was powdered.

I don't remember being hungry, no, I kind of grew up that way. Just like today I can probably go maybe two days without eating, you know? We grew up poor, remember there were sixteen of us [children] in my family, so . . . we were definitely poor. People can talk about poor [but] they can't even match what we went through.

Parents would have to sit up at the chapel area in the front; there was a waiting room out there. They would have a limit on that too, you could only have like two families that could come and you'd get what we'd call "goodies." I can't remember what was in it, candy and whatever else kids liked back then. It wasn't much, because my dad couldn't bring me things; we didn't have the money. He couldn't even come and visit us. One year, I think me and Bob and my sister Yvonne, we stayed there all summer [so the staff could] teach us how to work. So, we worked with the cows and corn and trash and cleaning buildings and paint. We did all that stuff to learn how to work. The worst thing I ever went through in my life. I didn't know what pay was, because we never got paid.

I think it was Owen Red Bear and me and I can't remember the other one. I think it was Jerome, and I think it was Dale Adams, I can't remember, but we ran away. You've got to remember that Tekakwitha is only about two miles from Sisseton, so we ran across the field. I don't know why;

we could have gone on the road, I guess, but we ran through the field and went home and got back to the house. So happy to be . . . . my mom lived in town . . . so happy to be there. My mom says, "What the heck are you doing here? How did you get over here?" I said I ran away. So she called my dad. My dad was working on the highway. He came in madder than hell. Mad. Whipped me, spanked me, took me back to the orphanage. The Brothers beat the hell out of me again, so I got beat up twice in one day, for no reason. Don't even know why I ran away. Yeah, I don't know, we had no place to go I guess. I don't know, that's why I never ran away [again].

We had chores. Floors, mop floors. Clean the toilets, hated that. Sometimes I'd go wash dishes. Clean up outside. No matter how cold it was outside, when you had to go outside and play you had to go outside and stay outside. You don't come in; they send you out at one o'clock [and] you can't come back in again until, I'm not sure, 3:30 or whatever. So you're out there freezing . . . we looked like a herd of cattle all bunched together in the corner out of the wind. It was colder than hell, and we'd have to stay out there; we had no choice.

I didn't speak any English. I got caught in-between a couple of times because we spoke fluent Dakota at home, you know, but when you have to switch over you learn in a hurry because you get beat, and that's not a joke. They talk about a long time ago—my grandpa used to say, "Oh yeah, we couldn't say nothing in Indian." It was hard because then when you'd leave you'd go home, and Grandpa and Grandma and everybody they'd say [speaks Dakota]. Yeah, then we'd have to change or watch ourselves, what we would say, because if you would say something to somebody else that talked fluent Indian like my cousins, you'd get a slap in the head while you're standing in line; then you just realize what you did, you know? Shouldn't have said that; yeah, they did it, they got us, scared the hell out of us.

The only problem I found out is when I tried to go between going from St. Peter's School to Two Point High School, the public school. That's where I ran into a lot of racism, real bad. The racism was bad because we talked with an accent. If you speak real Dakota, and you say it, it sounds like you are uncivilized or something. In English class, old Miller, the teacher, a white boy . . . I had to do a speech. It was a requirement. So I started to read a little story I made up, you know, everything's made up back then anyway. The kids started to laugh at me, so I quit. I stopped talking. As I started walking away—I left school—I was walking out of the classroom and he grabbed me and told me—old Miller, he's probably dead, dead and gone — he pulled me back, pushed me back in and made me stay in the room. All the kids were still laughing at me. The next chance I got, I took off. I went home and again, my mom sent me back. That's when I quit. Then I got in trouble, stealing. I wanted to get sent to Plankinton. I wanted to go to reform school because I didn't want to go to Sisseton.

St. Peter's in Sisseton. Yeah, that's a Catholic school, seventh and eighth grade. So when I got in trouble, about five of us for stealing, three of them they sent to Plankinton, [but] they kept me and Jim Barker; they kept us there and they said, "Where are you guys gonna go? Wanna go back to school? Wanna go to Flandreau?" Well, [they] asked because [our other option was] to go to jail. I said, "OK." Those were my Flandreau days. Flandreau was another problem too. Oh God, I can't remember how old I was, fourteen or fifteen, or somewhere around there fourteen or twelve?

I guess I would describe it by saying it's pretty much like the Catholic school, same thing, only thing is the matrons that work in the dormitory take care of all the kids. There were guards. At night — they ride horses — so if you run away, they run you down, rope you, and bring you back. That's what this one guy said, they drove him back, they drove him back to the dorm. They caught him right in the alley, and he was trying to jump across the river or down that way, [but] they caught him. Yeah, on the horses, they caught him and they drug him back. Never to run again. I ran away from there later on. Me and John Hill, Irving Cook, stole a car from a farmer, jumped in and went all the way back to Sisseton. Made it home; told my mom, "I'm not going back to Flandreau." She said, "You guys go to Stephan then."

All right. Went to Stephan then. Catholic. Yep, I finished up tenth grade. I was supposed to be in . . . I don't know what grade I was supposed to be in. I thought it was eleventh grade. They gave me enough credits or whatever, and I graduated in eleventh grade from Stephan. Then I went on relocation, went to Oklahoma for a little bit. Came back, went to Oakland. Came back, got remarried. Came back, went to Minneapolis, got divorced, got remarried after that, and that was it . . . got an education. I worked in a warehouse for Great Wire Electric for a long time, and I said, "That's a god damn puppet, sitting in this basement every day." I was interested in what's going on in this world. I wanted to know because I, like now, I watch MSN-BC all the time and [I'm] always into news stuff. I'm always interested in current events. So I decided I'd go back to college and go to school.

So I tried. Graduated from Minneapolis Community College. I don't know what year it was, a long time ago. And then I went to school at Metro State University in St. Paul and got a Bachelor's degree.

I was working for the Coop Clinic, the Community Health Care Center. I was there for about eight years. Then a job came up at the University of Minnesota, the Mental Health Unit. Adolescent Mental Health unit was hiring, because they wanted to hire an American Indian because a little girl name Sarah, fourteen years old, committed suicide, and they found out they had nobody employed there that could meet the needs of Indian clients. So they hired me. I worked there nineteen years. And I seen it all. Boy, I've seen them kids come in. There was a gang, there was a gang area then, in the '70s, '80s, really bad, just a lot of bad things. I see kids come in, stand and look in the window and cry, and turn around, sit down, and start talking straight-faced. That's how it was. But I was a good guy though; I could talk to anybody. I could have parents come in ready to beat the hell out of every white provider they could run into until they met me. Then they would sit down, and I would always have something in common with these guys. I'd know everything about them. I'd know who their dad is, I played basketball with their uncle, you know? Red Lake and Cass Lake. So anyways, I got to be real good at that. Then I expanded over to Mental Health. I went over to Chemical Dependency, too, so I worked in both areas. Next thing you know they started calling me for the adult Mental Health unit, and that's, if you have ever been in a locked facility before, it's a trip for the first time. I went down there and they gave me keys to the North building.

"What kind of guy?"

"I don't know," [they said]. "You're going to have to see him; he's tall though."

I'm scared, and I'm coming in; he opened his door, you go in and it shuts behind you, you hear it clang behind you like you're going to jail or something. Then this other door opens up and, well, he's sitting over there in the waiting room, so I walk over and I said, "Oh, the river's up; It's nice and pretty." And the guy was sitting and looking up, and he gets up—he's about six feet four—he's got a headband on. He looked like he just came back from Wounded Knee or something. Holy cats, what am I going to do?

I told him to sit down. I was talking Indian, and I told him to sit down. I forget where he said he was from, but anyway, we started talking, and he was telling me all these problems. He said, "You know these people think

I'm crazy," he said, "Shit, I just lost a family member," he said. "I'm really sad. I'm just trying to make things go."

When I'd go in that building all the adults, they'd have ribbons and flowers in their hair, and some guys would be standing there saluting the flag all by themselves. I said, "Oh my God"; I couldn't get used to [that] one, that part, but then they'd form a smudge, so that's when, I was pretty good at that.[43]

I started getting involved in my culture when my son Terry was born in 1970. He started dancing in 1973. In 1973, [he] wore his first bustle.[44] Nathan Thompson made the first bustle for him. So that was kind of the start of it; I was getting more involved in the language. I remember Danny Seaboy dancing the Grass Dance out in Oakland one year, 1965; it was a long time ago. We had our own drum group in Stephan. I don't recall who was in that group, Melvin Hawk, Alvin Cantrell, Crow Flies High boys, Danny and Norman, I think they both passed away, too, didn't they?

The older one is Howard. I can't remember which ones are alive yet. I think it's just the boys and maybe their mom. I knew all of them, and they all knew me. When I go to New Town now I have a whole bunch of [people who know me], Murphy and everybody knows me, John Charging and Wade and all the Baker boys. When I go to Fort Totten it's the same thing; I got a lot of people that know me over there, too. I go to pow wows and basketball, Red Lake with Willie and all of them, the Strongs, the Cooks. I was at a pow wow with my granddaughter, and she said, "Grandpa take me over to this stand." They had little gifts, you know how at pow wows they have little knickknacks and toys and stuff; she wanted to go over there. Every time I'd start going so far someone would talk to me, and we'd shake hands and visit; she was standing there waiting and she'd keep pulling on me. We'd go so far and stop again, somebody would stop, well anyway, we got over there and she wanted an umbrella. I said, "No, I ain't getting that"; that thing was $29, and . . . and her grandma, my wife, said, "Here." She gave her $15.

"No," [my granddaughter] said, "I don't want to walk with Grandpa because he knows too many people . . . You have too many friends, Grandpa."

---

[43] The smudging ceremony is a smoke bath that removes negative energy, improves mental health and spiritual well-being, and heals.
[44] A bustle, generally bearing eagle or hawk feathers and originating from the Plains region, is a traditional part of a man's regalia worn in dances for competition and exhibition at pow wows.

I've got diabetes. I have nerve damage in my left shoulder, I have shoulder replacement on my right side, I had hip replacement on my left side. I think my heart's OK. I can't see out of my right eye, but other than being kind of crippled, mentally I think I'm pretty damn stable.

Yeah, I think we all had problems with alcohol and drugs at one time in our lives. When we started out, we used to think alcohol was fun, and for some people it was. I always liked to say it was fun for me, because I went through that too, but I quit using in 2007. I don't keep track of that. I was just told because my stepson Brian, he was a Sun Dancer, he started, [but then] he stopped, too, so I always kind of say, "because of you, I stopped drinking." So we take credit, we give each other credit. But I quit then because the place I worked at, Charles Hall . . . with the youth—they had group homes there—one of the guys I worked with was a real good work-er, but he got a DUI, so they had to let him go. I said, "Damn, I'd never want that to happen," and for that reason I quit. Although I've never had a DUI in my life, just the thought of it, that . . . if anybody says, "Why did you quit using?" that would be one of the . . . but, health-wise, I just quit. I don't know, I'm not into drugs, never was into drugs, never. I've been in and around people, a lot, but I guess, what do you expect, with sixteen . . . living siblings, many of them have been in and out of prison. A lot of them have been fired, drinkers, smokers, some of them went into drugs, some of them I think have now even tested meth. Kenny doesn't drink, my brother Roland doesn't drink, I don't drink.

I don't know how we call it, Indian religion or how do we describe that. I believe in the Indian ways. I believe in our culture. We burn sweet grass all the time in our house, sage, a lot; we do it a lot for our own healthy ways. This is my thing about the Catholic Church: if I'm to ever die, I don't want no damn priest around me. That's exactly what I would say, and I don't. Too much lying, too much [hypocrisy] that I ran into. Saw my uncle and he said that same thing: "When I die, want no wasicu around me." So I guess, I feel that way. When I do pass away, I'd like some friends of mine to talk, friends I knew a long time ago, some that can speak Dakota. I'd love it because I can understand Dakota 110 percent. But because I don't have the ability to practice it a lot I [am] semi-fluent, 75 percent. I can say whatever I have to. I know every word there is, you know? And spelling, we never were a written language, so what the heck. I think it would be harder for Ojibwe; I think the words are longer than heck.

At Wahpeton I was in the seventh grade, but it was just a short stint, really, I don't even have that much experience about it because all I know is I always felt like it was a bunch of bad kids there, I mean disciplinary things. I think it was scary . . . I didn't want to be there; that's why I chose to go to St. Peter's instead, because there I think I can handle them, although I'd get beat around a little bit there, too, at St. Peter's—mostly by staff and some white kids.

People would ask me, "What was your life like at St. Peter's when you were in the seventh grade or eighth grade?" Well, we would play baseball or basketball, or whatever, out there in the playground [with] some of my best friends, Neil Stapleton, Billy, there's two brothers. But then we came home from school—we walked, we had our house over here, there was one street in Sisseton called First Street all the way along, back in the old days it was called Taniga Avenue and all the Indians lived on that street on either side—anyway, when . . . I'd go that way towards the house . . . the [white] boys would go the other way, never ever to talk again until we got to the school; isn't that crazy? Those same friends that we played with and talked to would not associate with us until we got together on the playground. Covert racism, I'd say. We didn't go there and talk to them; it's not because my dad didn't want me to talk to them wasicu kids. He didn't want me to get hurt, because they would hurt me by saying something mean to me.

And you know, one experience about Sisseton, about that same age when you'd go home in the summer after Tekakwitha, I think I was about nine years old, my K'unsi—I called her K'unsi, my grandma; her wasicu name was Nancy, but to me, I'd just say "who's that . . . 'Nancy,' I don't know her. I just know that's K'unsi"—she would get a grant check, twenty dollars, twenty-two dollars, whatever they'd write checks for [speaks Dakota], [and she would say] "We're going to go eat now."

OK. I'm all happy; I'm walking with K'unsi, we'd come from her house all the way up to what we'd call the showhouse or the theater. We'd walk all the way down across the street [to where] there was a restaurant [called] Boyd's Café, an old brown building; it still sits in Sisseton right now. I don't know what it is right now. And then we would sit down. And we sat. And we sat. Nobody came to wait on us, nobody. Again, my grandma, K'unsi, picked that up right away. She felt it, covert racism was there, so we left. I've hated that place ever since; I've *hated* that place. Stavick's across the street was the store; same thing. Me and K'unsi went to the store, we walk in, here was this short white lady, whatever: "What do you need?" she asked K'unsi.

"We have to get something." She had a hard time talking so I would have to explain.

"Do you have money?"

We had to show our money, and this was in 1950-something, you had to show that you can pay back in those days.

"OK, what do you want?"

K'unsi told her what she wanted. I said, "She wants to get some food."

"OK, you got to go that way," because [the store] was divided; "Food's over there."

It was kind of like Walmart, so we went over there. We were watched over, especially Indians, they'd watch over us, and when you come out you had to go straight out again. You can't walk around in that store unless you have money. That's how they treated us.

So when they talk about Sisseton, there's getting to be more and more Indians there now, so I think Indians will end up taking over, I don't know when. There was racism there, a lot, and I've seen it all, so when it comes to feeling racism and covert racism, I've seen it, I've seen it a lot. My dad pulled into a gas station in Clark, South Dakota. We almost ran out of gas; we barely made it, we pushed up to the gas [pump], the wasicu guy that was in there turned off the machine. Back in the old days you had to take the numbers off when you turn it off. He said, "You'll have to come back in the morning." It was not even midnight, and he was locking up. So he made us sit there in that car. I always tell people you know we were in good hands; you know why? The cop must have come by about twenty-five times (making sure we didn't steal anything). They [usually] opened the pumps up in the morning at six o'clock, [but] they opened at about seven-thirty just to be hateful to us. All he needed to do was give us about a gallon of gas to make it to Redfield, then we would have made it, but nope. So I always say I know what racism is all about because I've been there, done that, seen that.

I have a granddaughter right now I'm raising, Katera, she's fifteen years old, she's right now with her aunt, my daughter up in Sisseton. [Katera] loves it on the rez, I don't know why. She goes to Shiloh; she's going to be a sophomore next year. She's doing really good. She's a B student and that's almost impossible at Shiloh, but she's doing it. She's doing good. She gets really upset with me when I get prejudice talking about black people or white people.

"People aren't like that, Grandpa."

I want to say, "Girl, if you only knew what I've been through you would understand." Apologies ain't going to help. [An] apology is saying something for something that you did wrong; it's still going to be there, that hurt's still going to be there. You can say you're sorry day and night, it's not going to help. I would think some kind of compensation for those people, not just myself, but I think somebody should pay for breaking my shoulder, or for whipping my back, and putting me through all this. I think the sorrow or the sadness I had to face, compensation for that.

Maybe I could have been a better student. Maybe I could have been a better person if I wasn't in that situation. Maybe I could have been a more smarter individual, got a better job, [without] that prejudice and discrimination and hate. But compensation not only just for myself as a person but something that I can share with my sons, with my kids and my wife. Be it physical even if it's compensation through money, whatever.

The main thing I would like to see . . . I just went and visited my granddaughter in Wilmot; there's a shelter there . . . an elderly home over there. My granddaughter Alissa works there, so I went to visit them. Jonas Graves was there; he was at the boys' school when I was there. He's sitting there like a vegetable right now. John Red Day can't really talk anymore; he was there. There was an older lady there that sits there looking at you listless, like . . . why are they in that situation right now? Is it because what the boarding school did to us? Did Tekakwitha put us in those situations that we didn't get the proper care, the help that we needed?

I think so. I think they could have changed things. Jonas could [have become] a lay person; [he] used to go around and do things for people, help them. I mean, those were the people that should get that help. [The schools] should be held accountable for that, and the only thing that hurts—organizations like the Catholic Church—is money, that hurts them the most. It's like the government, what hurts them the most, and I think that if we can help those people out, these homeless people . . . a lot of those guys have been to Vietnam, a lot of them have been fighting for their lives coming back uneducated, really lonely, not only sad from Vietnam but sad from what happened to them in the boarding school. Stuff that's happened to me . . . I think, I wasn't . . . I didn't have to go to Vietnam, but why, the trauma that we *had* to go through at the boarding school . . . it's just indescribable.

You just can't put it, can't pinpoint what it did to us. Just an apology and a hug is not going to help. It's only going to make it worse. So you turn around and say, "well, what's going to hurt the Church?"

All the money that they make—the Catholic charities played a big part, sold my son, my brothers—nobody [else] made nothing out of that; the church made all the money. I used to sit in that boarding school, in the classrooms, and stuff envelopes of all these things, all these envelopes . . . here, this one's to Washington, DC, this one here is to Kentucky, this one here to Europe or something like that. Envelopes, we'd fold these things up and push them in there and lick them; we didn't have [a choice], we did that . . . we'd stuff envelopes to sell ourselves. I used to tell people: "We sell ourselves." That picture, the little Indian boys, little Indian kids stuffing in help-this-poor-Indian-kid-out [messages]; we sold ourselves. Tekakwitha did that. Yeah, they did that to us.

I'm sure my picture appeared in many of the [mailings] . . . because there would be times when the nuns would take pictures of us guys sitting together and holding hands . . . we're sitting on the dirt . . . it was always some really bad scenery it seems like, you know? Just like, my mom has a picture of my three brothers with white shirts on, and we're hugging. It looked like it came from the orphanage; that's what we used to joke about, but yeah, we did sell ourselves. We sold ourselves and didn't even know, we didn't even know what we were doing. The biggest part I find with all of the people in Sisseton that were involved with Tekakwitha, you have to remember, were predominantly Catholics. [There were other] churches: Episcopalian, Protestants, Jehovah's Witnesses, name it. And I've always said to myself, half of those people in Sisseton from all of those other districts did not give a damn about Tekakwitha. They don't care because they never had to go there. If you're having a funeral at Old Agency, that's the tribal office, if you're having a community center, a funeral, what church does he go to?

One of the things I always find is a lot of people don't really care because they weren't [sent to Tekakwitha]. Some of them went to Bishop Hare's School in Rosebud, some of them went to St. Elizabeth over here in Ft. Yates, a lot of the ones that [were] Episcopalian, they go to those schools. Predominantly all of the boarding schools over there were Stephan and St. Joe's, all the Catholic ones; there was quite a few of them.

Being alive makes me happy today. My dad passed away at the age of fifty-seven, and I'm sitting here at the age of seventy-four. I'm thankful.

If I've got a little finger that hurts I think about all the people sitting in a wheelchair that can't walk, then my finger don't even bother me. I think a lot about the things I do have: I got a wife and I got a granddaughter and I got a son with me in Bismarck, not with me, but living in Bismarck-Mandan. They take care of me. If I should ever, if my time ever comes, and it's my time to leave, I think I would be in good hands. I've got my daughters and I will have fifty-eight grandkids. Fifty-eight grandkids! They can sing, they can dance; my girl can sing—church hymns, prayer songs, she's good at them.

I didn't raise my kids Catholic. No, no, like I said, when I got away from there, when I got educated, that was my biggest bias was that Catholic Church. So much things that . . . I just say this: I'm telling my granddaughter, there's an accident when kids survived, they're all talking about this thing—God is with him, Jesus is with you, took him in their hands—Oh really? What about those fifty-eight people that died? You know? I sound like Bill Maher right now, but anyway that's my little . . . look at things kind of open-mindedly, and I'm lucky. The only reason why I'm here today at this age [is that] I have a mission. I don't know what it is yet . . . I'm thinking, I think it's coming, [but] when? I don't know.

I hope it don't come right away, but when my time does go, I told my family—my granddaughters know, [even though] they don't want to hear about it . . . my granddaughter will not listen to me when I talk like that . . . I can't even make plans—I said I even made my own memorial song to sing, because I compose. I compose all the songs for [my son] Terry for Eyabay; I was the one that put all of those words in his songs. I told Joe Many Bears, you know him too, yeah? [He] said how in the hell, how did the elders come up with those damn songs anyway? I just now figured it out: it's you. They pointed at me, and I said, yeah, I did a lot of them. Terry would make trips in Arizona somewhere, make a song over the phone. Because they'd put the tune out, and I put the words on it and we'd go back and forth and get it done in that night, they sang it in Sunday School [or] Saturday night—the boys in that room, they'd practice, and they sang it. I said it's pretty good. I corrected, I edited a couple of words, and that's it. It was beautiful when it came out.

Well, I mean with Terry and what he did, it was so good, and my other son, he can sing almost as good as Terry, but no, he can't compose like Terry. Terry has that hidden talent, the talent you can't describe. Everybody says that about him. I miss him a lot.

I'm not so much worried about myself. Like I said, I'm a survivor. It's been a lot of years. I put in a lot of time. I'm more worried about my people close to me. I get sad when I hear people have died; that's what I'm worried about. I know my cousin out in Montana, he just died . . . I feel sorry for [his wife] and wonder how she's doing. I hope she comes to the pow wow next weekend. She's so fun, too. There's a young boy . . . he came up to me one time; he was at a special [event]. He called my name, and he gave me a Star Quilt at Fort Totten, and I just knew my son—he liked Terry, he idolized Terry—anyway, a couple years ago he gave me a Star Quilt, and today I just read something on Facebook and he lost his little brother. I feel sad about that, bad stuff like that. I wish for the best for them. I want people to enjoy themselves.

As far as my stress, I can deal with it; nothing bothers me. See, my granddaughter is Princess Prairie Island; [in] two weeks—not next week, the week after—we're going over there, and she's giving up her crown, so I have to get money together. We're picking up a bunch of t-shirts for her, as a matter of fact, this afternoon. That's what I'm looking forward to. I mean, that's what makes me happy. Tekakwitha's not there no more, the building's gone [and] it's a playground now. This is what bothered me when I saw that: how can they play over all the hurt and pain that went on on that land? Above that ground? And how many of those hidden graves are up in there someplace?

There's a little grotto-type thing there; some people said there's some graves over on the side, I don't know. Yeah, that's sad. Just the thought of it over there makes me sad to know that they should have made a memorial out of it instead. You know? Memorialize all those people that survived that, the ones that passed away and the ones that are still alive. That would have been kind of nice, but a playground? I don't know, I have a hard time with that. Right now the people that don't know, they don't have no idea what that was like a long time ago. They're having fun now taking their kids over there, playing around, walking around, swings and everything. I guess it's OK, I don't know. For me personally I think it's sad.

I'm doing this [interview] willingly because I need it; I need to have that done, I wanted to tell somebody, I've been wanting to do that. You know, I just hope word would get out that . . . we talked about how the Catholic Church treated us. I'm your witness; I was there. I was there. They got scrubbed, I was there. They got DDT powder dumped all over them . . . and I'm the one that got whipped. [It's] not trivialized. It's not romanticized . . . it's real. It happened. I survived because I'm Dakota.

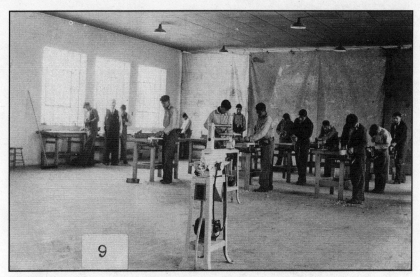

Carpentry class, Flandreau Indian Boarding School, SD.
National Archives at Kansas City.

Mechanics class, Flandreau Indian Boarding School, SD.
National Archives at Kansas City.

RATTLESNAKES!

In December, just before Christmas, I drove to Green Acres, a tribal housing project on the Turtle Mountain Indian Reservation west of the town Belcourt, to interview Tommy Davis (b. 1946), a former student at the Pierre Indian Boarding School, South Dakota. Although early evening, by the time I arrived it was dark and had begun to snow lightly. I had not been to this reservation housing project before and was grateful for his directions as I passed East Cluster and Eagleview housing projects, finally arriving at Green Acres and locating his modest home "next to the house that is lit up with yard ornaments." We sat at his kitchen table during the interview, while Tommy served hot black tea throughout the evening. At the time of this interview, Tommy is seventy-two years of age, retired. He is Turtle Mountain Pembina Chippewa. Pembina means high bush cranberry. Both of his parents are Chippewa/ Cree. He is divorced, has four sisters and eleven children, one passed away. Tommy maintains his first languages, Chippewa and Cree, and would easily slip in and out of each language, translating what he said. Without prompting, he immediately launched into his family history before being sent to boarding school.

I was born in Belcourt. My grandpa Colin Davis named me after Thomas Little Shell. He had an old white man friend named Duane. So, he named me that, Thomas Little Shell and Duane. We had a beautiful home north of Poker Hill, way up far before you leave the reservation. Way in the woods. My grandfather built the house. A basement on top of the ground and a structure on top of the basement. The basement was where all the activity took place, [with] the cook stove and the big homemade table with benches. It always smelled like fresh bread and wood smoke. The lake was down below the hill about maybe three hundred yards. We hauled water from there and they would boil it for purification. We used that for drinking, cleaning, washing clothes. Mom and Grandma would take the wash down to the lake with the scrub board and a brick of soap and go down there and wash clothes.

We hauled wood. They would start hauling wood about August, before the leaves fell, because you could find the good seasoned wood, the dead wood when the leaves are still on. We used horses with chains, put four or five logs on a clamp, and pull them out of the woods. We had a big hay rack; they load that hay rack full like that and haul it to the house. Mike Poitra used to help. Frank Gladue used to help. Frank had an old beat-up kind of tractor. I can remember this thing, had a big blade on it and a big long belt. Rrrrrr, they would cut wood together. Lasted through the winter. I watched them do that.

He had cows, so I learned how to milk when I was about five-and-a-half years old, I suppose. Tried it anyway. Helped make cream, separate it. Cleaned the barn. A team of horses was your transportation, and they were treated like people. Their stall cleaned, fed, watered—had to break holes in the ice to water them.

It was a beautiful life. It was so much survival skills and understanding that we didn't need nobody, didn't need no government, we didn't need no BIA. We didn't need no nothing. I see that was so good for everybody; there was love among our families. The best thing you could have was a good neighbor. That kind of living, that's the way it should have remained. Maybe someday it will come back the way things are going. But I feel bad for our young people. They have no survival skills any more. They wouldn't know what to do if [the] electricity [was cut] off [laughter].

When I was four or five years old, I slept between Grandpa and Grandma. I don't know, they just took a love to me. They had a small bed for me. Then my grandpa made a little bed out of oak [laughter]. He taught me a lot of things. I tried to copy him. I remember one time they had an old car there. They were trying to start this old tractor to cut wood. I watched them siphon a little bit of gas with a hose. I had to go try. I got sick; me, I swallowed a bunch of gas, and I remember they made me drink a can of milk. Puked all over, vomiting all over.

All medicinal things were done by herbal understanding. I remember one time one of the girls got poison oak. Papa went down by the lake. I remember he brought back a big bunch of these blue flowers; they looked like little bugles. Little purple, blue flowers. He boiled them, and I can't remember what he put in there with the little flowers, and he put it on my auntie all over and the next day it dried up all of that liquid from the blisters. Honest to God, I saw that with my own eyes.

We lived a beautiful life. We had no vehicle. I remember when the old battery radio came out. My grandpa got one. You could only listen to it for a little bitty while, twenty minutes, before the battery died. He used to listen to Porky Charbonneau's Ranch House out of Winnipeg. It was a fiddle hour. My grandpa Bill was one of the best fiddle players I ever did hear. Bill Davis, Koomish's grandpa—that was my grandpa's brother. Don Messer was a famous one, Andy Desjarlais. But me and my sister, when we first got that radio, we'd hear these people talking. We went in the back and tried to see if we could see these people. Like a TV thing, tried to see these little, those little people in there [laughter]. It was interesting, that kind of life. We were poor, but we were rich in other ways.

My mother worked at San Haven for twenty-six years, I believe. My father worked just about anything. He worked Bethlehem Steel. He worked in construction. He fought two wars—the European Theater and the Pacific Theater. When he came home from the war, Carl St. Claire and Trottier and him caught the train as far as Rugby. In those days, Rugby had a taxi-cab service there. They caught a ride, paid the cab as far as Yellow Corner, ten miles south of Dunseith, as far as the taxi would take them. They were in full uniform. They had their ribbons and all their medals. They went into the tavern there, the Yellow Corner, that was the name of it. They wanted to have a drink. There was a sign there that said, "No Dogs, No Indians Allowed." They turned them down. My dad said, "We were stuck in this place, ten miles from home. We didn't know nothing. We kind of got angry. Told them we just got done fighting your damn war for you guys. We marched across Europe and I was in the Philippines and you can't even get us a beer?" They got kind of rowdy, I guess. They called the sheriff. They waited for about a half hour, I guess, and the sheriff got there. He asked them, "What's the trouble boys?"

"We just want a drink. We just got off the train. We were in the war."

"Get in the car," he says.

My dad thought they were going to jail.

"I'll go talk to these guys to see what's going on," the sheriff said. He went in there, and pretty soon he come out. He had a package. He brought them guys a six-pack and a bottle, a mickey of whiskey. And gave them a ride to Dunseith.

I always think of those things about my father, from his boarding school stuff. How tough it was for them when he was in a boarding school. He said if you weren't an athlete or exceptionally good at something, you were treated like second-class citizenry. I always remember that. Same time they were trying to terminate my people. In 1953, the Termination Era came in, and the one who was president at that time was the guy that was his commander in the European Theater, Dwight Eisenhower. My dad hated Eisenhower after that, and excuse my language, but he said, "I marched across Europe for that son-of-a-bitch, and he's trying to terminate my people. You're never going into the service, Tommy." He said, "Never. Don't you ever. I fought enough for *all* of my family. When they get to the reservation line, fight." That's what my father told me.

He was also the vice-chairman of the tribe here in 1954. He went on the Relocation program. He assigned his position from District Four to his nephew, Robert Wilkie. We went on to Relocation. I was probably seven years old going on eight. I had never been out of Rolette County. I think we went to Bottineau one time in my life before that. They took us and put us on a train in Rugby. It took us three days and three nights. On the fourth morning we got to San Francisco. We got off the train. We didn't know we walked out of the depot onto a ferry. The next thing I know, we went to look outside [and] we were in the middle of the Oakland and San Francisco Bay going towards Treasure Island! Scared the hell out of us, me and my sister. We had never been in that much water. We see this city coming, [and] here we ended up in San Francisco. I had never in my life encountered such a culture shock, I will say. At the time I didn't understand it, but as I got older and I started to think back on these things that happened to us because we were Natives.

I had never seen such racism. We were put in schools. The first school we were put in was a Catholic [school] called St. Junipero Serra. We had to dress in little blue slacks, white shirt, sweater. It was all regimented. Everything was militarized. We could hardly talk English good. Chippewa and Cree I talked mostly. My grandfather [speaking Chippewa], his names mean Flat Man. My dad's father was a Chippewa from White Earth. My mother and my grandmother actually spoke pure Cree, but also spoke Michif, depending on who they were with. So, we spoke a lot of broken English—mudder, fadder, brudder—all that kind of stuff. We got to the school, and there was a young boy there, he was a Sioux boy, named Stanley Twigs. He said something to me in his language. I suppose he was in the same position, the same condition as me about all this relocation stuff. So, these nuns, they took us in and made us stick out our hands, and they give us five cracks with a little bamboo stick on each hand. They busted my blood vessels on my one hand, they went purple.

When I got home, and my father got home, I showed him what happened. My father was a guy that didn't take negative about his kid right away. "Where were you, you must have been doing something wrong." My father was not like that. He understood, he had been around the world, he understood this. On the third day he took us out of that school. They put us in a school called Marshall. There must have been about seven to eight hundred kids there. It was a melting pot of nationalities. A lot of immigrants, Russians, Germans, Japanese, Hawaiians, Polynesians, Mexicans. And there was only four Indians in that whole school. The textbook we had showed an Indian man in a drawing. He had ahold of a woman by the hair and was hitting her on the head with a hatchet. So, from that moment on we were the most hated people in that school.

For about a month straight after school, me and these two Indian boys had to fight, fight, split lips, black eyes. Just young kids, seven or eight years old. The racism and the hatred that textbook showed—[the students] just turned on us. Even the immigrants were kicking us until we met a guy named John, a Chicano guy. Morales was his last name. He was an older man, John Morales. He had a boy that went to school there; his name was Celestino Morales. He took us home. He protected us and he walked with us to get us out of that schoolyard. "You have to get some gang together to protect yourself, you guys," he said. So, I was introduced to street gangs at eight years old. I became a pachuco at eight years old. There was big gangs, black shoes and white shoes were black groups. There was the pachucos. Everybody had a gang. It was survival. That's where I learned about racism and prejudice and things like that. I learned how hard it was being an Indian in this country.

Finally, my father took us out of there and we ended up in Hunters Point, which was a housing project right down by the Naval shipyard. Once again it was a melting pot of diverse nationalities, but they were more sensible, they were more getting along together. They had more understanding, for some reason. This went on '54, '55, and '56. In 1956 we had that big earthquake. We were in school, and the building started rocking and plaster started falling. We got under our desks. It was about 11:00 in the morning, just before lunch. When the earthquake was over, the tremors and all that, they turned out all the students to go home. On our way home— [me and] my sister Phyllis, the oldest one—we had to walk way around different places because the earth was cracked and opened up. You could see down in these big crevices. We finally got home, and the back porch where my mother hung clothes was all gone. The clothesline, the concrete, the back porch, everything was gone. The earth had separated that close to my mother. My mom was mad and crying. Dishes smashed all over the floor. She called the Bureau of Indian Affairs and told them, "I want to go home with my children." They tried to discourage her from it. She said, "I'll take my children and walk down the interstate and call the newspapers and tell what you done to me and my kids."

They finally arranged to bring us home. She left my father over there. Then we became a broken home. This was in early '57. When we got home of course, well, before she could get a job, she had to apply for assistance and help. My grandma and them were trying to get her work at the San [San Haven], find her work, and here come the Bureau of Indian Affairs again. Although we were living in Dunseith most of the time, half, part-time, they exerted their jurisdiction over us and said that we had to go to boarding school.

The superintendent got ahold of my mother and said, "We're going to take Tom to boarding school right after Christmas." Most of the time I spent with my grandfather, Colin Davis. He couldn't understand that. [Speaking Cree], he used to tell her. "Why are they doing this? He belongs here. He should live here with us, my grandson," he told her. She said, "What can we do? They're the Boss Farmers, what can we do?"

Well, they came and got me. There was a guy from the Pierre boarding school come got me in a station wagon.[45] I was ten going on eleven years old. We went to Fort Totten and picked up another student. His name was Joseph. Same thing there; his grandmother was an old traditional grandma, crying for her son. Joseph had braids down to his waist. You could tell he was being brought up in a very traditional way. When we got to Pierre boarding school that night, they gave us both bald heads. Why, I don't know. Right straight to the barber shop. Joseph, they just cut his braids off bald-headed and threw them in the garbage. And you know, he never recovered from that . . . he became a drunk. Even at the school he sniffed glue, gas. It destroyed him. They pretty much tried to do that with me. I don't know what the Creator did for me, but I mean, he wouldn't let them break my spirit, no matter what. It was the most horrible experience. And I've been in prison in my older days from that boarding school experience. It was worse than the prison that I was in. I hated. It was hatred in my heart for almost all mankind and all of what it stood for.

---

[45] The interviewee is referring to Pierre Indian School, now known as Pierre Indian Learning Center.

When we got there it was one of the most drab places I've ever seen. It reminded me of a warehouse. A warehouse of human beings. There it was so quiet and noise free. Everybody was scared to make a little noise. Kids, they all stared at you, wanted to fight you within half a minute after you got there. Different ones wanted to try you out. Then of course after you got your bald head, they ridiculed you, made fun of you. Where I come from, the bush Indian, we didn't take that; we fought. We were good fighters, tough. We had to do that there.

Oh, a human being can never express that hurt and loneliness you felt. There is no way you can relay that to another person. To get out of you what was in you, how you felt. How you missed your home, your mother, your father, your grandparents, your sister. Just being home. I wanted to commit suicide. I wanted to kill myself. I was so dispirited. I felt worthless, useless, nobody loved you. Nobody cared. You just have this emptiness. You don't care if you can get by the day or whatever. You get up about six o'clock in the morning. You have to go wash. On Monday, Wednesday, and Friday you had to go take a shower before going to breakfast. You had a woman matron sitting there when you come out of the shower, and you had to go in front of her and go like this [demonstrates lifting a towel above his head] and twirl around. I don't care if you were fifteen, sixteen years old, or ten years old. Make sure you were clean. They gave you a toothbrush and some powder in a can to brush your teeth. After you did that, [you] went to a clothing room [where they] gave you clean clothes on Monday; on Friday got [another set of] clean clothes, because [you] had to wear clean clothes Friday, Saturday, Sunday, until Monday [laughter]. So, they gave you jeans, long johns, socks, shirt, t-shirt, and that is what you wear. Had to get dressed, be done by 6:30. No time to goof around. Then you went downstairs [and you] had to do calisthenics. Do about fifteen minutes of stationary run, side-straddle hop, then you had to duck walk, get in a line walk like a duck all the way around. Come back, stand in line. Get counted. Then they take you to breakfast. Had to make your bed. Had to flip a quarter. If you didn't, they grab the mattress and pull it all over. If you persisted in not fixing your bed right, you had to put what was called square corners, spread same way, folded back on your pillow. If quarter didn't bounce on bed, [you] didn't get to go to the movies or go to town. Had to be on the pick-up gang—first thing in morning go outside and pick up all the garbage—called that the pick-up gang [laughter], you had to do it.

Everything you did was in military form; you had to march. You had to take everything they gave you on the tray even though you couldn't eat it. It wasn't good food. Homemade bread for a long time until started making deals, I guess, with a bakery truck. When I got there, they were still going out to the barn, Moses and them, at 4:00 in the morning; go out there and milk cows, because they had a farm going. Take milk downtown, pasteurize, homogenize it, and that's what we drank at the school. So, it was kind of self-sufficient in that way. Well, that was nuts. Could have left these guys home to help their dad, family farm at home. We ate cornmeal mush, Farina. That kind of stuff. Raisin rice, lot of that, and figs, ugh! Round figs like that. I remember I couldn't eat them. And that Chasing Crow came down, he took them and he forced them right down my throat. Puked right there. He slapped me around and made me go get things and clean that mess up. Course that spoiled other people's meal too. But this guy was mentally deranged, something wrong with him. He was shell shock; he was WWII veteran. He had a Jeep. In the morning when it was nice, even when there was snow, he made us run a figure eight. The building was like this [gestures], and we had to run all the way around in this figure eight and come back. He had a Jeep and he had a dog named Rocky, a boxer that followed him like this with that Jeep. He'd buy us some time. I remember that dog. He bit a guy named Wilson Guardipee, Blackfeet guy from Browning, Montana. He bit Wilson really bad, and Wilson kicked him, and Chasing Crow got there and he knocked that kid out cold. Right there in the snow and just drove off with his dog and left that kid there like that. [The kid] got up later, but [Chasing Crow] knocked him out, knocked him cold, *boof*. That's the kind of experience I had in boarding school.

There was very little time for happiness. Moses and Robert's little brother, Larry, was in the little boys' building right across the basketball court; they had a cyclone fence. That little boy used to cry to see his brother, and they wouldn't let him go see that little boy. So that little boy started peeing in bed. I suppose it was all the stress. While we were all lined up, they made that little boy carry his sheets to the laundry to embarrass him, pissy sheets, you know. I mean it was Nazism. I would say that. I think I could imagine what they did to the Jews.

So many died there when I was there, young boys. Sniffing gas. They'd just do anything to escape. They'd hold themselves like this [demonstrates with hand around his neck] and choke themselves and blackout, hyperventilate; they choked themselves until they blacked out. Anything to escape where they were. If there was a vehicle or any kind of machinery, they would sneak and take the gas cover off and sniff that gas. We lost a lot of them. Ronald Quilt was one of them kids. Their brains blew from that lead. Ronnie died in the hallway. Started hemorrhaging. He died, bled to death. We all saw it; we were in the day room, had a TV in there. We get to watch Boo Boo and Yogi Bear. I remember someone said, "Look, Ronnie fell down." We all ran out there. He was—blood was coming out of—he was hemorrhaging. From that lead they said, from that gas.

There was a few that died in their room after, too. One of the Kidders. One of the Grass Rope kids. I think they had one of those paupers' burials. A lot of them. A lot of them kids didn't get to go home for the summer, too; they didn't have no place to go. They had to stay there year-round for that torture. I suppose that really got to them.

They were trying to keep me there the first year. My grandfather raised so much hell with the superintendent here; he was ready to drag him out of the BIA office and give him a lickin'. They wouldn't let me [leave] until the last day. The last morning Turtle Mountain was loading up and going to Fort Totten. We had Wahpeton, Fort Totten, and us going on one bus. Quite a few from Fort Totten and Sisseton and Belcourt. I was so dejected, sitting at the bench in front of Dakota Hall. All of a sudden that guy came out and said, "Tommy, grab your stuff. They said you can go." Oh my God, I just got in and didn't even take my suitcase or box of stuff, the hell with it. But they made me go back again [in the fall] right here.

They had a racket of what they did with our kids. It was an economic thing for the schools, employees, workers. Rarely did you see white people inside of the dorm where we were housed as kids. It was always Indians in the dorms. I never did see a white man in there in any of the schools that worked in the dorm. There were teachers when you went to school in the day. Never did see an *Indian* teacher. All white teachers. All this time I went to school there never did see an Indian teacher, never. I saw a guy that was a child molester. He kept a little boy in his room with him right there. They never did a damn thing about it. He turned that little boy, his name was Blinky, he was from Fort Peck, his last name was Larocque, Robert, Bobby, and this guy from Fort Totten, his name was Peltier, he did that to that little boy. They knew it. But how could you say? Those are the horrors that people don't ever know about those places.

They started trying to make, I imagine, some reparations, some re-forming. As tribal leaders I would say, especially from South Dakota, from

Cheyenne River. Really vocal people, Peter Condon. It really hit when Frances Red Bear got killed running away. It brought a lot of attention to that school. He's the one that rolled the milk truck. They had some of those people started getting really vocal. There was a Chippewa guy there—his name was Richard Heisler. He was humane to us. Very protective of us kids, especially us Chippewa guys. He told Chasing Crow one time, "I'm going to knock you the fuck out, just like that, if you don't leave these little Belcourt kids alone." But after Heisler left, they double-downed on us then. This guy was sick. He needed medical attention. Mental attention. He was always after these young girls, too. All of a sudden, you'd start seeing him giving special attention to certain girls there. Giving them rides to town. He [got] a nice car, a '53 or '54 Ford, nice gray one, two-door, two-door hard top, kind of a classy one. Dual pipes on these cars trying to attract attention, that's the way he was. I remember him doing that.

Our days were work. My last year there, most of us worked the pick-up gang, picking up garbage, having to clean all the vehicles that belonged to the staff. Take a pile of wood over here and move it over here, and then days later move it back to where we took it from in the first place. Things like that. There was just no rhyme or reason for why they did that. A guy from Belcourt, Elmer Landry, he became the head boss in the kitchen my eighth-grade year. He took Clifford Chase, Roberta, and I and made us steady helpers in his kitchen, us Belcourt people, to kind of protect us. A little short guy; we called him Elmer Fudd. So, we go in there early in the morning, help him with big vats, whatever we're going to cook. We got a potato peeler, but before that we got to peel by hand. Finally, they got hooked up with a baker downtown. Then he'd give us two packs of rolls every time the bakery shop came, so we always had something to make a couple of dollars with. We'd sell a roll and little bit of instant coffee for a quarter. So, we became entrepreneurs. We had money to go to town. You had to have two dollars and fifty cents in your account or in your pocket to go to town. I also earned from Mrs. Eckleburger. She'd take me down-town and we'd rake her yard, me and Robert. Clean her garage, wash her car, windows. In snow time, she brings us down there and we'd shovel her walkways. She had one of these little lawn mowers that you push [laughter]. She'd pay us three, four dollars.

We get to go to downtown on Saturday and get little things we needed. We'd always buy one of those things of Folger coffee to keep our little business going over there. Go to a movie. Only twenty-five cents to go to a movie. Line up after the movie's over and get back on the bus. Things like that.

Oh yes, we were hungry, especially on the weekends. The cooks didn't come do a lot stuff on the weekends or long holidays, like here at the retirement home, same thing [laughter]. Déjà vu there! I remember some of these kids were so hungry, and some of these kids were big and needed food. I remember these kids from Winnebago and kids from Holy Rosary, Rosebud; [if] we didn't eat our fat, they wanted it. They'd roll it in their bread and eat it because they were so hungry. Some of them would break into the kitchen. I never did, but they did. They'd steal whatever they could get their hands on. Mostly bread and if they had lunch meat. If they had cakes that would just about all be gone by the time got through serving line. Leftovers, rather than give to kids, [the staff] threw in a big barrel, wait for the big dump truck to come around. It was tough.

A lady named Ms. McGee, she was one of the women that would make us put our towels over our heads and make us spin around in front of her. I think she was kind of weird. What she used to do—way south of us about half a mile was the Missouri River—she makes people run down there and go break a willow, had to be certain length, and bring it back and turn around and give a whipping with it. Make us run after our own whip. She made me run one time. When I went down there . . . I was lucky I didn't get bit by snakes, rattlesnakes. I was running down there, and got close like that, and I looked like this and there was a bunch of them. They must have been breeding, and I jumped like this. I think I walked in the air, honest. I went right above them. And here I was on the other side and I was thinking how the hell am I going to get back over there. So, I start throwing stuff at them. Pretty soon they started going away. I made sure that there were none there, and then boy I took off. But I brought her back my switch. She waited until we put our pajamas on to give us our lickin'. That was cruel.

They did things like that to us. Make us kneel on brooms. I kneeled on a broom one time from about one o'clock on Saturday until 4:30 going to dinner. And every time I tried to bend back, he'd kick me in the ass, make me kneel on it. That Chasing Crow and the other guy Eugene Fritz. When I stood up, I could hardly stand up, my tendons were just, oh God. It seemed to me they enjoyed that, because they're always disciplining children that way. There is no hope of getting anything good out of them. There is no way you are going to make them a better student or a better child to go home to your mom and dad. They sent a bunch of broken people back to our homes is what they did.

Then you try to figure out those people that I met there. I'll say 94 percent of them even to this day are nothing but druggies and drunks. I understand that. Try to bring it to the attention of people who could do something about it. They have no hearing, like what they did to Custer, them Cheyenne women. I saw that stick they stuck right through his ears. And they said in that museum the reason they did it was he wouldn't listen while he was on earth here, so they didn't want him to hear when he met the Creator either, they wanted him to be deaf. That's kind of like what it was down there. The BIA office was right there on campus, right down at the end . . . next to Lakota Hall. Call down there and you get a lickin'. Guys used to sneak out of the fire escape and go across into the girls' building. Nobody give a damn, just the way it was. You had people that were seventeen, eighteen years old in the eighth grade. Grown men and women. So, it was not a good place.

There were, I would say, my first years there . . . my teacher was a guy named Mr. Burke . . . He was a pervert. All he tried to do was play around with these little girls. That was constantly what he would do all through class. He was just a real gross guy. Of course, in those days you were taught writing and all the subjects from one teacher. No doubt he was doing that because sometimes when the girls would ask to go to the bathroom, he'd leave with them. And he'd be gone all the time, and of course the kids would start acting up and throwing stuff and goofing around. They'd come back, and everything would be the same. That was on my seventh-grade year. Mr. Burke used to hit people, too; he'd slap you around. I saw him slap people sitting by the wall. He'd slap them, blood be on the wall, then he'd make them go get brown paper towels to wipe it off. It's just, ah, you got used to it, you didn't think about it anymore, it was just something that they did. The damn people. I was lucky in my eighth-grade year I got Mrs. Eckleburger. She was such a nice lady. She took a liking to me and Robert. We were both smart.

There was the Birds, Gordon Bird was there, Doreen. They were there in school with us there, too. They all went to school in Pierre. Grey Owl girls were there. High Elks, Eagle Speakers. Some from New Town. There were cowboys. They were allowed to build a bucking horse. Had their bucking rigging. Had two guys pulling on the springs this way and this way. Then they had to stop . . . one guy busted his nose, had to take it down.

We had to go to church, be punished if you didn't go to church, didn't get no recreation, no privileges. If you were a Catholic you met with the priest, gave you nine Hail Mary's. You'd be praying all day. They were mean to us, too, the priests and nuns, they were not just all angels themselves. I'm sure that one priest that was there, I'm sure he molested some of those kids. I don't know. I told them I was an Episcopalian to get out of that church. They had a little church on the other side, Episcopalian. They gave you candy to go there. It was kind of a nice little church. They say nice things. But that Catholic thing was, the nuns were mean. They resented us for being there. That they had to come there and do whatever they do. It was like pulling on one of them guys' ears so hard they tore it right there, it was bleeding. Tear your ear, can you imagine that? What a pain like that for a seven, eight-year-old kid? Would have to have his ear tore because of that, kicked around like a God-darn dog. There should have been a child welfare program way back there, I would say. There should have been something like that to make sure these little Indian kids were protected

When I was locked up in prison, there was a priest there. His name was Father John I. Murray. He tried to get funny with me. I reported him. Then he tried to be nice to me, tried to get me into Boys Town. He wanted me to go to Father Flanagan's Boys Town. I could see what he was trying to do. Get private interviews with him. He was trying to get funny with me. I told him, "I'll knock you out." Tried to feel me up. I told him "I'll hit you! I'll knock you fuckin' out." I was a pretty tough kid. I'd fight before grown men in that place. I reported him. I reported to a guy named Mustache. I said what he tried to do. But he could never interview me again. Never come around me. Even the guards took an interest in me since I was such a young kid. But they were proud of me because I was a good athlete. Yah, he tried that one time.

One of the nuns around here tried that when I was in high school, here in the high school. She would come there after school, and after practice we were all sweaty; she was trying to rub me up and feel me. Trying to take me to have milk and cookies. I was sixteen or seventeen. That's when I got all that trouble and went to school here. I never did say who she was. I'll take it to my grave cause she's a good friend of mine now. I know what she was trying to do then. But nothing happened.

Some of the things when we were down there, too, is how they treated the small kids. And how I could look at these little kids when they come into the chow hall. You could see the hurt in their eyes, the little kids. It made you mad, you wanted to do something, you just wanted to get violent like, and I'd see these little boys and girls, five, six years old. Big blue marks on their face, slapped. You know nobody's going to do that . . . it's got to be them sons-a-bitches that were doing it. I saw that. All of a sudden, we were a little bit angry. We reported it to Eckleburger, people that would listen, we'd tell them. I don't know if she ever did report any of that. We tried to find somebody—maybe Elmer did, I don't know, Elmer Landry.

I learned how to be a good yoyo guy, I could make a yoyo walk, do little tricks with it. Make spaghetti with it, they call them sleepers, throw 'em out, bring back, around the world. I learned how to do all that. We'd all sit outside and listen to music on the radio and there was one lonely song, "Are You Lonesome Tonight?" All these kids would write those songs on the back of their jackets and get slapped around because they did that. One guy put on there that song "Lonely Blue Boy," by Elvis, and he put that on his back there; boy he got a beating. The matron beat the hell out of him. Washed his jacket, couldn't get it out because it was that clothing marker. But that's about all we had to do.

We never got to use the basketball courts because the good players hogged it. They didn't have baseball, or softball. They had track. They'd take the older kids, fifteen-, sixteen-, seventeen-year-olds, like high school kids. They couldn't compete in high school, but they could go run. I mean, we had some fast runners. That Kenny Fly, the one guy from Standing Rock, that sucker, hey, he could've been another Billy Mills. Eltwin Grass Rope was another one. Them guys, Herbie White Bear, them guys were speedsters.

For fun, there was not too much. In our class day, we had one hour of shop, and I got to be really good in shop. I made some pieces that went to the state fair in Sioux Falls, some coffee tables and stuff like that. I did my own lathing on the lathe, my table legs and all of that. A guy named Mr. Matteson, he took a special interest in me. He taught me how to do wrought iron and I made a coffee table with glass on it. Wood trimming to hold it. They sent it to state fair and I wanted to give it to my grandma and I never did see it again. He was careless with glue, as if he wanted kids to steal it.

There was nothing cultural; they wouldn't allow it. Me and Robert, we were talking over there one time [speaking Cree], they heard us. They had big brown soap, a big bar, they called them GI soap. They made us wash our mouths with that. Stick [it in] our mouths, had to put water in there. Rubbed it on our tongue. Took that soap and wet it down. To do a good job, you had to make bubbles. Had to make lather, work it until it lathered up. Had to hold it in there for a little bit, then you could wash it out. Just once they did that to me. We were careful about it. Moses and Robert, they spoke pure Chippewa, those ones. Their ma came [and] visited them one time. She tried to take Larry home, but they wouldn't let her. Kweken, they called her, Flora Dionne. That was her kids, Robert, Larry, and Moses. I think Moses passed on in Wolf Point. That Moses was a nice guy, full of hell. Joked a lot. Larry was kind of serious. They all died though. Larry died of alcohol; Robert died of alcohol. Their Indianism was beaten out of them, destroyed on them. I was just lucky they couldn't do that to me.

They didn't like us, the matrons, because we were Chippewa boys. There was only [a few] of us there from Belcourt: Moses Dionne, Robert Dionne, Larry Dionne, Clifford Chase, myself, and a young small girl who became a psychologist, Markel Vivier. They hated us Chippewa people. I think the war that went on for centuries between the Lakota [and] Dakota people and the Ojibwe [and] Anishinaabe people carried, and to this day, 2018, it's still there. I know that for a fact. But in them days it was the matrons that did this. They didn't like us because we were good-looking kids. We had nice wavy hair when it was long enough. We were popular with the girls. The girls liked us because we were good looking, I guess, I s'pose, I don't know, we never really gave a darn about it, it's just the way it was.

They did a lot of things. They kicked me. Crushed discs in my lumbar in my back. A guy named Melvin Chasing Crow . . . he was one of the boys' head advisors there. We were lined up in the basement with our pajamas on for a night count. And I don't know, I don't really remember if I did anything wrong, I don't think I did. There was "gunzling," you know, goofing around, you know, gunzling. They walked behind you and counted you. And when he got behind me he just kicked me. He called it "splittin' your cheeks." He hurt me so bad I had to crawl into a locker room and lay there. I was hurt so bad, and he got scared that he did something bad. They had to carry me off to my bed. Couldn't go to school the next day. That was like on a Friday. On Saturday I couldn't go to town. We had a town day. Couldn't go to the movie on Sunday. But, Robert Davis and his wife . . . they came to visit their daughter Doreen. She was working at the BIA office there on the boarding school campus. And that was my grandfather's brother, Robert. My grandpa has asked him, "[Speaking Cree] Check on Tommy," to see how I was doing. So, they made them take me to go have dinner at Doreen's. She had a BIA house on campus. And I could hardly walk. I was all humped over and I went there. My uncle Robert, he seen that [and asked], "[Speaking Cree] What's the matter with this guy, Do-

reen?" . . . I told them what happened. "[Speaking Cree] Tomorrow, I want
to report what they did to this little boy. Want to report it. You hear me?"
he told her. "[Speaking Cree] We always go toward our blood," he said. He
told her he was giving her hell. So, she did. She reported it.

About three o'clock that afternoon I was in my bed yet, I couldn't really walk. They come and got me. The same guy that came and got me two
years before, he took me to the Indian hospital in Wagner, South Dakota.
They were going to fix me, my back. What they did instead, they put me
under ether. When I woke up, I had a little pan that looked like a kidney
underneath my mouth. They took my tonsils and my adenoids out to hide
and cover up what they did at that school to me. When I woke up there was
a nun standing at my bed. I could hardly talk, my throat was so sore, all full
of blood and smell, stink, and ohhh, half-crazy from ether yet.

"Where you from?" she said. "I see your name here, Davis."

I told her I was from Belcourt.

"What's your dad's name?" she said.

"Daniel Davis," I said.

"That's my cousin," she said. Sister Anthony Marie, from the Tekakwitha Convent. That's how they covered that up.

I ran away from school in my seventh-grade year and part of my eighth-
grade year at least eleven times. Trying to get away from there. Angry at
them. The last time I ran away there was a guy named Robert LaRocque
from Wolf Point, Robert Dionne from Belcourt, and myself. Kenny Cain,
James Kidder, and Francis Red Bear from Bullhead, South Dakota. They
went across the river into Ft. Pierre. We stayed on the north side of the
river, going north. They stole a milk truck, rolled over and killed Francis.
When we got caught, we went back, and they were getting ready to have
a viewing of the body in Pierre at a church. We went, and his face was
crushed, a net over him. I never did run away again from that school. I became a straight-A student. I was taken under the wing of Mrs. Eckleburger,
the eighth-grade teacher. She was wonderful; she loved us. I won every
scholarship there was. I even took Home Economics. I was really popular
my last part of the year, from January on to graduation.

To haunt me, this man, Chasing Crow, he saw us sitting outside, sitting
on the swings just talking. It was still cold out, could see your breath frost.
All of a sudden, a student came. "Chasing Crow wants to see you." We
went inside. It was only three, four days before graduation and pictures.
My hair was nice wavy hair. He gave me a bald head. My mom had sent

me a nice little suit, shoes, necktie, suit jacket. I had to sit at the end of the bench of my class with a bald head. Just had to get the last kick into me again.

What's ironic about it, you know, I hated this man, anger with this man. I thought if I ever met him in my younger days, I might have killed him. About five, six years ago, I was still working for the tribe and I had to go to Pierre for a huge Water Coalition meeting for the tribe. I took Billy Morin with me; he was my best man at my wedding. Always been a close friend with him. So he wasn't doing nothing so I took him with me to keep me company. We drove down there. When we were registering, I showed them my ID, where I was from and all of that, who I represented. This guy that was taking registration was a Godfrey, I think Calvin Godfrey was his name. He said, "Are you Tommy Davis?"

"Ya," I said, "that's me."

"You remember me," he said. Then he said his name Godfrey, and I said, "Ya, I remember you." He said, "I always used to say if I ever saw Chasing Crow, I was going to beat the shit out of him," he told me.

"Ya," I said, "I felt the same way."

"Well," he said, "I saw him the other day. He's a wino, he's laying around there behind these bars out here. Skid Row, he's a skid row bum. I didn't have the heart. If you want to see him, just go there in the afternoon, you'll see him out in the back drinking, all these old winos."

So, I told Billy when the meeting was just about done, I said, "Let's go, I want to take you out to the Pierre boarding school, I want to go look at it." At the same time, we went by that bar. Sure enough, there he was. I prayed for him. I didn't have it in my heart. The Creator was [giving Chasing Crow] what he deserved. It came back to him like that.

I went to that school. It's all different. Nothing even similar to when I went to school there. Lakota Hall, Dakota Hall, all gone. And they got separate satellite cottages where the students are. Really different. I asked a lady there to get my graduation picture from 1960, and I don't know I never did hear back from her. I don't know if she even still works there. That lady said we never throw . . . we have pictures that go way back into the early '50s late '40s, she said.

[I remember] they had us [sitting] in a horseshoe [shape]. I was sitting at the end in a suit, necktie, looking good. But this is what [Chasing Crow] he did to us. He used to write—like a cue ball—he put an eight on my head. He was a great artist. He just loved doing those things to us Chippewa guys. Finally, Moses talked to him one time. [Chasing Crow had] hit Robert, nose bleeding and everything like that. So, Moses talked with him. Then [Chasing Crow] beat up Moses, but, you know, what could you say. He was . . . one of the boys' [attendants]. Moses tried to protect his little brother.

I never took my anger out on that; I just tried to get out of there. I tried to run away so many times. If caught we had to wear big tennis shoes about size twelve, bib overalls, skin heads, bald heads to the skin. They tried to ridicule you any way they can. I think the more they tried to ridicule me the more they liked me, the students. They liked me. I was a good athlete, even as a young boy. I was taught the basics of stuff in California at these athletic camps for children. We learned basketball, baseball, football, all the basics, all these things, and I was good at it. But he would never let me play basketball although I was one of the better athletes there. One of the Chippewa advisors there, named Richard, he got there and took over most of the coaching stuff. The last half of my eighth-grade year I made the first five on the basketball team, and I got to play with Herbie White Bear, Shelby White Bear, Benny Many Ribs, or, Four Dance now. We had one hell of a basketball team. We were beating ninth-grade teams. That was only after that Chippewa guy got there, Richard, but it was quite the deal.

I went to Flandreau the next year angry. Still angry about what all had happened to me all these years at that boarding school. The first thing happened when I got to that school was one of the advisors, named Andrew Zephier, hit me and made my nose bleed in front of everybody. Why, I don't know. So, I ran away. Me and Clifford Chase, another guy from Dunseith. We ran away. Here we got downtown, and it started to snow bad. It was the last part of October. [We found] an old shed; we kicked the door and went in there to get out of the cold. There were some other boys that ran away; they came in there. There was some Crows, and they were in there.

I told Clifford we better go back. So, we got back to the school. They knew we were gone, and they were waiting for us. We had to report in. Here the next day the sheriff come up to the school and got us. Moody County. They took us to juvenile court downtown. No lawyer, nothing! Went before a guy named Judge McCracken. He sent us to the reform school in Plankinton, South Dakota, for kicking that door in [laughter]. We had to go to a reformatory in Plankinton. We were there, and when you get there you are what you call a Seven Day Grub. Then you become a Rookie. Then you become an Explorer, then you become a Pilot. When you become a Pilot you're eligible to go home. So, we worked our way up to that, and Clifford went home before me. I worked in the kitchen, because I was a good cook. Worked under a guy, Mr. Johnson. I worked my way up. My mom already has sent me clothes to come home with. She had already got notice that I was coming home. I got letters that verify that I'm on my way home. Here, that Sunday morning, a lady named Mrs. Shultz, that runs the dining hall, it was her job to have her girls take the skin off boiled potatoes for potato salad. She tried to make me do that. I took the little paring knife and threw it in there to stab a potato and instead it hit on the floor. She took off running and got the assistant, I would say the warden, came back, slapped the hell out of me. I told him Mr. Johnson told me to go back to my cottage. "You're not going back," he said, "You're going to start from a Seven Day Grub." And I was on my way to go home! So, they brought me back in the main building. That same night me and a guy named Warren Filbert from Lower Brule, we kicked out the window, and we ran away. We got a ride all the way to Chamberlain by a trucker at a truck stop.

The next morning—he had twin brothers that went to school at Chamberlain High in town—so we went [and] found them. They gave him the keys to the pickup. We took the pickup and were on our way to Sioux City to find his mother. [The law] start chasing us and they flipped us over, rolled over, the sheriff of Trip County, South Dakota, and some other law enforcement. We rolled that pickup. We're lucky we didn't get hurt. Warren got sent to the military. A judge named Walter gave me five years in the state penitentiary in Sioux Falls, South Dakota. I was fifteen years old. I was five foot seven or eight inches tall, about one hundred fifty pounds. He gave me five years in the prison.

They took me down to a prison in Sioux Falls. I got there at suppertime, and they made me go to the supper. All these Indians, they were so mad at that judge for what he did. They were hollering at me, "Hey! Does your momma know you're here? Does your momma know you smoke?" and all kinds of things like that. That's where I met my Indian culture. I met a guy named Eugene Spotted Wolf, spiritual leader, and Walter Cree from Dunseith. Both of them were very spiritual [in] Indian ways. And I had these athletic abilities. I was taken under the wing of a guy named Ken Taylor, Richard "Dicky" Byington, Wally Thornton, Jessie Zimmerman. They made a man out of me. They made me fight. Don't anybody try to mess with me. By the time I was sixteen, I was the starting shortstop for the prison. That's how good of a baseball player I was. I even had the Minnesota Twins come look at me and try to get me parole to South Carolina to the Rookie League. They refused to parole me.

Of course, when I got out of there I went on a rampage. I was almost eighteen. I did two and a half years and they paroled me. I came home up here. I ended up running into Norman Swain and all these outlaws up here. I think I was only out about three months and I end up in trouble with these guys. I got seven years in Bismarck. The youngest one! All these guys got three years. They put all the blame on me. They gave me four to seven. I had to do my four years before eligible for parole. So, I did six years. By the time I was nineteen years, I came home. I got paroled to my uncle Fritz Monnette, who was the housing director. I started school here. I was a good athlete. The coach was already grooming me to be able to play basketball. That was January. I was the student manager. Here, Willard Champagne, Ronnie's dad and one of the Marions, Clark's family, wrote a letter to the chairman of the high school athletic association, who was my catcher in the prison. But anyway, he wrote back to them. He didn't think it would be fair to other high school kids for me to play high school basketball, because I had played college level basketball with these prisoners and stuff like that. But they refused to let me play.

Ya, they did that, and one day they called me in and Coach Thorfinnson said, "Tom, Mr. Malaterre is going to ask you to leave school."

"Why," I said, "I'm a good student."

So, I went in there and met with Mr. Malaterre.

"Tom," he said, "This is not a situation for you here."

I'd been working with Mr. Roy Lafontaine over at the Bureau of Indian Affairs. He was head of employment for the BIA. They put me in a school in Denver. I went down there for surveying. Although when I got there, they didn't have any surveying availability. So, they tried to put me in welding. Ruin my eyes. So, I went to work in a luggage company. I was good at sewing and running stuff like that. I made good money repairing Samsonite luggage. It was almost a year before I came home.

You were asking me about these fellows in prison about the cultural part of it. Prior to that I had learned a lot about culture already from my father. In 1951 he took me to the old Round Hall. He was one of the veterans that was going to be in the Grand Entry. At that time that Round Hall was sacred. The pipe bundles were brought there. They didn't have the big traditional dancer bustles and all of that in those days. The Fancy Shawl dancers. They had one man that brought the Grand Entry in. He was called the Eagle Belt dancer. Louis Cree was the Eagle Belt dancer. It's a big leather belt that goes around your waist with one tail that goes down past your ankles. A wide piece of leather goes in the back, like a loin cloth, and on that breech clout was these eagle feathers. He was the only one that would lead the Grand Entry, and behind him came the Grass dancers like Joe Great Walker and those guys, John Henry, Lawrence Henry, all these guys that dance, Joe Fayant. I was just about going on six years old. The drum I saw there, and I remember them all. I was just fascinated by these singers. My dad knew them, too. I remember we would go hunt rabbits with those people. He'd bring me to drop them off. My father was good for them like that. And then that drum group, Sam Standing Chief Sr. was their lead singer. Their second was a guy named Pat "Blind Man" Deschamp. He's the composer of songs. He made all their songs. Their . . . second singers were William John Henry, Tom Kakenawash, Howard Kanewah, who danced hoops and sang at the same time. There was Thomas Cree, Norman Johnson, Joe Fayant, Alic Machipeness. They had a big drum group. I remember before they started everybody had to be quiet. They brought these bundles out unrolled them, Charlie Cree and them. They prayed with a pipe for them. [Speaking Cree] they talked, they would pray. I learned that. There was a Sun Dance that same year. My father was to go to the Sun Dance behind St. Mary's church. The Sun Dance was put on by a woman named Agnes St. Claire. There was Carl's mother, and she wanted to thank the Creator for bringing her son home from the war. I got to go to that.

I got to see people pierce. Quality things at a young age. So, when that came to me when I was prison, it became familiar to me. I knew all these things even when I went on relocation. I knew these things when I went to that boarding school in Pierre, South Dakota, that is why they could not break me. I already had that knowledge. Then when I met these guys in prison that were really into that kind of thing, our culture, the understanding of the way of Manitou. That straightened me up, made a man out of me. That's why I'm so fierce for my children. That's why I would never live with a woman that abused my kids. Or that would drink. I raised my own kids most of them by myself, because of that. I didn't want them to go through life watching me combat with alcohol, drugs. I want my kids to be clean.

The only time I ever drank I got in trouble, so I never drank. Of course, during the '60s I was a flower child, I tried a little bit of marijuana, tried a little bit of this and that, but I never did like it. I never was somebody that would even think of enjoying using it daily, daily, daily, every day. I had my things I did. I tried acid one time and I hated it. I laid below a tree and that thing was talking to me. The veins were pumping like this [demonstrates] and I was thinking, gee this is the way this thing works, too. I never did want to do that again. I smoked a little bit. You get older and you grow up you don't need stuff like that. You have a lot of good things that you take care of with your life, your kids, grandkids. Things like this, research, I had a good job. I was a tribal planner for a lot of years. I have a high regard, I pray every morning here.

I want to write a book called *When the Fiddle Met the Round Hall*, because from there, I saw this collision of cultures. I saw this thing with my own eyes as a young boy when they opened them bundles with their pipes. Beautiful pipes. I pray. And here then, you know, I seen women cry when we pull rope, when we pull skulls. I saw all of these things. I remember before we went on relocation in '54, my father was so mad. He came, and he was arguing with these Peltiers, Edward Peltier, Joseph, and those guys, Ben Decoteau.

"You guys," he said, "you desecrated that place," he said. "Those guys won't even go back there," he said.

They started having fiddle dances and they started bootlegging. They just would never bring their bundles there, they just let that thing . . . I've always said that what they did, and they were having a tough time as it was to have these things, Indian way, because they were already being harassed by these guys in Belcourt, the church and everybody was after them about . . . you're going to have to go underground to do these things. These guys here, what they did, no respect for the bundles and the pipes, the ceremonial things. The great things that happened in the Round Hall there. The important meetings about our land and the things that went on in there.

Me, I been adopted into the Great Walker family from the time their boy Butch got killed. Joseph and them adopted me when [he] got killed. They come found me one day and said they were lonesome for a son. I've been with them ever since. Even when he was dying, he called for me. I was in Fort Totten when he died. But before that he had called me and had me pray for him in our language. He wanted me to read this book, Anishinaabe Bible. It's about a way of living with the Creator; it's like a Bible. *[365 Days of Walking] the Red Road.* It all came back to this. He said, "Your heart has an eye. More important than these [our two eyes], trust this eye, when you can see through the eye of your heart [speaking Chippewa], you'll know it's honest, it's true."

This old man, Joe, is like my father. I was close to him. We hunt together, showed me how to trap. He taught me about my culture, how to sing songs. I have a lot of songs I made that these guys don't sing. Word songs [speaking Chippewa]. The Creator wants us to do these things. I make songs like that. I even make woman songs like [speaking Chippewa]. I make songs because I have the language [speaking Chippewa] the Creator gave us to use. Them words, I tell Timmy and them, use these words. They don't know how to compose. Dave Ripley knows, he always wants me to sing songs. I made Victory songs. "[Speaking Chippewa] Chippewa people you are victorious. You dance, this is your dance." They taught me those things. I made all the drums for the Great Walker family, five of them.

I made a big drum, an octagon. Like the Round Hall. It's a thirty-inch drum. A guy offered me five thousand dollars for it. I told him it's not for sale, belongs for this little boy, Justin. The old lady always wanted me to name a drum after the Butte St. Paul. It says on there long before Father Belcourt named this the Butte St. Paul, it was always known as Otahkaha-wakowin. Otah means here. Katahwahkowin means See Far. From Here I See Far. She always wanted me to shorten it. Sees Far. She wanted a name for that drum. She said there is four hills here like this. One on that side going north of Bottineau, toward that little town, Maleta; there's one back here over on the other side, St. John. And there's this one here by Azure's hill and the butte. She said they had men up there almost all the time, watching so nobody would come on up. Then they had one on the other side of Pembina going toward Winnipeg. They watched for the Sioux, could see the dust. It was a spiritual place, fires and prayers. They go seek vision up there. There was over thirty people that froze to death at the butte.

She was so mad because that guy started farming. They must have dug up all the bones. I went there with my father when old John Lilly lived there. The St. Pierre's. They had houses there, when you went in there before you get to the second road, there was houses there. All around this way on the outside. They drank out of cans, their tea was in tomato cans, washed out [laughter]. I saw all of that.

I lived in three log houses in my life when I was young. Dirt floor. The first one was behind the San [San Haven] when my mother and father lived there, called Chaseville. Then we move up Poker Hill. There's Christmas trees there now 'cause my dad and them planted trees all over there now. Then we lived where St. Anthony Church is here. Right around the bend . . . there's a place they call—in Michif—they call it a flowing well, and we lived alongside it there. We used to haul our water, put on a sleigh in cream cans.

But also there was about fifteen to twenty Assiniboine killed there. They were ambushed by the Standing Chiefs and others. They were using it as a war trail, killing settlers, stealing cattle. Here, the military was going to come from Fort Totten to punish the Indians up here, so they got together to protect them from the army. They killed all them Assiniboine's there. They ambushed them, big slaughter. After that, that's when they had that big Sun Dance over there on Buffalo Lake. The military record I read said 1,100 dancers they had there. A general had sent [soldiers] there because they thought [it was] going to be another Custer thing, all these Indians. They went there.

There was a story told to me, too, about a young boy and his father. This boy and his father were sent out as scouts to go find these buffalo herds. The carts were coming; they were looking for the buffalo. The boy and his father got to that hill, Buffalo Lodge, the buffalo were on the north side. They camped on this side with his boy waiting for the Red River carts to get there. This little boy was anxious, no patience. He kept wanting to kill a buffalo. His father kept telling him not to do that. When they went to sleep, that little boy snuck [out] early in the morning. I guess that man heard a shot, but his boy wasn't coming back, wasn't coming back, wasn't coming back. He went back there, and he found his boy all mangled up. One of them bulls killed him. And he was telling me, that's the moral I want you to understand. Pay attention to your elderly people, listen. See what happen[ed when] this boy didn't want to listen. He lost his life, hurt his family. Broke the hearts of his father and mother. I talk to my grandkids like that, stories like that. I was told that.

I go pick medicine there. I used to take Francis Cree to go pick all over. He's my godfather. He gave me my [Chippewa] name, Young Thunder, that's my name. I had to go through sweats, Sun Dance with him, fire keeper, before all of that, get my colors. I was pretty close to him. I was one of his medicine finders. [Speaking Chippewa] I was his piercer.

The people don't know these things about me. I don't want them to know these things. For you to do it like this, fine. I was taught to be humble about traditional ways, not to brag on me. I was brought up this way; if you don't understand what a Sun Dance man is in there telling you in their language, don't go. They can learn, sit with the elderly. I taught young boys how to pray. I taught them how to say certain things. They don't let us teach in the schools. Although the damn boarding schools tried to kill us and everything. Now today . . . we learn all these things, all these valuable things we have as people.

You can't learn what we learned out of a schoolbook. You have to be shown that, be involved with someone with that knowledge. You want to learn how to make a sweat lodge, ashtum, I'll show you. Want to learn how to pray with a pipe, what it means four directions, ashtum, come on. Want to learn how to make a drum, ashtum.

So what do you do, you feel discriminated upon. And then I feel like a salt shaker in the cupboard. Whenever they need somebody to come in and show that there are Indians here, they call me, put some salt on me, then put me back in the cupboard [laughter]. I feel like a salt shaker. When they had the military come, the big military doings, National Guard, big doings up there at the casino, they needed somebody to pray in their language. What I did for the military, Okitchita, I did it for them. I went [and] prayed a long time.

What they used to call New Year's [speaking Cree] . . . we're going to have a good time here. My grandpa and his brother King Davis, they would have at least three, four days of celebrating, eating, and visiting on this side. On my father's side [speaking Cree] they would go a whole week, seven days. One thing I seen him do, all his kids and adult grandchildren would come to my grandpa's house. They would all kneel down one at a time and he would bless them for the year and [give] a good preaching about being good. Don't [speaking Cree] do things like that; don't abuse kids. Things like that all of them. I don't care if they were fifty years old, they went [and] knelt before my grandfather and he put his hand on [their] shoulder and he'd pray and bless them and they'd get up and kiss him. I think that meant a lot to my father, uncles, aunts. His grandkids.

I can honestly say those people were not bad people. I never did see them do or hear of them do anything bad. They always were good to their families. Work hard, never scared to work at anything, butchering, hauling wood, cutting hay, whatever it took, they did it. Good hunters. My father was excellent; he was an infantry man. He knew lots about guns, taught me to shoot, one shot, don't suffer animals [speaking Cree]. You kill them; that's the kind of compassion we were brought up with. Watching these New Year's things, the respect he had for Grandpa and Grandma. They were the core, they were the center of our existence those days. A lot of it happened on those days; Easter same thing. Holidays there was just a lot of things about religion. But also, a lot of stuff about cultural things, too. They were all Catholics except my grandpa. He was more traditional that way, him. But my grandma was a Turcotte, was very, very religious. My father same thing, my mother. When they split up, they never got divorced because it was against the church. They died like that.

But I remember all those things. Christmases were small. We got an apple and orange in Grandpa's big long socks that came up high above the knee, look like oatmeal. We called them oatmeal socks [laughter]. They used to put them over their shoes and tie them up here when they go hunt rabbits, that way you don't get snow inside of your shoes. We did that, and holidays were very special. I remember them [from] when I was very young.

I was baptized because I was told I had to do it by my grandpa and grandma and my dad and my mom. I never did consider myself a Christian that way. I believe in the right for them to have the right to believe whatever they feel good about it themselves. But I always thought I got more understanding and more spirituality out of my Indian ways. It had more meaning to me after I did the ceremonies and Sun dancing, sweat lodge, and things like that. They became more, I would say, more engrained in me when I learned how to talk and pray. I don't touch nothing in this house, I wash my hands. I don't touch nothing in the morning when I get up. I pray first. Open that window, I have my stuff here, my sage and sweet grass. I don't do nothing until I thank the Creator for seeing the ceiling [laughter], my grandkids, grandparents.

There're all kinds of ways you can pray. You never pray the same way. I always start off [speaking Chippewa] . . . I pray like that. I thank the Creator every day. I pray for the soldiers [speaking Chippewa] to come home again, ones that are sick. I pray [speaking Chippewa] for them old people and those kids that are running away and being slaughtered over there. I pray for them Chippewa, don't let anybody kill them anymore. I also pray for those that went home already, that passed away already. I tell the Creator to help them [speaking Chippewa]. I do that every day of my life. I teach my grandkids to do that—they are learning. This little boy comes here. I teach him a word every day.

"What was the first word you ever learned, Papa," he told me.

"Kiya! [laughter]."

"What does that mean?"

"Don't!"

That was the first word, I remember they would tell you that.

Over here they talk Michif, over there on this side Anishinaabe. I was pretty lucky. I had good mentors. I had Emma Great Walker, Alma Wilkie, Mary Cornelius, not that I didn't love my grandmother and my mom. They loved me just as much as them. There was a different relationship we had. I always respected my maternal mom and grandmother just as much as I love them. They grabbed me when I was wild [speaking Chippewa], they made me think. Alma was a great mentor for me. She stood by me no matter what kind of trouble I was getting into. She saw something in me. When she needed to do something, she'd always come get me. So, I was always close to her about it. Mary Cornelius taught me how to fight. Don't take nothing. She took me to Washington, DC, on treaty marches. I walked all the way from Pennsylvania on the treaty march. I walked all the way down Pennsylvania Avenue to listen to Fritz Mondale tell us our president was over in Germany talking about civil rights [laughter]. We walked with all these twelve Sun dancers that carried the pipe all the way from Sacramento. These traditionalist Japanese people carried this one . . . day. Dick Gregory, Jane Fonda, Oren Lyons, got to know him. Went and sang on this drum with them guys, he was one of the guys that [would] talk with us. He had the mic for a long time, talked about good things. He's kind of comical. He said one thing that made me laugh. He said you have to have compassion for the white man; you don't have to try and understand their foolishness, he said, but you have to try to deal with them, he said. They're the only people I know, he said, that will pee upstream, run downstream, and drink it [laughter]. Cracked me up when he said that.

And then Paul Little, he was my uncle. I got his drum when he was dying. I'm making a little drum for a boy here. All red. [Singing with a drum] I actually started learning [to sing] from Eugene Spotted Wolf and those guys in Sioux Falls. I started running around with Boy Joe Fayant, Pat Fayant. I know just about all those old songs; I can sing them by myself if I have to. That's one thing I'm proud of about that, I don't care where I'm at, I can get up there and do it.

Nowadays, ah, well, I have a heart problem. I have a lot of back problems. Had to go through painful myelograms. That's how I discovered that these discs were done to me at boarding school. I knew something was done there, but they put me in the university hospital in Minneapolis and they did these myelograms on me. They shoot needles, big long needles, they go way up to the top of your neck and they start down and shoot dye and they can't use no sedative because they're by nerves; the only way they can tell getting close to a nerve is by our reaction, so they don't do that. They went all the way down. After they did all of this, they wanted to put two discs inserted in me. He said it was only a 50/50 chance that it will work. I can't guarantee that it will work, he said. Your two discs were crushed at a young age. I told him what happened. He said that's what happened, that guy kicked you and crushed them, you were too young. So, he put me in a girdle for six months, one of these big girdles. He made me get up on my toes, watch my diet, don't eat lots, keep your muscles on the side of your backbone hard, that'll keep that thing from moving. And when they move . . . if they do touch, you'll end up in the hospital on Demerol for eight to ten days. You just can't come out of it, you can't move. Even to move your leg is just like [it] kills you. I fell one time and I hurt myself with my daughter, my little grandson, and scared them. They couldn't move me. They had to come and slide a deal under me, the ambulance, pick me up that way. They knocked me out on Demerol for about nine days, couldn't eat. Was on IVs. I think that for going on the sixth day I didn't get to eat. I was starving, I was so high on [medication], I could hear the bells up in there ding ding ding ding [laughter]. Even if they weren't doing it I could hear them. And then they come in finally and put a deal on me, whenever you feel pain just push the button. Well, I didn't know any better, after a while I was just pushing it; I damn near OD'd myself. Started vomiting and they had to turn me over, almost choked. Boy they caught hell them nurses. They moved that thing out of there. They come in and gave me a shot and put an IV in that thing there. I [have been at] the hospital quite a few times because of my back. I have to be careful. I can't lift like I want, I can't walk all over like I used to, hunting and stuff like that as you get older. I'm still in good shape, don't overeat, try to take care of my body as best I can, luck I guess. Nobody thinks I'm old at all. Hope I can stay long, as long as my grandpas, in their '90s, my grandma, La See Do, 105.

My boarding school experiences affected my first children because I could see the militarized in me. You became like that, become overly [stern] when you say don't do this, then it was like don't do it or you going to be punished. Make them be too clean. I want your room clean. I want your bed fixed. Then I start to understand that I was starting to replicate what was being done to me in the boarding school. EJ and Danielle were the ones that got the worst of it, but after that I learned right away that I was doing that to my boy EJ. But he was good; he talked to me. Dad, you don't need to do that, I'll do it. One of them wanted to go to boarding school. I told them don't do it. You aren't going to like it. Well because Timmy and them were all down there, Jeff, Danny, they were all in that boarding school in Wahpeton. He wanted to go in the middle of the year like I did.

"You go, you going to be staying there until at least May, can't come home." Well, he was there only a month. Mr. Yellow Bird, I think was his name, called me. He said, "Your boy ran away, stole some bikes on the other side of the river. We caught him going up on the Breckenridge side. What do you think we should do?" I said, "Well, I want to talk to him." So, I talked to him.

"I want to come home, Dad," he said.

"Well," I said, "You made a decision, you're going to have to stand by your decision. I have to go to Aberdeen for the tribe, I'll come and visit you. How's that?"

"OK," he said. So, I kind of made it at least once or twice a month. I'd go see him at Wahpeton. Let the people know that I was going to buy him stuff, leave him money in his account, things like that. His brother Louis was there. They took good care of him, protected him. But he didn't like it and he never did want to go back again.

Ah, you know, I never did seek out psychologists, psychiatrists. I always turned back to the pipe. That right there. My relationship with my Creator. The counseling I got was from the Elders like Emma and Joe and Alma. The reinforcement of being a good person, a good man. Love your fellow man, don't lose who you are, don't go off the deep end, don't stray from the Red Road, all these good things. Don't turn down people when they ask you for help. Go to school, be smart, do your job, be proud. Those are the kind of things I got, that kind of counseling. I never did seek it out from professionals. When I was locked up, they sent one guy, his name was Dr. F. Luc Chou, from Yankton, I suppose the state hospital. They had to come in and give you an evaluation that's required of every prisoner. He came in and all these ink blots you know, what do you see here, see there. What does this remind you of, things like that. I did it with him. When he got done with me, he said, "You don't belong here in this place." Well, I know that, I told him. But all the other stuff for maintaining my daily thing, I owe it all to these old people, my mom, Dad, Emma, Alma, Larry, people like that. What they told me never left my brain. It's there. It keeps me above water. That's the best I can do.

Basketball team, 1927, Holy Rosary Mission, SD. *Marquette Archives.*

The drill, 1900, Holy Rosary Mission, SD. *Marquette Archives.*

WAKAN TANKA

I interviewed Erich Longie (b. 1953) in his office located on the Spirit Lake reservation. Erich works as the Tribal Historic Preservation Officer. Reflective, soft spoken, and sipping on tea, he sat for several long interviews after his office closed for the day. I knew Erich from our days at University of North Dakota while we completed our doctoral degrees. Erich is known nationally for his anti-Fighting Sioux logo activism.

I was born in Devils Lake, North Dakota, in 1953. During my infant and toddler years I lived in the East End. The East End was the eastern part of the reservation where my dad grew up. But most of my memories are out in Crow Hill, where my mom is from. My mom and my dad separated when I was a toddler. In Crow Hill, we lived in a two-room frame house; part of it was a frame house, part of it was log cabin with a porch attached to it. I remember it being warm and cozy. We had a kerosene stove, with three burners, which we cooked on. We always had a lot of dogs. We ran around in the woods, went down to the lake and swam all the time. We explored woods and hills within a five-mile radius and played many games to keep us occupied in the evening. I remember my auntie on my dad's side who stayed with us, we called her Auntie Abu. Abu is a Dakota word that is inserted in a lullaby Dakota mothers sing to their babies. "Abu, abu . . . go to sleep . . ." She used to sleep on the floor behind the kerosene stove; her takoza [grandchild] would sleep with her. They would talk nothing but Dakota all the time. It was a good life. I didn't have a care in the world.

I remember the older kids going to school and wondering where they went. One summer day my cousin Timmy, my sister Becky, and I—I must have been about four years at the time—went down to the lake to swim. When we arrived at the lake, we saw some smoke coming from where our house was. Becky said, "I want to go see where the fire is coming from." She looked worried when she left. Timmy and I followed her, but we took our time. Becky came running back and she was crying. She sobbed, "The house is burning down." We went running up the hill, and sure enough the house was on fire and there were people around it watching it burn. We lost everything in the house. No one died, but we lost everything.

That was a first major change in my life. We went from a nice comfortable house to sleeping in a tent for the rest of the summer. I remember the generosity of people; someone gave Mom a tent, and we put it up in the woods. There were a lot of us, six, seven of us, so we all couldn't fit in the tent, so most of us slept outside around the tent. People brought us clothes, cooking utensils, etc., which we stockpiled in the tent. People also brought food, which we cooked and ate outside. When it rained, we all tried to squeeze in the tent in an attempt from getting rained on. Due to this experience, when people talk about how fun it is to go camping, I don't see it as fun.

Eventually, another log cabin was built about one hundred yards from where the one that burnt down was. It was a one-room log cabin smaller than the old one. My older sister, my three younger brothers, and I slept up in the loft. The planks across the rafters extended about a third of the way across, and there was a little stairway built into the wall. We climbed up the ladder to sleep in the loft at bedtime. It was the warmest place to sleep in the wintertime, but it was also the hottest place in the summer. And that's what I remember of my first five years.

I think Mom went up to ninth grade. I don't think my dad went very far past the eighth grade if at all. My mom was very intelligent. She read a lot; although English was her second language, she spoke it fluently, but she spoke Dakota most of the time. I know a couple words [in Dakota], well, I know more than a couple words, and I can follow a conversation in Dakota if it is spoken slowly and English words are inserted now and then.

Mom raised ten children and did a good job. I had four older siblings and five younger siblings. My older brother, who was the oldest of the family, died of cancer; two older sisters died of liver failure, due to alcoholism; a third older sister died of a drug overdose; and my younger brother committed suicide, which was due to alcohol, too.

My auntie Alvina, who was older than my mom almost by twenty years, talked about boarding school at the old fort. She described it as a "bad place to be." She'd talk about students getting beatings, about freezing in the winter, and she mentioned a cellar where they put bad kids; she mentioned that once or twice.

We were very poor. We never had money for anything. We never had toys, we hardly went to town, we never had candy. We raised rabbits and chickens . . . we ate a lot of eggs. Every now and then we would skin a rabbit. However, it was hard to kill a pet, so my stepdad snared wild rabbits, which we make [into] stew. Always short on food, Mom would jump at the chance to send us to church because the ministers would say, "Send them to church, and we'll feed them sandwiches later." They would also provide transportation. For the most part, learning about Christianity wasn't all that bad, but I hated white people back then, for whatever reason, I just didn't like them, and the ministers were white people.

I finally figured out by the time I was eleven or twelve years old that Christianity, and how the Christian really behaved, was different. I realized there was really no true Christians in the world, just people who claimed to be Christians. Christians acted . . . opposite of what my mom taught me: never lie, to stand up for what is right, go help others, and to share what you have with people who don't have anything. By the time I was eleven or twelve years old, I rejected Christianity all together. I did love listening to Christian hymns though, and I continue to listen them to this day, a habit I kept hidden from everyone for years.

We had neither electricity nor running water, which meant we had a lot of chores to do. My older brother was already gone by the time I was eight, nine years old. The next three oldest were all girls. I had to do all the wood chopping, and my younger brother hauled the water. We would get off the bus and I would haul wood, saw wood, split wood, and carry it into the house. I made sure we had enough wood for the night and for the next day. My younger brother Mark, rest in peace, would haul water. Often, Mom would put the water pails in her trunk and go someplace, come here to Fort Totten or some other place, and fill up the water pails someplace and bring [them] home.

I remember when they tried to dig us a well, but they couldn't find any water. They finally struck water, but it was so deep it took two of us to pump it out. They dug us a water line from the pump to our log cabin and connected it to a tank in our house. I don't ever recall the tank getting full; it was so hard to pump the water. In the wintertime we melted snow, and that was our water, or we caught rainwater in the summer and that was the water we used. In the summertime, we swam all the time, so we never had to worry about staying clean. In the wintertime, every now and then, Mom would get out her great big tub and fill it up with snow, put it on the stove, and when it was full of warm water one of us would get in there and take a bath. I remember we always had a lot of impetigo sores back then, and

I think the reason was because there was not enough water to take baths. I've still got scars on my legs from them. We hauled or pumped water and sawed and split wood until we moved to Fort Totten, when I was around fifteen years old.

For the most part, I remember my childhood as a happy time. It was tough; we wished for toys, we wished for better food, new clothes and stuff like that, but it was still a good life. Probably the happiest time is when Mom was [cooking on] Sundays. Mom would always manage to get a chicken Sunday dinner. We would go to church and then we'd get off the minister's van, and she would have chicken dinner all ready. The whole family would sit at the table and eat. Those Sunday dinners were probably the happiest times. But then again, you know, it was a different time; our family was close, and we all loved and respected each other.

We had cousins who lived over the hill from us. Together, we ran around Crow Hill all day, went swimming in summer, and sliding in winter on cardboard. There were tough times, too, when there wasn't enough to eat, the log cabin was hot in the summer, cold in the winter, but mostly, I remember my life during that time as happy. Man! There are times when I miss those days.

I've lived on the rez all my life, except when I went to boarding school when I was in high school and when I served in the Marine Corps. [The boarding school I attended] was called Benson County Agricultural and Training School [BCATS]. I'd stay at BCATS during the week and then come home for the weekend. My experiences with the white man's education began here at the old fort in 1959. I was in kindergarten class, and I remember it was really a scary experience. We lived out in the country; we didn't see very many people. We were loners out there. All of sudden I was thrust into this crowd of strange children, and the teacher was a black woman. I couldn't figure out why she was black, because I had never seen a black person before. Everything was so strange, and she was mean. The second year they closed that place down, and they built a new school and Miss Daggs kept me in kindergarten for a second year. By then I kind of figured out that Miss Daggs, as mean as she was, kind of favored me, even though she would still beat me with a ruler every now and then. Here's why: one day when I was home sick on my birthday a little after 12:00, the school bus comes over the hill and pulls up beside the log cabin. I'm wondering what the heck is going on? My entire class got off the bus along with Miss Daggs, who was carrying a birthday cake. They all stood by the window and sang happy birthday to me. Mom went outside and Miss Daggs handed her my birthday cake. She [Miss Daggs] kept me for another year; altogether I spent three years in her classroom, and then she promoted me straight to third grade, having me skip second grade.

They put me with a teacher called Mrs. Reynolds, who was really mean. She slapped me hard once because I wasn't paying attention. She would pull our ears, or grab us by the shirt and jerk us around, or shake us and yell at us. I don't seem to recall it ever bothered us very much because that's kind of how life was back then. We were always fighting with this person or that person, therefore, physical violence was kind of a way of life for us, especially from the teachers. Although the teachers were mean they really couldn't hurt or scare us. They were not as bad as going out to the schoolyard and getting into a fight with somebody older and getting the crap beat out of you.

They became scared of us as we got older; I think they knew we remembered the beatings and wanted to get even. So, they were really careful how they treated us in the upper grades. I remember one teacher would run to the door all the time. He was the seventh-grade teacher, and anytime something would happen in class, he would run to the door and call the principal . . . he was so scared of us. I remember there was an eighth-grade teacher, a Miss Stenjen, who was one of the nicer teachers . . . bringing me several shirts. I remember she would bring me clothes because my clothes were ragged. Mom never had any enough money to buy us new clothes.

By the time I reached eighth grade life was great. I had complete freedom because Mom by that time had married a white man, but he never really raised us and Mom just let me do whatever I wanted to. I was free to come and go and do whatever I wanted to do, and life was great.

After I graduated from grade school, I went to Maddock [BCAT]. It's a school thirty miles west of Fort Totten. When our high school closed down in '60 at the old fort, they had to ship the high schoolers someplace. Most went to Indian boarding schools, some went to Maddock. Maddock used the Johnson-O'Malley funds to bus Indian students to their school, where we stayed in dorms during the week and came home on Fridays. That all started in '61–'62, and by the time I started high school in '67 we pretty much knew Maddock was a boarding school. My older brother and two older sisters went there. My older brother dropped out, but two older sisters were really good students. They worked in the cafeteria after school, washing dishes. They would get paid every two weeks or whatever, and they would come back and give Mom money to go to the bingo and drink some beer, and they used that money to buy their clothes,

When I graduated from eighth grade, I had no idea what to do, so I enrolled in BCATS because my two older sisters had graduated from there. It was a culture shock to say the least. I'd never seen so many white people in one place at one time. It was strange. Looking back, they saw an opportunity to make some money off Indian students by bussing us over there, keeping us, and then they would get funding through Johnson-O'Malley because they eventually built a new school on the Johnson-O'Malley funds.

Maddock was a good-sized town back then. When I went to school there, we would start out with fifteen to twenty boys, and about thirty, forty girls. The school had a population of about three hundred students. At the end of each year there was only about five of us boys still in school, and about fifteen Indian girls. That's just the way it was. They just dropped out. Back then very few people went to school past eight grades. The only reason I went to school was because of my mom. It was both a bad time and a good time for school; it was bad in a sense because there was a lot of racism, [and] it was good [because] we kind of ruled the school . . . because the white kids were all scared of us. So we kind of did what we wanted.

The school divided the students into two groups. In one group would be us Indians and whom I always called the poor, or slow, white students. In the other group, they would put the rest of the white students. Whether it was math, science, or typing, the other group were always a couple chapters ahead of us. And, they never put an Indian student into algebra; they always put us in general math. I can't remember for whatever reason, but I took algebra in my sophomore year and I regretted it. I took it with a bunch of freshman white students, and socially it wasn't bad because I was older, and I was able to do what I wanted to in class. The white students were always laughing at me because I was rebellious, and the teacher couldn't control me. I can't remember, but I think I flunked it.

Indian boys were fighters back then. There were two brothers, Jack and Dean, and my goodness they were good fighters. I remember either Jack or Dean would—I wouldn't say they would pick a fight—but they were always ready and willing to fight at the slightest provocation. The white boys would yell at us when they went by in a car, and we would yell back. If the white boys did stop to fight, Jack or Dean usually beat the shit out of whoever was brave enough to take them on. That usually ended the harassment for a while. Every now and then throughout the year, there would be one or two fights which the Indian boys usually won. Personally, I never had any problem with any of the white guys, but I was an Indian and I stuck with my kind. But, I didn't like most of them, and I think they didn't like me, but I never had any real problem with them.

My sister started reading to us when I was in about the third or fourth grade up in the loft of that log cabin. She would read aloud books like *The Wizard of Oz* and *The Boxcar Children* and *Alice in Wonderland* to us. She was about four years older than me, and since there was no TV or anything, we looked forward to her reading books to us. That's how she kept us in line, too: "If you don't behave"—she used to babysit us—"if you don't behave, I'm not going to read to you guys tonight." It's how we all became readers.

Once I started reading, I wouldn't stop. Mom would tell me, "istima," when we would sit at the table using an old kerosene lamp as lighting, and read long past my bedtime. Istima means, "go to sleep" in Dakota. My younger brother read just as much as I did if not more.

As time went by, our lives became a little bit better and Mom was able give us money at times. My brother and I would go to town with Mom and we would each buy a couple books, maybe five books each, and then we would trade back and forth until we had both read the other's books. Every place I went, if somebody had a book, I would ask him or her for it. I didn't care what subject it was, I read it. The worst thing about grade school was they had a library, but they [never] let students read the books in it, much less check them out. I actually went in that library to get a film projector. I remember seeing rows and rows of books, and I just wanted to read them so bad. When we would line up for dinner, it would be right across from the library. Man! I would stand there wondering what kind of books were in that library. I just was dying to get my hands on those books, but they never once opened it up to us students.

Every time I would go visit Auntie Alvina, I always had a book in my pocket, and when I'd take it out to read she'd say, "One of these days you are going to be a great man because you carry a book around with you wherever you go." When I was a teenager, Mom would always tell me, "You're going to make something of your life, you're smarter than these guys, you're not going to be like these worthless Indian men, you're going to make something of your life." She told me that over and over again, and that was one of the reasons why I didn't drop out of high school. I didn't even try very hard to do the work in high school. I was just there just to go because of Mom, and because they really served us three square meals every day, which I never had before. When it came right down to it, Mom was the reason why I never dropped out of school.

In the dorm there was always chores. We had to make sure our beds were made, and I think we had to sweep the rooms too, which wasn't much work. The school fed us breakfast and supper in addition to dinner. When my sisters went to school there, they would get up early and help the cooks get ready, and then they would stay after supper and help the cooks clean up, too. They earned enough money so that they had clothes, and they gave Mom enough to go play bingo and buy some beer. Mom didn't work at a regular job, but she was always out hustling, trying to get some money one way or the other, and sometimes she would be gone for a couple days. Those were the bad times because we would get lonesome for Mom, although our older sisters were perfectly capable of taking care of us. Mom would go to the valley and pick potatoes, and she would be gone for a week or so, and that's when I would really miss her. Mom worked in the field a lot, she would haul bales, pick rocks—just like a man—and she would do other stuff to make a few dollars here and there.

From my perspective, the dorm was great simply because I had a real bed to sleep in. At home, I didn't have a bed. Instead, I slept on the floor on a mattress I shared with two brothers. At BCATS I actually had my own bed to sleep on, not only a bed, but also, I had blankets to myself, and it was warm. At home, the fire would go out in the wintertime and it would get really cold in the old log cabin. At BCATS there was a shower, running water, and the dorm master, whatever they called him, would bring a TV out in the hallway and we would get to watch TV. I went from a primitive log cabin to a dorm that had everything. So, to me the dorm was good, it was a good life.

I think there were six rooms with two bunk beds in each of them, about twenty-four beds in all. There might have been more . . . I don't remember ever those rooms [and] beds ever filling up. As I said earlier, at the end of the year most of those rooms would be empty due to most of the Indian boys dropping out.

We had a dresser, which I didn't use because back then I only had five pants and five shirts; that was it. I was there for only five days at a time, so I left my clothes in a suitcase. The room didn't have frills, but I didn't care: it was warm, it was clean, I had a bed all to myself. Maybe that's the other reason why I didn't drop out. Because coming from a one-room log cabin without electricity or running water, all those luxuries were great and the food was great!

We would get up at 7:30 and by eight o'clock we would go down to eat; from there we went to school. We arrived at school early, because back then school didn't start until nine, and then we had to go to our place in the auditorium where we sat in alphabetical order. I think that's how they took attendance. Then we went to our first class at 9:15. As, I said, I never really tried very hard in class. Plus, I needed glasses. I had broken my glasses, and I couldn't see. When I became a senior, I needed just three classes to graduate. Even without trying very hard, I managed to earn enough credit to graduate. I think you needed seventeen credits to graduate back then. By the time I finished my junior year I had fourteen credits, I think because I had flunked, I think five courses. I remember this one Indian guy saying, "how come you spend all that time in the library?" Library was also study hall. When you didn't have class, you would go into the library/study hall and sit at a table until your next class. Well, because I only had three classes I was always in the library. My senior year was a good time in many ways.

I missed thirty-two days during my senior year. By then I had started to drink hard, and lots of times I would get drunk over the weekend and not make it back to school on Sunday. Many times, I'd miss a whole week at a time.

During the summer, before my senior year, my sister had said, "Hobo Joe, you like to have your hair long; here take this," and she gave me a headband. I thought it was pretty cool, so I wore it all summer. At the end of the summers, Mom would always say, "You need a haircut before school starts, Hobo Joe." [One] time I said, "No Mom, I don't want to cut my hair."

"OK," she said, and I went back to school with my hair long. During the week, all the students, especially the white students, kept looking at my long hair. Heck, even some of the Indian students thought my hair was too long. Friday, right before the three o'clock dismissal, the principal called me in the office and said, "Erich, if you want to come back to school next week, you're going to have to get a haircut." When I went home, I told Mom what the principal had told me. She asked me, "Are you going to get a haircut?"

"No."

"Well, you've got to go to school."

I didn't say anything. When the bus came on Sunday, I didn't go to school. Tuesday came around and she said, "What are you going to do?

You can't sit around all day." By then I was kind of a juvenile delin-quent; we had moved from the country into town and I was always getting into trouble.

I said, "Well, take me back and I'll find out." When she parked in front of the school, I told her, "Wait here for me. I'll see what happens, if they kick me out I'll just go home. If they don't you can take me to the dorm."

I went to the principal's office to get a permit to return to class slip. When I walked in his office he looks up at me, didn't say anything; I didn't say anything either. I was standing there, standing there, standing there . . . pretty soon he reaches over and picks up a "return to class" slip, writes something on it, hands it to me, never saying a word. I took it, I didn't say a word either, and I went and told Mom, "Well, I get to go back to school."

She took me back to the dorm. I just let my hair grow all that year, and wore that headband. You know, the old hippie days [laughter]. Several years ago, I met an underclassman from BCATS. He told me that a group of boys wore their hair long the year after I graduated and when told to cut their hair they reminded the administration that I was allowed to wear my hair long the previous year. They were allowed to keep their long hair.

I went through the graduation ceremony. I was already an alcoholic by then. I was glad to have finished high school, but at the same time I wondered what I was going to do. Really, I had no clue what I was going to do. Years later, I realized that everybody has a plan after high school, and I didn't. I think my self-esteem was so low back then I really didn't think I was capable of anything after high school other than just working at labor jobs.

I started drinking at fourteen or fifteen. I was probably an alcoholic by the time I was seventeen. After I graduated from high school, the BIA sent me to Haskell. I wanted to be a welder. I had learned to weld in shop at BCATS. It was the reason I liked shop in high school, and I was a re-ally good welder. So, I wanted to be a welder. During the summer, I was employed by Sully's Hill National Park. After watching the park manager trying to weld a cow guard meant to go on the front gate, I asked him to let me try. He gladly turned the welder over to me. I welded that cow guard up in no time. It is still in place. Anyway, back to my story, they had me take a test and told me, "You're not going to be a welder. You can do better than a welder. We are going to enroll you in electronics." I went down to Haskell, and I hated electronics. At Thanksgiving, I was given five dollars and a bus ticket, and [they] sent me home. The next year I enrolled in Lake

Region Jr. College in their welding program, and nine months later I had a welding degree. I worked as a welder for Haybusters down in Jamestown after I obtained my welder's degree.

When I was fired from Haybusters after I broke into the bar, I started working at Sioux Manufacturing. They fired me there, too, but they would hire me right away because they needed workers. It was after one such firing when a good friend of mine Dan Cavanaugh, who grew up not far from me, said he was going to Fargo to get a physical. He was going to join the Marine Corps. He asked, "You want to ride along?" I had read—even in spite of my drinking, I still read all the time—about the Marine Corps and boot camp and how tough it was, so I didn't want to join the marines. But I had been thinking about joining the navy, so I said, "OK, I'll go with you." All the way down to Fargo, the marine recruiters and Dan talked to me about joining the marines. They finally talked me into taking a physical, and the next thing I knew I was signing my name on a paper that said I was joining the Marine Corps. So that's how I joined the Marine Corps. I'll never forget the day that I left for Marine Corps boot. I was so hung-over from being drunk for a couple weeks.

When we landed in San Diego, we were put on a bus, and a drill instructor came on the bus and started yelling at us: "You're in the Marine Corps now and your ass is mine." It was about 3:00 in the morning when we got to the Marine Corps training depot where they lined us all up on footprints painted on the asphalt. They would call us one by one to go into the barbershop, where they would shave our hair. My hair was long but it took no more than two minutes and it was all gone.

We finally went to bed at 3:30 and we were up at 5:30 for breakfast. The first couple days I kept saying to myself, "What the hell am I doing here?" After a couple of days, my resilience took over. Although it was tough, really tough, I was in good physical shape, had lots of endurance and I was only twenty-one years old, so the physical training never really bothered me. I just had issues with, you know, with the spit and polish part. My boots were never shined like they should have been, my outfit was never ironed the way it was supposed to be, and all this and that. But other than that, you know, it wasn't all that bad. In fact, there's a lot of laughs about it because things were so crazy. I learned right away just to follow the rules and I learned another thing too; if they don't notice you, they're not going to holler at you. One of the proudest moments of my life was when I graduated from Marine Corps boot camp. Forty years after leaving the marines, I am still extremely proud to say, I'm a United States Marine!

My mom suffered a stroke while I was stationed in Camp Lejeune, North Carolina, so I caught a plane home. My heart nearly broke when I went to the hospital and seen her. She went from about 190 pounds to just 90 pounds. It was just so heartbreaking to see her. I had been on the wagon prior to Mom's stroke, and I used it as an excuse to start drinking again. I wouldn't quit for another several years.

Who I am today is because of my mom. My mom always told me she said, "Joe, hobo, you're smart, you're really smart. When you grow up you're going to make something out of yourself. You're not going to be like the rest of these worthless Indian men around here. You're going to do something with your life." She told me that continuously over the years.

I was in five car accidents, five rollovers, and two head-on collisions in my life, but I will only tell about the last one rollover, so I can get to the education part. I was married to my son's mother, or I was with her, and we worked in Cando, North Dakota, at a pasta plant. We worked the swing shift. On paydays, we would rush to the bar, and we would have a couple beers and then we'd go back to Cando. On the Friday I'm talking about, as usual we rushed to the bar, drank several beers, and started going home. It was starting to snow and the snow was sticking on the ground, the car started sliding, and I lost control. We went into the ditch and hit a snow bank and slowly rolled over. Nobody was hurt; we rolled over so slow.

It was my fourth time I had been in a rollover. The next one would change my life dramatically. We climbed out and pushed the car back on its wheels. In the meantime, a pickup stopped and pulled us out of the ditch, and we drove home. The next morning my wife's brother and I jumped in a car with two other guys, and we went to Devils Lake, where we proceeded to drink all day. We were drunk all that Saturday, and on Sunday, I asked my sister's boyfriend, "Can you give me a ride back to Cando?"

He gave me a ride back home; on the way, we started bragging about our cars. When we arrived at my house, I jumped in my car and we drove to the highway and the race was on! It was in the spring of the year, when it thaws one day and freezes the next. This particular day was cold so all [the] snow that had melted the day before was frozen solid. I vividly remember my speedometer going past sixty, and the next thing I knew I was going sideways. Apparently, I had hit an icy spot, started sliding sideways, and then hit a dry spot and the car started rolling over and over. I broke my back in two places, broke my ribs, broke my shoulder bone, broke my ankle, tore the entire skin off the side of my face, and numerous other injuries.

From what I was told, I was thrown out of the car, but they were not sure if the car rolled over me. They put me into the car and took me home. However, the pain was too great and an ambulance was called. Once in the ambulance, I was rushed to Grand Forks . . . the doctor said I might not live through the night, and if I lived, I probably would not walk again. I made it through the night, but I couldn't move from the waist down . . . paralyzed from the waist down. Eventually I ended in the rehabilitation wing of the hospital where I had to do all that physical therapy. One day they pushed me into a room where all the stoves and stuff were at wheelchair level, and they wanted me to fry an egg. I refused. I said, "No."

I absolutely refused to fry an egg on that, so they sent me back to my room, and they said I was depressed. What they didn't know was I had made up my mind that I was going to walk again no matter what it took. I also knew it would be extremely difficult; therefore, I couldn't have any doubt in my mind. To me, learning how to cope in a wheelchair would only weaken my resolve. Therefore, I refused to learn on how to fry an egg in a wheelchair.

So, long story short, two years later, I was walking with crutches. Eventually I walked with a cane and then I was walking without a cane, even though I was partially paralyzed on my left side. However, I kept on drinking.

Three years after that I was lying in bed, drunk in some home, and I was thinking of what my mom said. My mom's words kept coming back to haunt me so to speak. So, I'm lying in that bed thinking, geez, here I am thirty-one years old, and I don't have anything, and my mom always said I was smarter than everybody, and I am smarter than most people but here am nothing but a drunk? That led me to sign up for alcohol treatment for my third time. I went to treatment for the third time, and I haven't taken a drink since.

I have always believed in Wakan Tanka. I know I went to church and learned about God, I know that. But, in my earliest memories I always believed in Wakan Tanka. Where I picked that up I don't know where, maybe from my auntie, I don't know. I know Mom and her sisters would talk Dakota all the time, and you know, that is where I probably learned it. I always knew that there was a being that was mightier than anything. Years later, I read a book by Luther Standing Bear. He said in Christianity there's a continuous battle between good and evil, and given time evil could take over, and the whole universe would be filled with evil. He said, "In our belief, there's never a doubt, good will always conquer evil."

I didn't know that back then because I didn't read Luther Standing Bear back then. I just knew my belief in Wakan Tanka was powerful and that's kind of what my belief is that pulled me through those tough times. And that's the reason why I quit drinking.

After breaking my back, I went to school for two years at our tribal college, although I was still drinking at the time. Then when I went to treatment for the third time, I sobered up and I came home and was hired at Sioux Manufacturing in July. Right before the fall semester started at the tribal college, my brother-in-law came up to me, and he said, "I need you to come enroll in a teacher preparation we have at the college." I asked why. I had just finished two years of college, while drinking no less, and now that I was sober and had a job, I didn't feel like going back to college. He persisted. Finally, I looked at him and asked, "Why me, Al?'

He replied, "Well, there's only two students at the college that got over a 3.0 grade point average and you're one of them."

I said, "Really?" That was hard to believe because I was drunk the two years that I went there to Little Hoop.

I switched to the graveyard shift at Sioux Manufacturing and attended classes during the day. After a year went by Al told me, "You have to go to UND."[46]

I thought, "Well, I will go and enroll in UND, and after a month or so I'll drop out. I'll come home, and go back to work at Sioux Man." But at UND I realized two things. One, Elementary Education was so easy I didn't even have to study. Two, I began to understand the importance of education. I really began to see how much better my life would be with education. The third thing is that they had a pool hall that I went to every single night, so with those three factors I stuck it out and graduated with a teaching degree.

I came back and taught third grade for three years. When I was going through my student teaching, my mom passed away, and what was the toughest, hardest thing was not to fall back to the bottle. When I was in treatment I had to go to different AA meetings, but I think AA does not work for Indians, for most Indians. It didn't work for me, but they have a

---

[46] The University of North Dakota, located in Grand Forks.

lot of wisdom in their sayings, and I kind of picked up on a couple of them. One of them sayings was, "life is tough, but it gets tougher if you drink."

When Mom died, I know if I drank, my life would probably be worse, so I didn't drink. I was happy teaching because I loved my teaching and the kids. People in the community looked up to me as a teacher. When I would go to pow wows—I was a pow-wow-goer back then—I'd run into people and they'd ask, "What do you do?" and I'd say, "I teach third grade," and they'd say, "Oh, really!" I really liked it.

A few years later I went back again, to [UND], for my Master's program. To be honest, I just did enough to get by. It wasn't the work was that hard; it was just the amount of work was more than I was willing to do, so I just did it enough just to get by. I eventually enrolled in a doctorate program. Classes were going good, I was finally getting in the swing of the course work, and then my seventeen-year-old son was killed in a car accident. My life come to a complete halt, I was so devastated.

I took a year off. When I took a year off, I lost all the advantages of being in a cohort. In a cohort, the classes are all lined up for you, and now I was on my own. That was tough and that is why it took me so long to complete my doctorate program. It was hard to take the classes while grieving for my son. We Dakota believe in grieving four years. But the advantages [of not being in a cohort] were there was fewer students in my classes and with fewer students I was speaking up more. I was getting more involved in the classes, learning more. Overall, I became a better student.

When I graduated, it was the proudest moment in my life. I arrived at the commencement and noticed I was last in line. How in the heck did that happen, I wondered? I thought we were to go in alphabetical order. When my name was called I walked across the stage to receive my degree. Then I walked over to shake the president's hand. He stopped me from walking off the stage.

"Wait here, Erich," he said.

I stood there on stage. The emcee—he was friendly to Indians all the time, Dr. Robert Boyd—took the mic and said, "You know the commencement speaker talked to me about people making a difference. What we have here today is the first person from his tribe to earn a doctorate degree, Dr. Erich Longie."

He said more but I don't remember his words. The audience gave me a standing ovation. Over the loudness of the standing ovation, I could hear my son war-whooping, and it was one of the proudest moments of my life.

I was diagnosed with cancer about nine years ago. I underwent thirty-seven days of radiation. I was tired all the time, but I came through it OK. After my last day of radiation treatment, I drove to Minot, North Dakota, and entered the North Dakota Pool Association State Singles Tournament. I ended up winning the championship in the "B" Division. At my check-up after my radiation treatment, the doctor concluded that I had five years to live.

In the months following my radiation treatment, my PSA numbers went down and according to the doctor, I was almost cured. He told me, "Maybe the radiation did cure you."

However, after a couple years my numbers started climbing again and this past summer they got to the point where they determined that there was a good chance cancer was growing in a different part of my body. They determined this because my cancer was found in a lymph node before my radiation treatment. They transferred me to the department where they just tried to hold the cancer at bay, to keep me alive as long as possible. It was sort of strange to know that that's all they were going to do is keep me alive as long as they could. While I was there, they ran all kinds of tests on me again, and lo and behold, they didn't find any cancer. Wakan Tanka was surely watching over me. So, here I was, listed as a Stage Four cancer for nine years and then all of a sudden, I'm right back to Stage 1. Talk about a sense of relief.

Last year I accepted a [Facebook] friend request from a woman I knew in my youth but hadn't seen in close to fifty years. She lives six hundred miles away and was recently widowed. One thing led to another, and pretty soon I was driving down to see her every weekend. The people who know me would know when I want something, or if I'm going to do something, or if I make up my mind about something, nothing gets in the way of getting what I want. I would not have a doctorate, I would never have fought cancer this long, I would never overcome alcoholism, and I would still be in a wheelchair if I gave up easily. When I want something pretty bad, I put on blinders and nothing distracts me until I have achieved whatever it is I want to achieve. Everything is irrelevant except what I want, and in this case, I wanted her. It didn't matter how many miles I drove, how tired I became, those are all irrelevant, and fortunately she began to feel the same way. We had our problems, but she said, "The Creator picked this time in our lives to be together," and she was absolutely right. So, I proposed to her and we got married—twice. Once by the white man's way and the other through a Dakota ceremony. Best decision I ever made.

I always did believe in what we Dakota call Wakan Tanka, the Great Mystery. I always knew that there was something there. When we went to church you know, the person that talked about God and Jesus was the same as Wakan Tanka; there was no difference as far as there being the higher power. In fourth grade, I would do my prayers every night, and I think I picked that up because at some point maybe Mom made us say prayers, and I just continued as I grew older. I began to realize that Christianity—although Christ did a lot of good things—did not follow Christ's teachings, and so I left the church, and so to speak, I rejected Christianity before I reached my teenage years. I didn't reject Christ's teachings; I rejected Christianity, because in my mind it was all hypocritical. The other reason was because I knew I was becoming a teenager, and I wanted to do certain things that would be frowned on that good Christians didn't do. I felt if I wasn't a Christian I could go out and do these things. So, I rejected Christianity, and began to live a life that brought a lot of heartache to me and a lot of other people. But all through those I never stopped believing in Wakan Tanka. I began to pray for a way out of a life of alcoholism, and I went to treatment three times and the third time I was thirty-one years old. I haven't taken a drink since then.

With prayer and determination, I've made it to where I'm at today. Everything I do, everything I face, all the good things that happen, I pray, and I give thanks for. All the challenges I face, all my fears, I'm able to face because of my prayer. I don't think I'm better than anybody else. I don't think I'm going to heaven and everybody else is going to hell. I just believe that Wakan Tanka listens to a person who prays if they are sincere and if they really want to change. If they're doing it for a good reason, and like I said, I knew right from wrong. Once I quit drinking, I quit doing a lot of wrong . . . but on the other hand, I am extremely arrogant. I do and say what I want; I don't care what people think. That's just the way I am. However, I often minimize my bad behavior because I know it's wrong.

What basically makes me happy is I'm able to open my eyes every morning. Some of the things that I went through . . . like when I broke my back and I wasn't expected to walk again . . . going back even further as a kid I had a horrible infection in my ear and they had to operate on my ear. I had another operation below my left shoulder when I was a kid, and I made it through that one. I was in five rollovers and two head-on collisions. So the fact that I am still here makes me feel extremely grateful, and I'm also grateful and happy for the gift that Creator gave to me. I feel that He gave me a lot of gifts, and probably the greatest gift he gave me was a quick mind. Because of my quick mind I'm able to do a lot of things that I want to do; I'm able to get a lot of things that I want to have; I'm able to accomplish a lot of things, so that's what makes me very happy. Basically, I feel like the Creator blessed me in many ways and continues to bless me. One example is, my grandchildren; I love my grandchildren beyond words, and they love me too. I just love spending time with them. They bring me a lot of happiness.

As far as BCATS, Fort Totten did not have a high school when I graduated from grade school so I went to BCATS. I had two sisters who went to Maddock and they both graduated from Maddock. When it came time for me to go to high school, I didn't want to go to a [regular] Indian boarding school, so I went to BCATS. I had family and relatives who went to Flandreau, to Marty, and you know all those Indian boarding schools, and even though they told stories about how good those schools were, I didn't want to leave home for a year. I'm glad I went to BCATS; some of the happiest days of my life were there.

They were carefree times because we were still in a log cabin when I went to school at Maddock. I would get on the bus from a log cabin that didn't have no electricity, no running water, nothing like that, and thirty minutes later I would be in a dorm that had all that, so . . . and they fed us supper. At home, I can't say we starved, but at times we hardly had enough to eat—going to a place that had all the luxuries, and three meals a day, was what made this little Indian boy pretty happy.

School was just a place to raise hell and have fun. I barely graduated; I always had D's and F's and C's. But, that was one of the happiest times of my life. On the other hand, there was a lot of racism there, too, and it negatively impacted me then and I think it still impacts me to this day. I learned that people didn't like me because of the color of my skin. I learned that even being nice to people, they still looked at you like you're a piece of shit. So, I began to develop hatred towards white people that I carried with me for a lot of years. And an incredible inferior complex, too, that I struggled with for many years because, you know, the white people, geez, they had nice clothes, and some of the kids had cars, and here I was just a little Indian boy from a log cabin with barely enough clothes to last a week. I really never learned anything as far as becoming mature, as far as learning things I should do later on in life. I was just there just to have fun you know, within the rules, without getting kicked out. But on the other hand, I did make some acquaintances at that school with some white people that are still in place to this day. Some of them are my Facebook friends. So, you know, that, in a sense, BCATS really added to my going down the wrong road after, because high school is supposed to get you ready for adulthood, and BCATS did just the opposite; it just didn't help me in any way at all. But it was a good time, I had, you know, my friends were there; there was girls, sports.

When I left BCATS, I was lost for many years until I sobered up and got back on the right track. And how I sobered up—I began to realize that, you know, I figured myself smarter than most people, so I think of some-body my age who was dumb as a rock, but yet they had a car and they had a house and everything, well, I had nothing. I'm smart enough to realize that it was the alcohol. I remember one particular morning I woke up with a hangover and Mom's words [about my potential for success] came back to me . . . [and] a few days later I got in touch with the veteran's in-service officer, and a few months later I went off to treatment at the VA and I have not touched a drop of alcohol ever since.

I mentioned earlier that Mom taught me right from wrong. Mom taught me all the values that I have today. Everything that I accomplished, ev-erything that I did was because of her. My biggest regret was that I didn't graduate with a college degree before she unfortunately passed away. On the other hand, she knew I was going to graduate; she was really proud of me, and I knew that I made her happy because I turned my life around. One night I came back from shooting pool and I jumped in the shower, and a dreadful feeling came over me, one of extreme loneliness. I showered, and I just couldn't shake that awful loneliness I felt. I went and checked on my kids, my daughter, and my sons, and they were all doing well. When I went and lay down to sleep, I just couldn't get rid of that lonely feeling. I went to sleep, and at five o'clock in the morning the phone rang, and when it rang, I knew what happened. It was my sister telling me that Mom passed away. As we were talking, she told the time when Mom passed away, and that was the time I was getting in the shower, when I started feeling that loneliness, and I felt her spirit leave, or she stopped to say goodbye before she left, and that's what made me so lonely. Her leaving was a big blow to me; it devastated me. It was several months before I could "get over it" so to speak. Mom was such a strong woman I never once thought about her dying. So, like I said, everything that I am today is because of her.

After a life of extreme highs and lows, one adventure after another, overcoming challenges, surviving horrible mistakes and bad decisions, I feel pretty really good right now. I was blessed with a good mother who taught me right from wrong; I believe I was blessed with the ability to think and think fast when needed, and a strong sense of self-honesty. Because of those qualities I am able to accept whatever comes my way. My biggest challenge right now is living with my cancer. Although, having lived with it for almost ten years, it doesn't scare me as much as it did before when they first told me I only had five years to live.

The main [reason] for the happiness in my life right now is due to meeting my current wife about a year ago, having a whirlwind romance, and the wedding of the century. She brings a lot of happiness into my life. In fact, we were just talking about it and I was telling her that being with her changed my way of thinking. You know, I'm no longer worried. I'm no longer scared of my cancer. I'm no longer worried about getting old. There's a lot of things I'm no longer worried about simply because I'm with her. I have a good life: I can shoot pool with the best young ones yet, I do a lot of traveling, many people respect me, I have great grandkids, an awesome wife . . . what more could this old Indian ask for?

PART III:

The elders told us we would not be free from this trauma unless we could forgive the unforgivable.

— Don Coyhis, Founder and CEO, White Bison Center for the Wellbriety Movement

Picking strawberries at Chemawa, OR. *National Archives and Records Administration.*

Boys in uniform at the entrance to Indian Training School, Chemawa, OR. *Oregon State Library.*

Author's grandfather Benjamin Lajimodiere and his sister Martha, Fort Totten, 1898. *Author files.*

MY HEALING JOURNEY

Sitting in a musty room at the Pacific Alaska Region National Archives in Seattle, Washington, I opened a file and held my father's Chemawa Indian Boarding School report cards and letters from home in my hands, and wept.[47] Carrying my request, the archivist had disappeared behind a closed door, returned, and gently laid a thin, gray, government file in front of me on the heavy oak table. It had been a year-long journey to find his school records, a journey that led from my home on the Turtle Mountain Indian Reservation in North Dakota, to Chemawa, Oregon. A journey that involved Don Coyhis and his White Bison *Journey for Forgiveness*, and my involvement in the National Boarding School Healing Project as an interviewer of boarding school survivors living in the northern plains states. This essay weaves the history of American Indian boarding schools into the story of my father's experiences at Chemawa Industrial boarding school.[48]

Historical Trauma

In researching boarding schools, I came across terms I had not heard of before, terms such as historical trauma, intergenerational trauma, collective trauma, multigenerational trauma, and unresolved grieving. Historical trauma—the term used most often by scholars of American Indian trauma—is conceptualized as a collective complex trauma inflicted on a group of people who have a specific group identity or ethnicity, nationality, or religious affiliation. It is the legacy of numerous traumatic events a community experiences over generations and encompasses the psychological and social responses to such events.[49] Scholars have suggested that the effects

[47] The Pacific Alaska Region National Archives is located in Seattle, Washington. For more information, see http://www.archives.gov/pacific-alaska/seattle.
[48] "My Healing Journey," revised and updated for publication in *Stringing Rosaries*, was first published in *Wicazo Sa Review* 27, no. 2: 5-19, University of Minnesota Press.
[49] Brave Heart, "Gender Differences in the Historical Trauma Response among the Lakota," *Journal of Health and Social Policy* 10 no. 4 (1999): 1–21; Brave Heart, "Oyate Ptayela: Rebuilding the Lakota Nation through Addressing Historical Trauma among Lakota Parents," *Journal of Human Behavior in the Social Environment* 2, nos. 1–2 (1999): 109–26; Brave Heart, "Wakiksuyapi: Carrying the Historical Trauma of the Lakota," *Tulane Studies in Social Welfare*, 21–22 (2000): 245–66; Brave Heart and DeBruyn, "The American Indian Holocaust"; Brave Heart, "The Return to the Sacred Path."

of these historically traumatic events are transmitted intergenerationally as descendants continue to identify emotionally with ancestral suffering.[50]

When I read that unresolved grieving is mourning that has not been completed and the ensuing depressions are absorbed by children from birth on, I felt like I had been punched in the gut.[51] Years ago, I had come across the term, "Adult Child of an Alcoholic," and was shocked to realize that it defined me. Once again, upon hearing the terms and seeing the definitions of intergenerational trauma and unresolved grieving, I thought, my God, that is me; it is my family, my brother, my sister, aunts, uncles, grandparents. Scholars have characterized this collective trauma as the soul wound.[52] The damage from boarding school abuse, loneliness, lack of affection, and subpar parenting is seen as a major factor in ills that trouble tribes today.[53]

One day, about a year before he died, I brought the documentary *In the White Man's Image* for my father to watch.[54] The video spoke of the government's attempt to stamp out American Indian culture, language, tradition, stories, and ceremonies. It reviewed the background of Captain Richard Pratt and detailed his educational experiment designed to transform the Indian into the white man's image. Pratt's first school, Carlisle, Pennsylvania, was profiled, and the second school, Chemawa, near Salem, Oregon, where my father was sent, was also mentioned.[55] The video documented the use of whistles, bells, bugles, military style punishment and daily regimen, the building of guardhouses on school campuses, kids dying of homesickness, disease, and poor nutrition. The narrator said that boarding schools left a legacy of confused and lonely children.

Following the video, and after a long silence, with head in hands, he said softly, "So that's what the God damn hell they were trying to do to us." The power and impact of his words slammed into me and I sat trem-

[50] Wesley-Esquimaux and Smolewski, "Historic Trauma and Aboriginal Healing; Duran, et al., "Healing the American Soul Wound."
[51] Brave Heart and DeBruyn, "The American Indian Holocaust." See also: Brave Heart, "Oyate Ptayela.
[52] For more on soul wound see Eduardo Duran, *Healing the Soul Wound: Counseling with American Indians and Other Native Peoples* (New York: Teacher College Press, 2006); Duran, et al., "Healing the American Indian Soul Wound"; [Smith, 2007]
[53] Duran, et al., "Healing the American Indian Soul Wound." See also Smith, *Soul Wound*; Marie-Anik Gagne, "The Role of Dependency and Colonialism in Generation Trauma in First Nations Citizens: The James Bay Cree," in *International Handbook of Multigenerational Legacies of Trauma*, ed. Yael Danieli (New York: Plenum Press, 1998), pp. 355–72.
[54] *American Experience*: "In the White Man's Image," TV series documentary, 1988.
[55] See Patrick Michael McKeehan, "The History of Chemawa Indian School" (PhD diss., University of Washington, Seattle, 1981); Burton C. Lemmon, "The Historical Development of the Chemawa Indian School" (master's thesis, Oregon State College, Corvallis, 1941); James Alan Smith, "To Assimilate the Children: The Boarding School at Chemawa, Oregon, 1880–1930" (master's thesis, Central Washington University, Ellensburg, 1993); Cynthia Straughan, "Indian Education and Acculturation: The Forest Grove Industrial Training School, 1880–1885" (honors thesis, Pacific University, Forest Grove, 1991). Also SuAnn M. Reddick, "Chemawa Indian Boarding School: The First Chapter," a paper read at the Pacific Northwest History Conference in April 1996.

bling, fighting back tears, unable to say a word, unable to comfort. He had never learned, throughout his entire life, about the government's assimilation policy, why he was stolen, why his hair was shaved off, why he was beaten for speaking Cree and had Christianity forced on him. This was his soul wound.

Now I understand that my father suffered all of his life from undiagnosed post-traumatic stress disorder, both from his days at Chemawa Industrial School and the horrors he saw fighting the Japanese in the Aleutians during World War II. My brother, sister, and I are the first generation of survivors of boarding school horrors and human rights abuses. We've all struggled with emotional or drug and alcohol issues and so have our children. We are trying to break the cycle with our grandchildren. I am only now grieving the unresolved trauma that my parents and grandparents went through. I also have a deeper understanding of why my parents and grandparents parented in the manner that they did. Their only parenting model was the strict military-style corporal punishment they experienced at boarding school, combined with a total lack of love and caring experience there, along with the absolute forbiddance of tribal cultural traditions.

My Father's Story

The Turtle Mountain Band of Pembina Chippewa resides on a seventy-two-square-mile reservation located in north-central North Dakota, a few miles south of the Canadian border.[56] It is a tribe made up of Chippewa and Metis.[57] The Metis are a nation made of Cree, Chippewa, and French mix-bloods.[58] On my father's side is a relative, Louis Riel, whose mother was Julie Lajimodiere.[59] Riel was a Metis who led two rebellions against the Canadian government and was hung for treason in 1885. After Riel's death, my father's grandfather, along with many Metis involved in the last uprising, fled Winnipeg for the Turtle Mountains, settling there and intermarrying with my full-blood Chippewa and Cree grandmothers.

---

[56] The Turtle Mountain Band of Pembina Chippewa is a federally recognized tribe.

[57] Also Ojibwe, Ojibway, Ojibwa, Salteaux. Anishinaabe is the Chippewa language term commonly used.

[58] For more information on Metis see Gregory Camp, "The Dispossessed: The Ojibwa and Metis of Northwest North Dakota," *North Dakota History: Journal of the Northern Plains*, 67, no. 1 (2000); Jacqueline Peterson and Jennifer S. Brown, eds., *The New Peoples: Being and Becoming Metis in North America* (St. Paul: Minnesota Historical Society Press, 2001).

[59] For further information on Louis Riel, see Joseph Howard, *Strange Empire: A Narrative of the Northwest (Louis Riel and the Metis People)* (New York: William Morrow & Co., 1952); Maggie Siggins, *Riel: A Life of Revolution.* (Toronto: HarperCollins, 1994); George Stanley, Louis Riel (Toronto: McGraw-Hill. 1963).

The reservation was formed in 1892 as the result of an agreement in-
famously known as the Ten Cent Treaty in recognition of the amount ne-
gotiated per acre.[60] Chief Little Shell III refused to sign the agreement.
Starving, he left with his family and other band members to find buffalo in
Montana, eventually reaching the Bear Paw Mountains, or Rocky Boy. The
three-man McCumber Commission then handpicked a Council of 32, made
up of sixteen full-bloods and sixteen mix-bloods.[61] Facing starvation, and
under the threat of being removed to White Earth, Minnesota, this council
signed the agreement.[62]

My father, Leo Joseph Lajimodiere, was born on the prairie of southern
Saskatchewan in the summer of 1916. His parents were traveling by horse
and wagon from the Turtle Mountains to visit family. Born premature, one
of his grandmothers had to take milk from a nursing horse to feed the new-
born baby boy. When he was two years old, his mother died in the 1918 flu
epidemic, leaving him and a sister to be raised by their father. Instead, he
gave them to separate families. My father, Leo, was raised by an older full-
blood Cree couple. He was raised in a small log cabin, speaking only Cree.
In an interview I did with him before he died, he told me that a tribal Indian
agent would come by every now and then, checking for kids to send to
school. Whenever his adoptive parents would spy the agent coming down
the road, they would tell him pimbastah, run! Leo would jump out a back
window and hide in the nearby aspen and burr oak tree grove surrounded
by tall red willows until they would call to him ashtum noshishim, come
grandchild. They did not want him stolen and sent away to school. By the
time Leo was nine years old, his father had signed off at the agency to have
him sent to boarding school, and the old couple was threatened with having
government food rations denied and going to jail if they continued refusing
to give up my father.[63]

---

[60] See Keith Steven Richotte, Jr. "We the Indians of the Turtle Mountain Reservation . . . Rethinking Tribal Con-
stitutionalism beyond the Colonialist/Revolutionary Dialectic" (PhD diss., University of Minnesota, 2009). For
further information on the Turtle Mountain Band of Chippewa see John Hesketh, "History of the Turtle Mountain
Chippewa," in Collections of the State Historical Society of North Dakota, vol. 5 (Bismarck, ND: State Historical
Society of North Dakota, 1923; Stanley N. Murray, "The Turtle Mountain Chippewa, 1882–1905," North Dakota
History (Winter 1984); Verne Dusenberry, "Waiting for a Day That Never Comes," Montana: The Magazine of
Western History 8, no. 2 (1958); Les LaFountain, Orie Richard, and Scott Belgarde, "Who Am I: A Guide to Your
Turtle Mountain Home," Turtle Mountain Community College, http://www.turtle-mountain.cc.nd.us/community/
propeace/resources/WhoIAm.pdf.
[61] Ibid.
[62] Ibid.
[63] On March 3, 1891, Congress authorized the Commissioner of Indian Affairs "to make and enforce by proper
means such rules and regulations as will secure the attendance of Indian children of suitable age and health at
schools established and maintained for their benefit." Congress addressed the issue of enforcement, authorizing the
Indian Office to "withhold rations, clothing and other annuities from Indian parents or guardians who refuse or
neglect to send and keep their children of proper school age in some school a reasonable portion of each year." The
Statutes at Large of the United States of America, vol. 26, p. 1014 and vol. 27, p. 635. This policy was reaffirmed in
Education Circular no. 130, 15, January 1906, OIA.

The Final Solution to the Indian Problem

On March 3, 1819, the US Congress had passed a mandatory education act. Government officials believed that forced attendance would eventually assimilate Indians into the lower strata of society. Through education, the so-called "Indian problem" would be resolved.[64] Richard Henry Pratt, a staunch assimilationist, had been a frontier Indian fighter before becoming an educator. He liked Indians, but had no use for the culture. He never questioned his belief that civilization must triumph over what he viewed as savagism.[65] Arapaho, Cheyenne, Comanche, and Kiowa prisoners at Fort Marion became subjects in Pratt's newly devised civilization education experiment. The prisoners were introduced to reading, arithmetic, and Christianity in a classroom setting and worked part-time at odd jobs in Saint Augustine. Encouraged by his successful experiment with the prisoners in Florida, he campaigned for off-reservation boarding schools and was allowed to found a school in 1879 at the site of unused cavalry barracks at Carlisle, Pennsylvania.[66] A Civil War veteran, he organized his school along rigid, strict, and often harsh military standards. His battle cry, "Kill the Indian in him, and save the man," is well known throughout Indian country.[67] A year after Carlisle was established, Pratt's friend and fellow Civil War veteran Lt. Melville Cary Wilkinson of the US Army, traveled to Forest Grove, Oregon, to begin the second boarding school following in Pratt's rigid military formula. The school was moved south to a site close to Salem, Oregon. He named the school Chemawa.[68] He became the superintendent from July 21, 1879, to October 15, 1882. A "rabid Congregationalist" and self-described "ranting religionist," Wilkinson was well-known to the local townspeople as a religious zealot.[69] Before his Chemawa years, he was also known for his unprovoked attack on a group of Palouse Indians, comprised mostly of noncombatants, camped near Wallula, Washington. He had "seized control of a Gatling gun and unleashed a firestorm so deadly that when the shooting finally stopped men women and children lay in every direction."[70] In a bit of irony, Wilkinson was killed in a Chippewa uprising at Leech Lake, Minnesota, in 1898.

---

[64] Adams, *Education for Extinction*.

[65] For more on Pratt's policies see *Battlefield and Classroom: An Autobiography by Richard Henry Pratt*, ed. Robert Utley (Norman: University of Oklahoma Press, 1964).

[66] Sarah Kathryn Pitcher Hayes, "The Experiment at Fort Marion: Richard Henry Pratt's Recreation of Penitential Regimes at the Old Fort and Its Influence on American Indian Education, *Journal of Florida Studies* 1 (7: 2018): 1-4.

[67] See Pratt, Official Report of the Nineteenth Annual Conference of Charities and Correction, 1892, p. 46.

[68] Cary Collins, "The Broken Crucible of Assimilation: Forest Grove Indian School and the Origins of Off-Reservation Boarding School Education in the West," *Oregon Historical Quarterly* 101, no. 4 (Fall 2000).

[69] Ibid., p. 469.

[70] Ibid., p. 470.

Forced Removal

I can only imagine the terror my father experienced as he was literally torn away from a loving home and the only parents he knew. Then nine years old, speaking only Cree, and having known only the prairie and gentle hills of the Turtle Mountains with its fresh water lakes, subsistence hunting, trapping, and fishing, with no previous formal education, he was put on a train with five other terrified kids from the Turtle Mountains, one of which was his older sister, Lillian, also taken from her adoptive parents. If he spoke Cree, he said, "the white matron traveling with us would slap me, shouting something at me I had no way of understanding." Bewildered, he waited until she was asleep before he spoke with his sister.

Chemawa: "Happy Home"

After a journey of "three days and three nights" away from the northern plains, over the Rocky Mountains, and a thousand miles from home, the children stepped off the train and were escorted through a black, arched, gabled gate that proclaimed "Chemawa Industrial School."[71] Leo was immediately separated from his sister. For the next four years he was only allowed to see her intermittently, catching glimpses of her across the parade grounds. His hair was cut and deloused using kerosene, which "burned like hell." A photo I have of him, titled "The Little Boys and Their Foster Mother, Miss Semanski," shows the military style uniform that all boys were made to wear—a dark blazer, tie, knickers to the knee, long socks, and lace-up boots. He said it was made of wool and terribly scratchy. That night he was sent to a crowded dorm where he cried himself to sleep along with many other little boys, two to a bed. My father said in his interview that over the years boys would die in their sleep. When I asked how, he said, "They died of loneliness."[72]

Beginning early the next morning, a strict regimen of bells and whistles controlled his every waking moment.[73] The children were marched ev-

---

[71] Although the exact meaning of the name, Chemawa, is not too clear, it is said to come from the Chemeketa Tribe and means Happy Home. See Chemawa Indian School: A Case Study of Educational Failure. Retrieved from http://www.myspace.com/lehmanbrightman/blog/372632876. January 1, 2011. Other names attributed to the meaning of Chemawa are Our Old Home, True Talk, and Gravelly Soil. There is little on record to substantiate any of the meanings.

[72] Organic failure to thrive can be caused by psychological, social, or economic problems within a family. Separation from parent(s) is one of the risk factors. For more information, see "Failure to Thrive" http://www.lpch.org/DiseaseHealthInfo/HealthLibrary/growth/thrive.html.

[73] An observer interviewed for the *Evening Telegram* said about Chemawa, "Everything in the institution is arranged and carried on with military precision. The children . . . rise by a bell, bathe by a bell, sit down at table by a bell, go to prayer by a bell, take exercise by a bell, go to bed by a bell, and, for ought we know, snore by a bell and dream of bells." *Evening Telegram* (Portland, Oregon), August 31, 1880.

erywhere. The little boys practiced marching drills. He said he marched "carrying a small wooden gun."[74] English was beaten into Leo, who struggled for a year to learn the language. Shaking his head, he told me, "I just couldn't learn that language." He was forced to attend church, "Not a choice," he said. Following Pratt's model, the military atmosphere of schools was reinforced by a strict discipline policy; corporal punishment was incorporated along with a court of older students to maintain discipline.[75] Pratt believed in having as few rules as possible, but those that existed were rigidly enforced.[76] By 1890, the official position of the government was that corporal punishment should be resorted to "only in cases of grave violation of rules." Superintendents were permitted to inflict corporal punishment and even to imprison students in on-campus guardhouses.[77]

One day Leo told another boy that he thought the headmaster and dorm matron had a "case" for each other, meaning they liked each other. An older boy overheard and reported him. His punishment was the dreaded gauntlet. Leo was made to lie over a bed while two boys held his arms and feet. All the boys lined up behind him and were handed a leather belt embedded with studs. Each boy had to hit him across the back, buttocks, or legs as hard as they could. If one of the boys chose to hit gently, he would have had to take my father's place. His flesh torn and bleeding, my father told me he passed out from the pain and woke up in the school's infirmary. He was there for two weeks, sleeping on his stomach while his back healed. His flesh eventually healed, but the emotional scars never did. He told me about a Browning Blackfeet boy that died from the gauntlet. He said, "His kidneys had ruptured." I wonder if my father had been forced in line to hit the boy, leaving him with the horror of thinking he had helped kill him.

Students at Chemawa were responsible for campus maintenance, construction, and repairs, and raising and caring for crops and livestock. The school was not given enough funds to support their size, so students were exploited to work in the large fields, gardens, and barns, and to maintain the buildings.[78] Leo worked in the large onion field near the school. He was also assigned to carpentry, a job that he did for the rest of his life. In this

---

[74] Pratt believed by constantly marching and drilling, the clocklike, mechanical movements on the drill field would carry over to other areas of student behavior. See Adams, *Education for Extinction*.

[75] Henry Sicade, a student at Chemawa, said, "Under Captain Wilkinson the discipline was patterned after army discipline; the boys were divided into four groups with four sergeants in charge of each group. These had corporals or assistants under them. When one offended he was brought before a court martial of the disciplinarian and the four sergeants and if found guilty was given his sentence by them." Henry Sicade, quoted in Washington County News-Times (Forest Grove, OR), January 5, 1928.

[76] Carmelita Ryan, "The Carlisle Indian Industrial School" (PhD diss., Georgetown University, 1961).

[77] Annual Report Commission of Indian Affairs (ARCIA),1890, clii; Adams, *Education for Extinction*, ch. 4.

[78] Child, *Boarding School Seasons*.

manner, Pratt's vocational emphasis was successful. My father worked as a carpenter and foreman until his retirement. Although he worked as an engineer in the army and taught math for a while after the war, it was carpentry that he returned to.

The Returned

After four years, Leo and his sister were returned home. No one met them at the train station. Hitching a ride to the reservation, he stood at the front door of his birth father's house, since the old Cree couple had died while the children were at boarding school. There was no joyful reunion. His father had remarried. Leo was introduced to his new mother, a stranger. As Leo and his sister stood by the door, his father announced, "Oh! The kids are here!" His father, also a total stranger to him, told him to come and kiss his new mother. His sister complied, but Leo refused and his father struck him. He was then assigned to sleep outside in a tent.

After four years of regimented schedules, bells, marching, and now speaking only English, Leo found himself unable to fit in and was sent to Fort Totten Boarding School on the Fort Totten reservation, near Devils Lake, North Dakota.[79] Named in honor of Brevet Major-General Joseph Gilbert Totten, the brick fort was built in 1868 to protect settlers in the area from the Dakota (Sioux), and then later manned by the cavalry to protect the mail trails and the surveyor parties working on the border between the United States and Canada. Two and sometimes three companies of the 7th US Cavalry were stationed at the post, with Custer visiting from Fort Lincoln. In 1890, the last of the soldiers left the fort and it was turned over to the Bureau of Indian Affairs to be used as a boarding school until 1959.[80]

Now a national historical site, with the Pioneer Daughter's Museum and a bed and breakfast, Fort Totten also houses an ignominious cellar where boarding school students were dropped from a trap door into total darkness for discipline.[81] When I asked my father about his experiences at Fort Totten, he refused to speak at all. He had told me horror stories of his

---

[79] Now officially called Spirit Lake.
[80] The Spirit Lake Dakota People, published by friends of Fort Totten Historic Site: 2000.
[81] I was allowed by the Fort Totten Historical Society to have an escorted tour of the school places and rooms not accessible to tourists. Through my National Boarding School Healing Project interviews, I had heard of this cellar. Not one of my interviewees would accompany me to look for this room. Under the boys' dorm is a cavernous basement, not mentioned in any of the literature of the fort. When the boarding school was closed, the school came under the direction of the Fort Totten tribe. A hole had been punched through a wall made of huge stones and cement in order to put in updated water pipes. On the other side of the wall was this dark, dank room; the only possible access was a trap door. The trap door is in what would have been a headmaster's bathroom. I believe this is the cellar of which I was told. One interviewee said her father was put into the cellar for refusing to speak English. She said, "He didn't care. He sang Chippewa songs at the top of his lungs!"

war years, fighting the Japanese in the Aleutians, his beating at Chemawa, but he maintained silence on his time at Fort Totten. Elders from Fort Totten have since told me he was most likely sexually molested there, an interview question I had never thought to ask. After a short stay there he ran away, returning to Belcourt. Still unable to get along with his father and stepmother, who turned out to resent him—she threw a knife at him, and his father barely missed him with a pitchfork—he hopped a freight train in Rolla, a small town seven miles off the reservation, and headed west. Changing his name to Joe Harper, a combination of Joe DiMaggio and *Harper's Magazine*—he worked the dude ranches in Montana, breaking broncos. He joined the Civilian Conservation Corp, working in the Grand Tetons of Wyoming, and then signed up for the army after the attack at Pearl Harbor. He returned home to the reservation after the war, wounded in more ways than one.

He married my mother. Drinking became a way to numb feelings, and he became a verbally abusive and violent alcoholic, beating her and my older brother often, and whipping us girls with a belt that left welts. Mom was often the brunt of his abuse, suffering loss of hearing and requiring stitches in her scalp. While inebriated, he would often state over and over, "I just want to be a man, not a fucking Indian." I'd ask Mom what he meant, and she would only shrug. Perhaps Captain Pratt's "kill the Indian, save the man" policy?

In reflecting back on his life, I now ask myself when could he have learned parenting skills.[82] The fact is, he was deprived of a loving family and instead raised with rigid, harsh military-style discipline. He always said the army was a piece of cake after his boarding school experiences.

Chemawa Today

The old water tower can still be seen from Oregon's I-5. I turned on Indian School Road, drove past the empty guard post, and followed a shady tree-lined drive to get to the oldest operating boarding school in the United States, celebrating 130 years as a school.[83] The old white wooden buildings had long been replaced by brick. A hand-painted sign said, "Chemawa—since 1880. Home of the Braves." I parked and walked up to a large totem pole in front of the school. A plaque said, "The Indian-in-the-Moon Totem

---

[82] Initial work suggests that impacts may include impaired family communication. [Wardi 1992]; on stress around parenting, see. Brave Heart and DeBruyn, "The American Indian Holocaust."
[83] "Chemawa History," www.chemawa.bie.edu/history.html.

Pole, donated to Chemawa in memory of the lost children of Chemawa and to all the past school board members and students."

As of 2005, the school serves ninth through twelfth grades. In the late 1970s, Chemawa moved to this new campus, with most of the original buildings being destroyed.[84] I'm greeted by the school principal. We chatted for a bit about our common experiences as principals in the Bureau of Indian Affairs system. He then mentioned that the school still housed a ledger that lists students attending the school during the years my father was there. I was led upstairs to an office where the ledger sat on top a filing cabinet. A female staff member rested her hands on the ledger, looked at me, and quietly asked, what year? I said 1925 and held my breath as she opened the large ledger and began paging through the years. And then, there he was: Leo Joseph Lajimodiere, 1925, Turtle Mountain Agency, Chippewa, nine years old.[85] The moment suddenly and unexpectedly washed over me. His stories of loneliness; his beatings; hunger; laboring in the onion fields, barn, and carpentry shop; his loss of his language, culture, traditions, ceremonies, and spirituality were suddenly made all the more real, powerful, and overwhelming by seeing his name carefully typed into this boarding school ledger. I found myself sobbing in front of a stranger.

The Cemetery

I didn't ask for, nor was I offered, a tour of the campus. I was more interested in what the campus looked like when my father arrived. The original campus site is about two miles from the current school, and I was driven out to it by a maintenance worker. He pointed out that a tree farm covers the original footprint of the school. He dropped me off and promised to return in an hour. I welcomed the quiet and was glad for the sunny, warm day.

Looking out of place next to the trimmed neat rows of small fir trees was the school's cemetery, the only remaining physical evidence of the original school. Enclosed by a fence, it was unkempt and untended. Huge tall pine trees stood in sharp contrast to the neatly rowed young ones surrounding it outside the fence. Small plaques—made by students after a Bureau of Indian Affairs school maintenance worker bulldozed the original headstones—lay flat in the tall grass, some covered by a tangle of weeds

---

[84] Chemawa Indian School web site. http://www.publicschoolreview.com/school_ov/school_id/91607. Retrieved 1.20.11.

[85] Whether ethnically Cree or Metis, students enrolled in the Turtle Mountain Agency were listed as Chippewa.

and wildflowers. How many unmarked graves are there? Clear pinesap coursed down the trees' bark like bitter tears, the trees' roots tugging at the plaques.

I searched out the names of students that had died and were buried during the years my father was a student there. Had they been his friends? How did they die? Were they ill? Did he watch them being beaten? Were there funerals for these children? Assigned to carpentry, did he have to make the coffins for these children?

I walked across the narrow paved road and stood on the train tracks where my father and his sister would have arrived. An older Native man driving a beat-up car, stopped, got out, and walked up to me. I introduced myself, explaining why I was standing on the tracks. He said his father used to be the conductor for the train that brought kids to the school. He ducked his head down and said, "It was so sad; crying, screaming, scared to death, them kids." Shaking his head, he got back into his car and drove slowly away.

White Bison's Wellbriety Journey of Forgiveness

The White Bison Center for the Wellbriety Movement has offered healing resources to Native America since 1998.[86] Through its founder and president, Don Coyhis (Mohican), White Bison offers sobriety, recovery, addictions prevention, and Wellness/Wellbriety learning resources to Native American communities nationwide. During the summer of 2009, White Bison began a seven-thousand-mile healing journey, called the Journey of Forgiveness, across the United States to help raise awareness of human rights violations along with historical and intergenerational trauma caused by boarding school abuses. The journey took White Bison to twenty-four boarding school sites, where the group recorded stories of the elders who had attended the schools. The group began its journey at Chemawa, Oregon, a boarding school still currently in operation, and the second boarding school established in the United States by Wilkerson. White Bison ended the journey at Carlisle, the first boarding school established in the United States by Richard Pratt.

Coyhis and the group invited boarding school survivors to tell their stories in a safe environment, where counselors and therapists were available in another room if needed. They carried with them the Sacred Hoop

---

[86] White Bison Center for the Wellbriety Movement, http://www.whitebison.org.

of one hundred eagle feathers. Elders had placed the four gifts of Healing, Hope, Unity, and the Power to forgive the unforgivable into the hoop. In reflecting on the journey, Coyhis said:

> The stories were unbelievable. We now know that what was done to the children in these boarding schools is directly tied to the social issues we are currently experiencing in our communities. We call this Intergenerational Trauma. The elders told us we would not be free from this trauma unless we could forgive the unforgivable.[87]

I participated in a White Bison session held on the White Earth Chippewa Reservation, Minnesota, and listened to elders tell stories of abuse at a boarding school located on the reservation and at other boarding schools throughout Minnesota and North Dakota. At the end of the day, Don invited all of us there to take tobacco, sprinkle it on the hoop, and forgive. Forgive the horrors, forgive the perpetrators, and forgive the headmasters, matrons, priests, nuns. Forgive our parents, aunts, uncles, brothers, sisters. Don asked me to help dance the large hoop of one hundred eagle feathers out of the room to the sound of the drum. This was the time to forgive my father. To forgive the unforgiveable. With tears streaming, I held the hoop and felt no weight, nor the tug of the other three helping to dance it out. Perhaps my father helped carry the hoop that day.

***

The archivist rustled quietly up to where I was sitting and offered a box of tissue. She made me copies of my father's academic school records and letters from home. I then gently closed the file.

While Wilkinson and Pratt were contemporaries and viewed by themselves and others of their era as heroes and enforcers of assimilationist policies and laws, I see them as having worked the tools of ethnic cleansing. The genocidal policies these men carried out were aimed at the destruction of the essential foundations of the lives of American Indian students. Their objective was the disintegration of culture, language, spirituality, health, dignity, and even the lives of thousands of children attending Chemawa, Carlisle, and many other Indian boarding schools on and off reservations.

My father's story is just one of thousands. By 1931, 30 percent of Indian children in school were in boarding schools, and it is estimated that

---

[87] See White Bison Center for the Wellbriety Movement, "Boarding School Apology Initiative: Grassroots Strategy" at http://www.whiteboson.org.

two-thirds of Indians have attended boarding school at some point in their lives.[88] Their stories need to be told and the human rights violations documented. There are a lot more files that need to be opened.

---

[88] Adams, *Education for Extinction*.

APPENDIX A

American Indian Boarding Schools by State
Compiled by Dr. Denise Lajimodiere
Updated July 2021

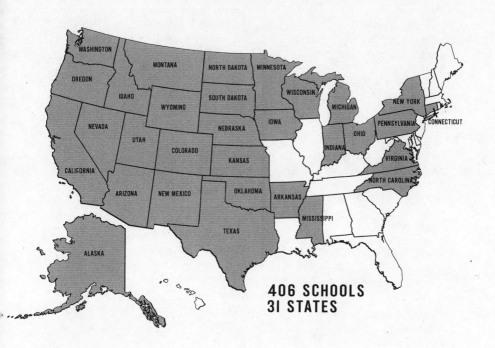

406 SCHOOLS
31 STATES

ALASKA (41)
Anchorage
Anvik Boarding School
Beltz
Bethel
Brevig Mission Orphanage
Chooutla
Cooper Valley
Covenant High School
Douglas Island Friends Mission School
Eklutna (Tyonek)
Fairbanks

Friends High School
Galena
Holy Cross
Jessee Lee
Kanakanak
Kenai Peninsula
Kodiak Aleutian Regional
Kosorefsky
Moravian Child's Home
Mount Edgecumbe
Nenana
Nenana High School

Nome High School
Nulato
Palmer
Palmer House
Pilgrim Mission
Pius Tenth Mission
Port Clarence Orphanage
Seward Sanitarium
Sheldon Jackson
Sheldon Jackson/Sitka Training School
St. Mark's Mission
St. Mary's
Victory Bible School
Wasilla
White Mountain
William E. Belt
Woody Island Mission and Orphanage
Wrangell Institute

ARIZONA (52)
Chinle
Colorado River
Crystal
Dennehotso
Dilcon Community School
Fort Apache (Theodore Roosevelt)
Fort Defiance
Fort Mojave Industrial School
Gila River St. Peter School
Greaswood Springs Community School
Greyhills Academy High School
Holbrook
Hunter's Point Indian School
Indian Mission
Jeehdeez'a Academy
Kaibeto Indian School
Keams Canyon
Kinlichee Indian School
Kingman Indian School
Leupp
Low Mountain
Lukachukai Community School
Many Farms High School
Marsh Pass
Naa Tsis'Ana Community School
Navajo
Navajo Mountain
Nażlini Community School
Phoenix

Pima
Pinon
Presbyterian Mission
Rice Station
Rocky Ridge
Rough Rock Community School
Sacaton
San Carlos
Santa Fe
Santa Rosa Ranch
Seba Dalkai
Shonto Indian School
St. Michaels Industrial
St. Johns Mission at Gila Crossing
Teec Nos Pos
Toyei
Truxton Canyon
Tuba City
Tucson Indian Training School
Western Navajo
Wide Ruins
Wide Ruins Community School
Yuma

ARKANSAS (1)
Dwight Mission

CALIFORNIA (9)
Fort Bidwell School
Fort Yuma
Greenville School
Hoopa
Round Valley Indian School
Sherman/Perris
St. Anthony
St. Boniface Industrial
St. Turibius Industrial

COLORADO (5)
Fort Lewis (now a college)
Grand Junction/Teller Institute
Holy Cross Abbey
Ignacio
Southern Ute

CONNECTICUT (1)
Foreign Mission School for Heathens,
    Cornwall

IOWA (3)
Sac & Fox
Toledo Industrial
White's Iowa Manual Labor Institute

IDAHO (6)
Fort Hall
Fort Lapwai
Lemhi
Nez Perce
Sacred Heart Convent of Mary Immalate
St. Josephs Normal

INDIANA (2)
White Manual Labor Institute
St. Joseph's

KANSAS (10)
Halstead Mennonite Mission B. School
Haskell Industrial Training School
Great Nemaha Indian School
Kaw Manual Labor School
Kickapoo
Osage Manual Labor School/ St.Francis
Potawatomi Manual Labor
Sac and Fox
Shawnee Mission Manual Labor School
Quapaw

MICHIGAN (5)
Holy Child School
Holy Name (Chippewa) Baraga
Mount Pleasant Industrial
Potawatomi
St. Joseph's Orphanage

MINNESOTA (16)
Cass/Leech Lake
Clontarf
Convent of our Lady of the Lake
Cross Lake
Graceville Convent of Our Lady
Morris Industrial
Pine Point
Pipestone
Red Lake
St. Benedict's Orphan School
St. John's Academy
St. Mary's
St. Theodore's

Vermillion Lake
White Earth
Wild Rice River

MISSISSIPPI (1)
Choctaw Central Indian School

MONTANA (16)
Bond's Mission School/Montana
   Industrial
Crow Agency
Cut Bank
Fort Shaw
Holy Family
Holy James Mission
Montana Industrial
Poplar Creek
Pryor Creek
St. Ignatius Mission
St. Labres Mission
St. Mary's
St. Paul's Mission
St. Peter's
St. Xavier's Industrial
Willow Creek

NEBRASKA (8)
Genoa Industrial
Iowa Industrial School
Omaha Indian School
Oto and Missouri Agency Industrial
Santee Industrial School
Santee Normal Training School
St. Augustine's
Winnebago

NEVADA (5)
Cason Training
Fort McDermitt
Pyramid Lake
Stewart
Western Shoshone Indian School

NEW MEXICO (26)
Albuquerque
Bernalillo
Chichiltah/Jones Ranch
Ch'ooshgai Community (Chuska)
Crownpoint Indian School
Dzilth-Na-O-Dith-Hle Community
   School

Fort Wingate Indian School
Jicarilla Apache
Lake Valley Indian School
Mescalero Apache
Navajo Prep
Nenannezed
Ojo Encino Indian School
Pine Hill
Pueblo Bonito
Pueblo Pintado Indian School
Ramona Institute
San Juan
Santa Fe
Shiprock
Southwestern Indian Polytechnic Inst.
St. Catherine Indian School
Toadlena
Tohatchi
Windgate Indian School
Zuni

NEW YORK (3)
Convent of Our Lady of Mercy
Thomas/Gowanda
Tunasassa Friends Boarding School for
    Indian Children

NORTH CAROLINA (1)
Eastern Cherokee

NORTH DAKOTA (14)
Bismarck
Edwards Mission
Fort Berthold
Fort Stevenson
Fort Totten
Grand River
Maddock Agricultural and Training
    School
Sacred Heart Mission
Seven Dolors Mission
St. Elizabeth
St. Mary (Turtle Mountain)
St. Michael's Mission
Standing Rock Agency Agricultural/
    Martin Kennel Standing Rock Indian
    Industrial School
Wahpeton Indian Agricultural (presently
    Circle of Nations)

OKLAHOMA (91)
Absentee Shawnee
Anadarko (St. Patrick's)
Arapaho Manual Labor and Boarding
    School (Concho)
Armstrong
Asbury Manual Labor School
Asbury Manual Labor School and
    Mission
Ayanabbe
Bacone College
Bloomfield Academy (renamed Carter
    in 1932)
Bloomfield Academy for Girls
Burney Institute
Cantonment Mission School
Cashe Creek Mission
Cherokee Female Seminary
Cherokee Indian Orphan School
Cherokee Male Seminary
Cheyenne Manual Labor and Boarding
    School
Chickasaw Manual Labor Academy for
    Boys
Chickasaw Orphan Home and Manual
    Labor School
Chilocco Indian Agricultural School
Chuala Female Seminary
Collins (Colbert) Institute
Coweta Mission
Darlington Mennonite Mission
Dwight Mission
El Meta Bond College
Emahaka Mission School for Girls
Euchee
Eufaula
Folsom Training School
Fort Coffee Academy for Boys
Fort Sill
Goodland Academy
Hillside Mission
Hominy Creek (St. John's)
Iowa Mission
Jones Male Academy (became co-ed
    in 1955, 1952 BIA, 1988 tribally
    controlled)
Kaw
Koonaha (Suesha)
Lone Wolf

Mekusukey
Mennonite Boarding
Methodist Episcopal Mission
Murray State School of Agriculture
(Murray State College)
Murrow Indian Orphanage
Nazareth (or College) Institute
Norwalk Academy for Boys
Nuyaka Mission
Nuyaka School and Orphanage
Oak Ridge Manual Labor School
Oklahoma Presbyterian College for Girls
Old Goodland Indian Orphanage
(Academy)
Osage Indian Manual Labor Boarding
School
Otoe
Pawhuska
Pawnee Industrial Boarding School
Ponca
Quapaw
Rainy Mountain
Red Moon
Riverside (Wichita School)
Sac & Fox
Sacred Heart New Hope
Sasakwa Female Academy
Seger
Seneca: Shawnee, Seneca, Shawnee
and Wyandotte Industrial Boarding
School; and Seneca
Boarding School; Wyandotte Mission
Sequoyah High School
Shawnee
Spencer Academy
St. Agnes
St. Agnes Academy
St. Benedict's Industrial School
St. Elizabeth School
St. John
St. Josephs School
St. Louis
St. Mary's
St. Mary's Academy School for Girls
St. Mary's School
Sulphur Springs School
Tulahassee Manual Labor Boarding
School

Tuskahoma Female Academy/ Choctaw
Female Academy
Wapanucka Academy for Girls (Allen
Academy)
Washita
Wealaka Mission (replaced Tulahassee)
Wetumka Mission (Levering)
Wewoka Mission Boarding School for
Girls
Wheelock Mission and Wheelock
Female Seminaries
Wichita Baptist
Yellow Springs School

OHIO (1)
Shawnee Friends Mission and School

OREGON (10)
Chemawa Industrial/Forest Grove
Grand Ronde
Kate Drexel or St. Andrews Industrial
School
Klamath (at the Agency)
Klamath Indian School for Boys
Siletz
Simnasho
Umatilla
Warm Springs
Yainax Indian Boarding School for Girls

PENNSYLVANIA (8)
Carlisle
Girl's Home of the Lincoln Institution/
Boy's Home
Holy Providence School for Indians and
Colored People
Lincoln Institute
Martinsburg
Ponemah/King of Prussia
St. Francis
West Philadelphia Industrial Boarding
School

SOUTH DAKOTA (24)
Brainard
Chamberlain (St. Joseph's)
Cheyenne River
Flandreau/Riggs Institute
Good Will Mission
Grace

Holy Rosary Mission/Red Cloud Indian
  School
Hope/Springfield
Lower Brule (St. Joseph's)
Marty (St. Paul's)
Oahe
Oglala Indian School
Our Lady of Lourdes
Pierre Indian Industrial School
Pine Ridge
Rapid City Indian City
Rosebud Sioux Indian School (St.
  Francis)
Sisseton Sioux Indian School
St. Elizabeth's
St. John's School for Girls
St. Mary's School for Girls
St. Stephan Immaculate Conception
Tekakwitha Indian Mission (orphanage)
Yankton Reservation Industrial Boarding
  School

TEXAS (1)
St. Margaret's Orphanage

UTAH (4)
Aneth
Intermountain
Ouray
Uintah

VIRGINIA (1)
Hampton University

WASHINGTON (22)
Chehallis
Colville Mission School
Cushman
Fort Simcoe
Fort Spokane Indian School
Makah

Male and Female Industrial School
Neah Bay
Nooksack
Okonagon
Puyallup
Quinault
Sacred Heart Convent
Sacred Heart Convent Academy
S'Kokomish
St. George's Mission
St. Francis Regis Mission
St. Mary
Stickney
Tonasket
Tulalip
Yakima

WISCONSIN (15)
Bad River (Odanah)
Good Shepard Industrial School
Hayward
Holy Family (Bayfield)
Keshena/Menominee
Lac Courte Oreille
Lac de Flambeau
Menominee
Oneida
St. Joseph's Industrial School
St. Mary's
Tomah
Weillsville Indian School
Winnebago
Wittenberg

WYOMING (4)
Fort Washakie/Wind River Robert's
Episcopal Mission for Shoshone Girls
St. Stephen's Mission Industrial School
Hayward Indian School

Since *Stringing Rosaries* was first published in 2019, more than fifty additional schools have been located and are now included in this list of American Indian Boarding Schools by State. Several entries on the first list, thought to be boarding schools, have since been deleted from the previously published list. Still, this updated list of boarding schools is not yet complete.

As an outside, international observer to Canada's Truth and Reconciliation process held in Whitehorse, Yukon, in 2013, I was asked by one of the commissioners how many boarding schools the United States had. Canada knew exactly how many they had. I sat silent for a long moment. I said, "I don't know." I realized, at that moment, no one had ever asked the US government, the Bureau of Indian Affairs, or churches how many schools they ran. Since that meeting, I have been on a mission to answer that question.

The National Native American Boarding School Healing Coalition has asked the BIA with no response. A Quaker researcher made available her findings of Quaker-run schools. I spent one week at Marquette University archives patiently culling through thirty-five sets of dusty files searching for boarding schools. Did I find them all? I doubt it. I am still searching other Christian denominations.

The research for US boarding schools is tedious, frustrating, painstaking, time-consuming. I would locate a document that would mention other boarding schools in the state or elsewhere, and I would be off spending hours and days searching for them. Government documents such as superintendents' school reports from the late 1800s were a gold mine, but also difficult to read with tired eyes. I would read long stories or news articles about a town or village before it mentioned a boarding school. People would mention a boarding school on Facebook or Twitter and I would search for more information. I saw boarding schools listed in photo captions, etc. Most records are scattered across jurisdictions, from the bowels of university archives to government offices, church archives, museums, historical societies, and personal collections, not to mention records that are lost or destroyed over the years, many to fires.

Once, my grandkids went dumpster-diving after a one-hundred-year-old neighbor died and her family tossed possessions into a huge dumpster. They found a scrapbook from the 1930s mentioning a boarding school the lady, as a Lutheran church member, had worked at in Wisconsin. I added that location to the list.

Adding to the difficulty of finding schools is the different names they went by such as Training, Industrial, Institute, Boarding, Agency, Mission, Indian school, Farm, Normal, Seminary. I have chosen to include orphanages. Some schools listed as orphanages, such as Tekakwitha in Sisseton, South Dakota, were indeed, boarding schools.

Schools also changed names during the course of their existence, causing me to list the same school twice unless diligent in my research. Some schools were listed under an agency, others were listed as "Agency school," adding more confusion.

Is the list complete? No. Is the research perfectly accurate? No. I appreciate any and all comments on the list.

I would like to acknowledge that the National Native American Boarding School Healing Coalition invited researchers to add to this list. I would like to thank Jaime Arsenault-Cote and Gezik Lajimodiere for their invaluable help researching these schools.

APPENDIX B

American Indian Boarding School Interview Protocol
Developed by the Boarding School Healing Project
Revised by Dr. Denise Lajimodiere, North Dakota State University

Interview suggestions:

– Introduce yourself. Tell why you want to interview them.
– Follow traditions of your tribe in requesting information from an elder. Offer tobacco, gifts, or whatever is your tribal tradition.
– Whether you interview a family member or community member, it is strongly recommended that a counselor or therapist be available to the survivor. As memories become unstuffed they can trigger powerful and overwhelming emotions.
– Show your recording device. Do a practice recording and play back so they can hear themselves. Wait until interviewee is comfortable before beginning the recording. Have available water, tea, coffee, snacks, fruit, sandwiches, being aware of possible diabetes issues.
– At beginning of taping, ask interviewee for permission to tape/video record session(s).
– Take notes while (s)he is speaking so as not to interrupt, then return to any further questions you may have on the subject. Let him/her do majority of speaking; you should speak very little other than asking, or clarifying, questions. Questions are not in lock step order, let the interviewee go in any direction they want. You can always bring them back to the question(s) later in interview.
– Allow several days or more for an elder as they may tire easily.
– Transcribe the interview and give a copy to interviewee allowing them to add or delete whatever they want. Give a copy of final transcribed interview to your interviewee. Some interviewees may not want to receive a copy of the interview, not wanting other family members to know what their boarding school experiences were. This is common.
– If you know you may want to use the interview for publication purposes, get written permission from the interviewee. Ask if they wish to remain anonymous; if so, assign a pseudonym.

- Listening to stories of survivor trauma, physical and sexual abuse can also result in secondary trauma for you the interviewer. Take appropriate steps to take care of yourself.
- Most important! Check in on your interviewee in the weeks following your interview.
- Please read through entire protocol before proceeding, you may wish to rearrange questions to suit your interviewee.

Part One: Demographics

Name_____

Age_____

Sex_____

Tribe_____

Mother's Tribe_____ Father's Tribe_____

Marital Status: Married__ Divorced__ Widowed__ Never Married__

Living: w/partner__ Single__ Single but in committed relationship__

Number of siblings_____ Living_____ Deceased_____

Number of children_____ Living_____ Deceased_____

Years of education_____

Schools attended_____

Employment: Fulltime__ Part-time__ Seasonal__ Unemployed__

Type of work_____

Parents' jobs_____

Part Two: Condensed Life History

- Where were you born?
- Did you move around a lot? If yes, can you tell about that?
- Are your parents alive? If no, how old were you when they died?
- Educational level of parents?
- Did your parents attend boarding school? Where? How long? Aunts or Uncles?
- Grandparents? Other relatives?
- Were you raised by your parents?
- If not, who? If in foster care, how long and how many placements?
- Did your family struggle financially when you were young?
- Was this hard on you? How was this difficult?
- Tell about your life when you were little – before age six or before BS
- Describe a happy time? Sad time?

Alcohol/Drugs
- Did you drink or do drugs while in Boarding school?
- If yes, how old were you when you started?
- How long?
- How did you get the booze or drugs?
- Do you remember why you did drugs/alcohol?
- Did your caretakers drink/drug?
- If yes, do you think this affected you? How?
- Do you drink or drug now?
- If yes, do you think your substance abuse is related to your experiences in BS? Can you tell more about this?
- If no, how long have you been sober/clean?

- Have you ever been in jail or prison? If yes, how many times, how long, and what for.
- Do you feel close to your relatives? Close to brothers and sisters?
- If no, why not?
- Have you lived your life on the reservation? If no, tell about when you left and why.
- Tell about your husband/wife/significant other/partner
- How long have you been together? How did you meet?
- Are you satisfied, somewhat satisfied, or dissatisfied w/ your current relationship?
- Tell about your children. How old were you when your first child was born?
- Are any deceased?
- Did they go to boarding school? Why or why not?
- Do you have any grandchildren?
- Do you want them to go to boarding school? Why or why not?
- Did you raise other relatives or children?
- Tell about the jobs you had.
- What one(s) did you especially like? Dislike? Why?
- Do you feel connected to your community? Why or why not?
- Do you participate in community doings? Probe why they do or don't
- What do like best about your family? Reservation?
- What would you like to change about your family? Reservation?

Boarding School Experiences
- Which boarding school(s) did you attend?
- Who ran your boarding school? The BIA? A church? Which church?
- Did you graduate from BS? Why or why not?
- How old were you when you first went to BS?
- Which of your brothers and sisters attended boarding school with you?
- Where did your family live while you were in boarding school? How far from home was your boarding school?
- How often did you go home during your time at boarding school? Did your parents ever come to visit you at school?
- How did your parents feel about you attending boarding school?
- Why did your parents send you to boarding school?
- Tell about your life when you were school-age
- How many years did you go to BS?
- Do you remember your first impression of the school?
- Describe what the BS looked like.
- Was there a fence around it? Did you feel confined? Could you freely go beyond the border of the BS? If no, why not?
- What was your daily routine like? What time did you get up in the morning? What did you eat at mealtimes? How long were in class during the day? What did you do in your free time?
- How old were you when you first arrived at BS?
- Do you remember being sad? Crying a lot?
- Did other kids cry?
- Did you have brothers and sisters there? Other relatives?
- Were you allowed to be with them much? If no, why not?
- Did you miss your family?
- How do you think this separation affected you?
- Did your family visit you? If yes, how often. If no, why not?
- Did you ever run away from the BS or think about running away?
- Did you have to go back to BS?
- Did you go home for the summer?
- Where did your family live while you were in boarding school? How far from home was your boarding school?
- What did you enjoy most about boarding school? What did you enjoy least about boarding school?
- Do you have any funny stories about your time at boarding school?
- Did you rebel against the matrons, head master, teachers, nuns or priests?

Physical Conditions
- Did you wear uniforms? If yes, what did they look like? If no, what did you wear?
- FEMALES: were you allowed to wear makeup? Jewelry? If no, why not?
- Was the food good?
- Did you get enough to eat? Did you ever feel hungry?
- Did you ever steal food? If yes, did you get caught? What happened?
- Did you have chores or a job at the BS? What chores/jobs did you do?
- Did you get paid or compensated for the work?
- Were you a part of the Outing program. Tell more about that.
- Did you take care of the younger kids?
- Do you ever remember being sick while at BS? If yes, what medicine did you take?
- Who gave you the medicine?
- Were the kids sick a lot at BS?
- Tell about the sleeping arrangements
- Do you ever remember anyone wetting the bed? What happened when this occurred?
- What did you do for fun? Did you play games? See movies? Go to town?
- Did you have good friends? If no, why not? Are you in contact with them now?

What Was Learned in School
- What was your favorite and least favorite subject in BS? Why?
- Who was your favorite teacher(s)/staff and least favorite teacher(s)/staff? Why?
- Did you go to public school as well as BS? If yes, how did the curriculum compare to BS?
- Was it harder? Easier? Did you feel behind in public school?
- Did what you learned at BS prepare you for work? Why or why not?

Loss of Native Language and Culture
- Did you speak your Native language as a child? Did your parents/caretakers? Other relatives?
- Were you forbidden to talk Indian at the BS? If yes, were you punished?
- How did this make you feel? Sad? Angry?

- Were you rewarded for talking English? How were you rewarded?
- Did students hide and talk Indian together?
- Were they ever caught? Were they punished? How?
- Did you feel that BS took something away from you? For example: your tribal culture, ceremonies, song, dance, learning traditional ways, individuality, and time with relatives,

Child Labor
- What chores did you do at BS? Like or dislike any chores?
- Did you get paid? How much? If no, why not?
- How often did you do these chores?
- Did you have any day(s) off from the chores?
- How old were you when you started the chores?
- Did the chores change as you got older?
- Did you often feel tired because of the work? Did this affect your school work?

Loss of Self-Respect, Self-Confidence, and Self-Esteem
- Looking back after all these years, how do you think that time in boarding school affected you? Have you experienced any personal problems that you link back to your time in boarding school? Can you elaborate?
- Do you think your experiences at BS affect how you parent your kids?
- Do you think it has affected your relationship with your parents? With your children?
- With your brothers and sisters? With your community?
- Do you think it has affected how you feel about yourself? Can you elaborate?
- Did the teachers or staff ever make you feel dumb? If yes, how?
- Describe a time when you felt ashamed of being Indian?
- What did you do to survive your experiences in BS?

Church
- Did you have to go to church? How many times a week or day?
- What happened if you did not go?
- Did you go to Sunday school or have Religious Studies classes?
- Did you like it? Dislike it?

Physical and Mental Abuse
- Do any of the teachers/staff stand out in your memory as being especially good or bad? Why?
- Did you ever witness teachers or staff mistreating the students?
- What kinds of things happened? For example, did any teachers/staff ever slip, hit, or push them? How often did this happen?
- Were there certain teachers or staff members who routinely mistreated students in these ways? Do you remember who they were?
- Were you ever mistreated? Did you remember who did this to you?
- How were students punished for misbehavior at your school? What effects did these punishments have on the students? On you?
- Were children ever physically punished in front of others?
- What kind of discipline did they use with the kids?
- When you were lonely or afraid, who comforted you? Did any of the teacher or staff comfort you?
- Did others kids beat you up?
- Did you beat up other kids? Why do you think you did this?

Sexual Abuse (Proceed very respectfully here).
- I know these things can be hard to talk about, but it's important for our communities to know about these things so we can better recover from them.
- Many priests and others are now being accused of sexual abuse. Did this ever happen to you or your friends in BS?
- If yes, how long did it last? Days, weeks, months, years?
- Do you remember who did this to you or your friends?
- Did you ever hear of other kids who were sexually abused? Can you talk about this?
- Who knew that these bad things had happened to you or your friends? At the time, who did you tell about these bad experiences? Did you ever tell your parents or teachers about these bad things? What did they do about it? How did you and your friends try to avoid such bad experiences?
- Who have you told about these experiences since you were grown? Have you told these things to a counselor, medicine person, healer, or therapist? Why or why not? Have you told these things to family members? Why or why not?
- Were any complaints every made? If yes, to who? What happened? What was the outcome?
- Did some students sexually abuse other students?

Health
- If you had to rate your overall physical health, would you say that you are in: very good healthy, good health, poor health or very poor health. Can you tell about that?
- Are there any factors that stand out that you think have contributed to your good and/or poor physical health?
- What about your mental health? Can you elaborate?
- What about your spiritual health? Can you elaborate?
- Do you have any ongoing health (physical, mental, or spiritual) that are attributed to your experiences at BS? Can you talk about that?
- As you think about your life, can you tell me about an experience that made you especially happy? Especially unhappy?
- What makes you happy at the age you are now? Sad? Can you elaborate?

Going Back Home
- Did you feel comfortable or uncomfortable once you were back home? Can you elaborate?
- Did you feel out of touch with your family? With your reservation?
- Did you feel that your parents abandoned you?
- If you experienced maltreatment in any form in BS did you react in any aggressive way once you were home? Can tell you talk about this more?
- Did you act out in any other way? For example, stealing, withdrawing from family, etc.
- Did your experiences in BS affect your relationship with your partner? Children? Other people?
- Did BS affect how you feel about White people?

Where to from Here
- For those who carry hurts from BS, what do you think is needed to help them heal?
- What would help you heal?
- What would help heal your reservation?
- Would you like counseling?
- What would you like to see happen?

End of Interview
- Thank participant and ask if they want to talk more (debrief—recorder off) or see a counselor, psychologist, priest, or spiritual leader.
- Remember, check on your family member often throughout the coming weeks as these memories may trigger other traumatic memories.

BIBLIOGRAPHY

Print Resources and Paper Presentations

Adams, David W. *Education for Extinction: American Indians and the Boarding School Experience, 1875–1928.* Lawrence: University Press of Kansas, 1995.

Archuleta, Margaret, Brenda Child, and Tsianina Lomawaima, eds. *Away from Home: American Indian Boarding School Experiences, 1879–2000.* Phoenix: Heard Museum, 2000.

Beiser, Morton. "Editorial: A Hazard to Mental Health: Indian Boarding School. *American Journal of Psychiatry* 131, no. 3 (1974): 305–306.

Brave Heart, Maria Yellow Horse. "Gender Differences in the Historical Trauma Response among the Lakota." *Journal of Health and Social Policy* 10, no. 4 (1999): 1–21.

_____. "The Historical Trauma Response among Natives and its Relationship with Substance Abuse: A Lakota illustration." In *Healing and Mental Health for Native Americans: Speaking in Red*, edited by E. Nebelkopf and M. Phillips. Walnut Creek, CA: Alta Mira Press, 2004.

_____. "Oyate Ptayela: Rebuilding the Lakota Nation through Addressing Historical Trauma among Lakota Parents." *Journal of Human Behavior in the Social Environment* 2, nos. 1–2 (1999): 109–26.

_____. "The Return to the Sacred Path: Healing the Historical Trauma Response among the Lakota." *Smith College Studies in Social Work* 68, no. 3 (1998): 287–305.

_____. "Wakiksuyapi: Carrying the Historical Trauma of the Lakota." *Tulane Studies in Social Welfare* 21–22 (2000): 245–66.

Brave Heart, Maria Yellow Horse and Lemyra M. DeBruyn. "The American Indian Holocaust: Healing Historical Unresolved Grief. *National Center for American Indian and Alaska Native Research* 8, no. 2 (1998): 56–78.

Brave Heart, Maria Yellow Horse, Josephine Chase, Jennifer Elkins, and Deborah B. Altschul. "Historical Trauma among Indigenous Peoples of the Americas: Concepts, Research, and Clinical Considerations." *Journal of Psychoactive Drugs* 43, no. 4 (2011): 282–90.

Camp, Gregory "The Dispossessed: The Ojibwa and Metis of Northwest North Dakota." *North Dakota History: Journal of the Northern Plains* 67, no. 1 (2000).

Child, Brenda. *Boarding School Seasons: American Indian Families, 1900–1940.* Lincoln: University of Nebraska Press, 2000.

Child, Brenda. "Runaway Boys, Resistant Girls: Rebellion at Flandreau and Haskell, 1900–1940." *Journal of American Indian Education* 35, no. 3 (1996): 49–57.

Coleman, Michael C. *American Indian Children at School, 1850–1930.* Jackson: University Press of Mississippi, 1994.

Collins, Gary. "The Broken Crucible of Assimilation: Forest Grove Indian School and the Origins of Off–Reservation Boarding School Education in the West." *Oregon Historical Quarterly* 101, no. 4 (Fall 2000).

Colmant, S., L. Schultz, R. Robbins, P. Ciali, J. Dorton, and Y. Rivera-Colmant. "Constructing Meaning to the Indian Boarding School Experience." *Journal of American Indian Education* 4, no. 3 (2004): 22–40.

Cooper, Michael. *Indian school: Teaching the White Man's Way.* New York: Clarion Books, 1999.

Creswell, John. W. *Research Design: Qualitative and Quantitative Approach.* Thousand Oaks: Sage Publication, 1994.

Denzin, K. Norman, and S. Yvonna Lincoln, eds. *Handbook of Qualitative Research.* Thousand Oaks: Sage Publication, 1984.

Dlugokinski, Eric and Lyn Kramer. "A System of Neglect: Indian Boarding School America." *Journal of Psychiatry* 131 (1974): 670–73.

Duran Eduardo, Bonnie Duran, Maria Yellow Horse Brave Heart, and Susan Yellow Horse–Davis. "Healing the American Soul Wound." In *International Handbook of Multigenerational Legacies of Trauma*, edited by Yael Danieli. New York: Plenum Press, 1998.

Dusenberry, Verne. "Waiting for a Day That Never Comes." *Montana:The Magazine of Western History* 8, no. 2 (1958).

Ellis, Clyde. *To Change Them Forever: Indian Education at the Rainy Mountain Boarding School, 1893–1920.* Oklahoma: University of Oklahoma Press, 1996.

Evans–Campbell, Teresa. "Historical Trauma in American Indian/Native Alaska Communities: A Multilevel Framework for Exploring Impacts on Individuals, Families, and Communities." *Journal of Interpersonal Violence* 23, no. 3 (2008): 313–38.

Favel–King, Alma. "The Treaty Right to Health. In *Royal Commission on Aboriginal Peoples*, The Path to Healing: Report of the National Round Table on Aboriginal Health and Social Issues. Ottawa: Minister of Supply and Services (1993), 120–27.

Hamley, Jeffrey. "Cultural Genocide in the Classroom: A History of the Federal Boarding School Movement in American Indian education, 1875–1920." PhD diss., Harvard University, 1994.

Hesketh, John. "History of the Turtle Mountain Chippewa." In *Collections of the State Historical Society of North Dakota* 5 (Bismarck, ND: State Historical Society of North Dakota, 1923).

Horne, Esther and Sally McBeth. *Essie's Story: The Life and Legacy of a Shoshone Teacher.* Lincoln: University of Nebraska Press, 1998.

Howard, Joseph. *Strange Empire: A Narrative of the Northwest (Louis Riel and the Metis People).* New York: William Morrow & Co., 1952.

Irwin, Marc. H. and Samuel Roll. "The Psychological Impact of Sexual Abuse of Native American Boarding School Children." *Journal of the American Academy of Psychoanalysis* 23, no. 3 (1995): 461–73.

Jacobs, Margaret D. *White Mother to a Dark Race: Settler Colonialism, Maternalism, and the Removal of Indigenous Children in the American West and Australia, 1880–1940.* Lincoln: University of Nebraska Press, 2009.

Johnston, Basil. *Indian School Days.* Toronto: Key Porter, 1988.

Lemmon, Burton C. "The Historical Development of the Chemawa Indian School." Master's thesis, Oregon State College, Corvallis, 1941.

Littlefield, Alice. "Learning to Labor: Native American Education in the United States, 1880–1930." In *The Political Economy of North American Indians*, edited by H. H. Moor. Norman: University of Oklahoma Press, 1993.

Lomawaima, K. Tsinina. "Domesticity in the Federal Indian Schools: The Power of Authority over Mind and Body. *American Ethnologist* 20, no. 2 (1993): 1–14.

_____. "Educating Native Americans." In *Handbook of Research on Multicultural Education*, edited by J. Banks, 331–47. New York: Macmillan, 1995.

_____. "Estelle Reel, Superintendent of Indian schools, 1898–1910: Politics, Curriculum and Land." *Journal of American Indian Education* 35, no. 3 (1996): 5–31.

_____. *They Called it Prairie Light: The Story of Chilocco Indian School.* Lincoln: University of Nebraska Press, 1994.

_____. "Tribal Sovereigns: Reframing Research in American Indian Education." *Harvard Educational Review* 70, no. 1 (Spring 2000): 1–21.

McBeth, Sally. *Ethnic Identity and the Boarding School Experience of West–Central Oklahoma American Indians.* Washington, DC: University Press of America, Inc., 1983.

McCabe, Glen. "The Healing Path: A Culture and Community–derived Indigenous Therapy Model." *Psychotherapy: Theory, Research, Practice, Training* 44, no. 2 (2007): 148–60.

McCormick, Roderick. "Culturally Appropriate Means and Ends of Counseling as Described by the First Nations people of British Columbia." *International Journal for the Advancement of Counselling* 18, no. 3 (1995/1996): 163–72.

McKeehan, Patrick M. "The History of Chemawa Indian School." PhD diss., University of Washington, Seattle, 1981.

Meriam, Lewis. "The Effects of Boarding Schools on Indian Family Life: 1928." In *The Destruction of American Indian Families*, edited by S. Unger. Washington, DC: University Press of America, 1983.

Mihesuah, Devon, A. *Cultivating the Rosebuds: The Education of Women at the Cherokee Female Seminary, 1851–1909.* Urbana: University of Illinois Press, 1993.

Murray, Stanley N. "The Turtle Mountain Chippewa, 1882–1905." *North Dakota History: Journal of the Northern Plains* (Winter 1984).

Noriega, J. "American Indian Education in the United States: Indoctrination for Subordination to Colonialism." In *The State of Native America: Genocide, Colonization, and Resistance*, edited by Annette Jaimes, 371–402. Boston: South End Press, 1992.

Peterson, Jacqueline and Jennifer S. Brown, eds. *The New Peoples: Being and Becoming Metis in North America.* St. Paul: Minnesota Historical Society Press, 2001.

Pratt, Richard, Official Report of the Nineteenth Annual Conference of Charities and Correction, 1892.

Regan, Paulette. *Unsettling the Settler Within: Indian Residential Schools, Truth Telling, and Reconciliation in Canada.* Vancouver: University of British Columbia Press, 2010.

Reyhner, John and Jeanne Eder. *Indian Education: A History.* Norman: University of Oklahoma Press, 2004.

Richotte, Keith S., Jr. "'We the Indians of the Turtle Mountain Reservation': Rethinking Tribal Constitutionalism beyond the Colonialist/Revolutionary Dialectic." PhD diss., George Washington University, 2009.

Riney, Scott. "Education by Hardship: Native American Boarding Schools in the U.S. and Canada." *The Oral History Review* 24, no. 2 (1997): 117–123.

Ryan, Carmelita. "The Carlisle Indian Industrial School." PhD diss., Georgetown University, Washington, DC, 1962.

Schurz, Carl. "Present Aspect of the Indian Problem." *North American Review* 258, no. 4 (1881): 45–54.

Siggins, Maggie. *Riel: A Life of Revolution.* Toronto: HarperCollins, 1994.

Smith, Andrea. *Conquest: Sexual Violence and American Indian Genocide.* Cambridge: South End Press, 2005.

Smith, James A. "To Assimilate the Children: The Boarding School at Chemawa, Oregon, 1880–1930." Master's thesis, Central Washington University, 1993.

Stanley, George. *Louis Riel.* Toronto: McGraw–Hill, 1963.

Straughan, Cynthia. "Indian Education and Acculturation: The Forest Grove Industrial Training School, 1880–1885." Honors thesis, Pacific University, Forest Grove, 1991.

Trafzer, Clifford, Jean Keller, and Lorene Sisquoc, Lorene, eds. *Boarding School Blues: Revisiting American Indian Educational Experiences.* Lincoln: University of Nebraska Press, 2006.

Trennert, Robert A. *The Phoenix Indian School: Forced Assimilation in Arizona, 1891–1935.* Norman: University of Oklahoma Press, 1988.

Utley, Robert M., ed. *Battlefield and Classroom: An Autobiography by Richard Henry Pratt.* Norman: University of Oklahoma Press, 2004.

Wesley–Esquimaux, Cynthia C. and Magdalena Smolewski. *Historic Trauma and Aboriginal Healing.* Ottawa: Aboriginal Healing Foundation, 2004.

Whitbeck, Les, G. Adams, D. Hoyt, and Z. Chen. "Conceptualizing and Measuring Historical Trauma among American Indian People." *American Journal of Community Psychology* 33, nos. 3–4 (2004): 119–30.

Yeo bah, A. "Education among Native Americans in the Periods Before and After Contact with Europeans: An overview." Paper presented at the Annual National Association of Native American Studies Conference, Houston, Texas, 2005.

Websites

"Boarding School Apology Initiative: Grassroots Strategy." *White Bison Center for the Wellbriety Movement.* Accessed 1 January 2011. http://www.whitebison.org.

"Chemawa Indian School: A Case Study of Educational Failure." Accessed 1 January 2011. http://www.myspace.com/lehmanbrightman/blog/372632876.

Chemawa Indian School. Accessed 20 January 2011. http://www.publicschoolreview.com/school_ov/school_id/91607.

LaFountain, Les, Orie Richard, and Scott Belgarde. "Who Am I: A Guide to Your Turtle Mountain Home." *Turtle Mountain Community College.* http://www.turtle–mountain.cc.nd.us/community/propeace/resources/WhoIAm.pdf.

Smith, Andrea. "Soul Wound: The Legacy of Native American Schools." *Amnesty Now*, Summer, 2003. Accessed 10 March 2010. http://www.manataka.org/page2290.html.

INDEX

Page numbers in italics reflect photographs.

ABOUT THE AUTHOR

Denise K. Lajimodiere's interest in American Indian boarding school survivors' stories evolved from recording her father and other family members speaking of their experiences. Her research helped her gain insight, a deeper understanding of her parents, and how and why she and her siblings were parented in the way they were. That insight led her to an emotional ceremony of forgiveness, described in the last chapter of *Stringing Rosaries*.

The journey to record survivors' stories led her through the Dakotas and Minnesota and into the personal and private space of boarding school survivors. While there, she heard stories that they had never shared before. She came to an understanding of new terms: historical and intergenerational trauma, soul wound.

She is haunted by the resounding silence of abuses that happened at boarding schools across the United States. She wants these survivors' stories told uninterrupted, so that each survivor tells their own story in their own words. The youngest survivor interviewed was fifty years old, and the oldest was eighty-nine. In the tradition of her Turtle Mountain Chippewa tribe, she offered them tobacco and gifts. She told them her parents' and grandparents' boarding school stories and that she is considered an intergenerational, someone who didn't go to boarding school but was a survivor of boarding school survivors.

The journey was emotionally exhausting. Often, after hearing their stories she had to sit in her car for a long while, sobbing, waiting to compose herself for the long drive back across the plains.

Lajimodiere is an enrolled Citizen of the Turtle Mountain Band of Chippewa, Belcourt, North Dakota. She has been involved in education for forty-four years as an elementary school teacher, principal, and professor, earning her bachelor, master's, and doctoral degrees from University of North Dakota. Denise recently retired as an associate professor from the School of Education, Education Leadership program, North Dakota State University, Fargo. She is one of the founders of the National Native America Board School Healing Coalition.

Denise is also a traditional Jingle Dress dancer, a writer (*Thunderbird* [North Dakota State University Press, 2017], *Bitter Tears* [Mammoth Press, 2016], *Dragonfly Dance* [Michigan State University Press, 2010], *His Feathers Were Chains* [North Dakota State University Press, 2020], *Josie Dances* [Minnesota State Historical Society Press, 2021]), and a Birch Bark Biting artist. Denise lives in a cozy cottage by a lake on the Turtle Mountain Indian Reservation.

Stringing Rosaries: The History, the Unforgivable, and the Healing of Northern Plains American Indian Boarding School Survivors has been recognized with multiple awards.

- One of three finalists for the 2020 Stubbendieck Great Plains Distinguished Book Prize
- 2020 Independent Press Awards, Distinguished Favorite in Cultural and Social Issues
- 2020 Independent Publishers Awards (IPPY Awards) Bronze Medal for Multicultural Nonfiction
- 2020 Independent Book Publishers Association—Benjamin Franklin Award, Silver Medalist in the Multicultural category
- 2019 Midwest Book Awards, Gold Medal in the Regional History category
- 2019 Foreword Reviews INDIES Finalist, History
- 2019 Midwest Book Awards, Silver Medal for Cover Design

ABOUT THE PRESS

North Dakota State University Press (NDSU Press) exists to stimulate and coordinate interdisciplinary regional scholarship. These regions include the Red River Valley, the state of North Dakota, the plains of North America (comprising both the Great Plains of the United States and the prairies of Canada), and comparable regions of other continents. We publish peer reviewed regional scholarship shaped by national and international events and comparative studies.

Neither topic nor discipline limits the scope of NDSU Press publications. We consider manuscripts in any field of learning. We define our scope, however, by a regional focus in accord with the press's mission. Generally, works published by NDSU Press address regional life directly, as the subject of study. Such works contribute to scholarly knowledge of region (that is, discovery of new knowledge) or to public consciousness of region (that is, dissemination of information, or interpretation of regional experience). Where regions abroad are treated, either for comparison or because of ties to those North American regions of primary concern to the press, the linkages are made plain. For nearly three-quarters of a century, NDSU Press has published substantial trade books, but the line of publications is not limited to that genre. We also publish textbooks (at any level), reference books, anthologies, reprints, papers, proceedings, and monographs. The press also considers works of poetry or fiction, provided they are established regional classics or they promise to assume landmark or reference status for the region. We select biographical or autobiographical works carefully for their prospective contribution to regional knowledge and culture. All publications, in whatever genre, are of such quality and substance as to embellish the imprint of NDSU Press.

We changed our imprint to North Dakota State University Press in January 2016. Prior to that, and since 1950, we published as the North Dakota Institute for Regional Studies Press. We continue to operate under the umbrella of the North Dakota Institute for Regional Studies, located at North Dakota State University.